CHILD RIGHTS, LEGAL THEORY AND SOCIAL ADVOCACY

Arguing for a democratic approach in authoritarian times, this book challenges the singular focus on age in identifying children in child rights. Even for the purposes of a benevolent rights regime, adopting a monist construction of child identity arguably artificially separates the law from reality, potentially foreclosing children's democratic deliberative agency in self-identification. The scope for a claimant to argue one's identity, or foundationally "I am a human being"; is an essential feature of other human rights, but such a contention is foreclosed when identification as a child is decided unequivocally by reference simply to age. Drawing on critical race theory's narrative method, and inspired by W. E. B. Du Bois' critique of identity construction through double consciousness, Professor Grahn-Farley advocates for a new theoretical approach of the child and of child rights, one that is cognizant of social interaction and democratic participation. This book will appeal to researchers in child and human rights, and to sociologists, legal theorists and activists. This title is part of the Flip it Open programme and may also be available Open Access. Check our website Cambridge Core for details.

Maria Grahn-Farley is Visiting Professor of Law at the University of Gothenburg (with tenure). She was one of the first children in the world recruited by Save the Children Sweden to participate in building an international child rights movement in anticipation of the adoption in 1989 of the United Nations Convention on the Rights of the Child. Grahn-Farley is a Harvard Law School graduate and has taught child rights and human rights for over twenty years, in the United States, Sweden and the United Kingdom. She is the coordinator of Human Rights Justification (HRJust), a Horizon Europe research and innovation consortium funded by the European Union.

Child Rights, Legal Theory and Social Advocacy

MARIA GRAHN-FARLEY
University of Gothenburg

CAMBRIDGE
UNIVERSITY PRESS

CAMBRIDGE
UNIVERSITY PRESS

Shaftesbury Road, Cambridge CB2 8EA, United Kingdom

One Liberty Plaza, 20th Floor, New York, NY 10006, USA

477 Williamstown Road, Port Melbourne, VIC 3207, Australia

314–321, 3rd Floor, Plot 3, Splendor Forum, Jasola District Centre, New Delhi – 110025, India

103 Penang Road, #05-06/07, Visioncrest Commercial, Singapore 238467

Cambridge University Press is part of Cambridge University Press & Assessment, a department of the University of Cambridge.

We share the University's mission to contribute to society through the pursuit of education, learning and research at the highest international levels of excellence.

www.cambridge.org
Information on this title: www.cambridge.org/9781009366960

DOI: 10.1017/9781009366953

When citing this work, please include a reference to the DOI 10.1017/9781009366953

First published 2024

A catalogue record for this publication is available from the British Library

Library of Congress Cataloging-in-Publication Data
NAMES: Grahn-Farly, Maria, author.
TITLE: Child rights, legal theory, and social advocacy / Maria Grahn-Farley, Göteborgs Universitet, Sweden.
DESCRIPTION: Cambridge, United Kingdom ; New York, NY : Cambridge University Press, 2024. | Includes bibliographical references and index.
IDENTIFIERS: LCCN 2023040868 (print) | LCCN 2023040869 (ebook) | ISBN 9781009366960 (hardback) | ISBN 9781009366939 (paperback) | ISBN 9781009366953 (epub)
SUBJECTS: LCSH: Children–Legal status, laws, etc. | Children's rights. | Social advocacy. | Social work with children.
CLASSIFICATION: LCC K639 .G73 2024 (print) | LCC K639 (ebook) | DDC 323.3/52–dc23/eng/20231002
LC record available at https://lccn.loc.gov/2023040868
LC ebook record available at https://lccn.loc.gov/2023040869

ISBN 978-1-009-36696-0 Hardback

For Astrid with all my love

Contents

Acknowledgments

There are many people to thank. I want to thank Laura Carlson for generously giving her time to comment on previous drafts and for encouraging me to keep going. Thanks to Didi Herman, Pierre Schlag, Pantea Javidan, Adam Gearey, Thomas Wilhelmsson and Astrid Grahn-Farley for comments on early drafts (all mistakes are mine). I also want to thank Harte Weiner and Joel Simundich for combined years of support and kindness. Special thanks go to the Child Studies department at Linköping University, and specially Karin Zetterqvist Nelson, Anna Sparrman, and Jonathan Josefsson for graciously commenting on the draft and generously sharing their own research. Thanks to Nirmala Pillay for engaged and engaging conversations on human rights and legal theory. Also, thanks to Max Lyles for thoughtful comments. Thank you to Cambridge University Press editor Deborah Renshaw for excellent editing support.

I have never properly thanked Duncan Kennedy for being an academic role model for all these years; this is my opportunity to say thank you.

Introduction

There was a time in Sweden when your name day – the calendar day dedicated to your name – was as important as your birthday in defining your identity. My own childhood began in that time. The names were highly regulated; each day of the year had a name associated with it, and parents were expected to give their child a name that had a name day. Women born on December 24 are often named Eve because it is the name day of Eve. My name day, for Maria, falls on February 28. In my second-grade classroom, you would find a flower wreath hanging on the blackboard. On your name day, the circle of flowers was moved from its upper-right corner of the blackboard to the upper center, and Ms. Frida would write your name in cursive in its center for the whole day for everyone to see that this day carried your name. For my maternal grandmother, it was her name day we would celebrate – that is, when a cake was baked. I cannot recall the teacher ever celebrating any classmate's birthday during elementary school. Today, children scarcely know their name day, and some do not even have a name day as names are not as tightly regulated, and new names have been added to the calendar that better represent the multicultural society that Sweden has become. I'm certain my daughter does not know her name day, and to be honest, I also cannot recall it off the top of my head. I only know that she has one because I made sure to choose a name with a place in the calendar. But what both of us would know instantly is her birthday. This is a cultural shift that has taken place just within my lifetime, and the shift has been so complete that it has all but erased any memory of name days, even for those of us who grew up with them. The shift has quite a significant meaning. One's name is a deliberate choice and even if it is connected to a special day, it is a day of choice and not just an accident of birth. A name has a history, but your birthday connects you to nothing but the Earth having orbited the Sun one full cycle. With the attribution of age, there is no choice. Fundamentally, this is what this book is about, how the child-right identity – constructed as a person under the age of eighteen – also reflects a whole new form of identity construction that is unique to children, an identity construction without agency. I call this construction monist, a construction that does not need a human act of annunciation to be created and where individual agency is made redundant for its meaning.

In this book *Child Rights, Legal Theory and Social Advocacy*, I explore four aspects of what I identify as a child rights theory of the posthegemonic liberal democratic era in which we now live. First, what are the overarching values of child rights? For example, everyone's equal freedom is an overarching value in the universal declaration of human rights, but when it comes to child rights specifically, it is unclear what overarching value might be governing their regime. Second, what are the qualifications necessary for a person to enjoy the rights under the UN Convention of the Rights of the Child, 1989 (CRC)? For general human rights, the criterion is to be born a human; the criterion for a child to be a holder of child rights is not as clear cut. Third, what are the means for these rights to be implemented within their specific social context in history and place? In this book, this place is Sweden. Finally, there is a tension between international child rights and national democracy in times when liberal democracy no longer enjoys a privileged, unchallenged ideological position within the West, leading to an examination of the relationship between authoritarianism and democracy as mediated through child rights.

Child rights, from their very moment of inception as a legal field through the adoption of the CRC,[1] have striven to disentangle themselves from social context. This book problematizes the very idea that child rights can be understood as free from the specifics of time and place, any more than they can be detached from the individual person claiming her rights. Neither can the role of the State be escaped. Place, time, and the State will continue to be the conditions upon which child rights gain their efficacy.

The writing of this book began in a Sweden that had declared itself to be a humanitarian superpower, and it ends in a Sweden that voted to national power a political party with roots in the neo-Nazi movement as the second largest party. By the time I had finished these last sentences, Sweden had abandoned its identity as a humanitarian superpower, replaced by extremist

[1] Convention on the Rights of the Child (hereafter CRC) (1989) adopted November 20, 1989, UN General Assembly, Resolution 44/25. Entered into force September 2, 1990 in accordance with article 49. As of April 2, 2023, there were 196 States parties and one signatory (The United States, the only nonparty to the CRC).

right-wing policies led by a government having decided to govern with the support of the Swedish democrats and their neo-Nazi roots. The Swedish self-appointment as a humanitarian superpower has been central to the Swedish self-image over recent decades for good and for bad, a self-annunciated identity never subjected to questioning and only praised.

A new European war is raging on Ukrainian territory, and major tension is expressed in the saber-rattling around the multiple centers of a new post-hegemonic liberal democratic world order that is becoming clearer as every day passes. Sweden changed its long-standing neutral position as a response to the Russian invasion of Ukraine and applied to join NATO together with its neighbor Finland. Finland's application to join NATO was quickly approved by its members. The Swedish application, on the other hand, met resistance from Turkey and from Hungary. Sweden become a full member of NATO almost one year after Finland. This idea of being a humanitarian superpower is sometimes seen as an expression of Swedish arrogance and was given as one reason why Hungary was unwilling to approve the Swedish application to join NATO.[2] As soon as human rights came with a cost in the form of Hungary withholding its approval, Sweden abandoned its claim to be a humanitarian superpower, revealing the shallowness of the concept. One would be hard pressed today to find anyone mentioning humanitarianism at all.

The Swedish example in this book serves to give child rights a place from which to begin the theoretical examination of their construction and the advocacy done in their name in this post-democratic new world. The political climate of the State in which child rights are to be implemented and applied matters for understanding the vulnerability of rights in relation to their dependency on the State. Eliminating that vulnerability by ignoring the antidemocratic wave sweeping the world, by enforcing States' own interpretation of the universal positivist claims of human rights, I argue, also risks undermining the democratic process itself. Child rights becoming more authoritarian does not resolve the often-embedded contradiction between forceful international human rights law and democracy. I am not proposing one without the other, but I am arguing for finding a relationality between the two; it is necessary to fully understand the local or national place where child

[2] A Swedish newspaper cites a Hungarian source explaining that the Swedish self-image of being "morally superior" is one of the reasons why Hungary has not have approved the Swedish NATO application. See Henrik Torehammar,"Kraven svider i den svenska självbilden [The demand stings the Swedish self-image], *Svenska Dagbladet*, March 29, 2023.

rights are to be applied in concrete cases when also preserving democratic legal processes within States.

Consequently, the narrative method is used here. This is a book written by a woman now in her fifties with a grown-up daughter. The book looks back at a lifetime in the child rights movement –having been one of its first children myself as I entered the field of child rights in anticipation of the UN adoption of the Convention now almost forty years ago and having spent my life taking part in creating an international child rights movement, as I moved between Sweden, the United States and finally a post-Brexit United Kingdom.

The objective of this book is to critically assess this development of child rights in order to further strengthen them. As an author, I have been inspired by the role critical race theory has served in revitalizing the civil rights movement, hoping here for such a revitalization in child rights advocacy. Derrick Bell, in his work as a celebrated civil rights lawyer, began an internal critique and self-examination of his movement's taboos and unexamined links between law and society. Critical race theory was initially seen as showing disrespect for the struggle and sacrifices the civil rights generation had endured in order to create a better world for the next generation. Some even thought it was a threat to the civil rights movement. Bell broke the taboo of the movement when he asked whether the legal struggle by the National Association for the Advancement of Colored People (NAACP) to desegregate American schools served the civil rights movement or the individual black children on whose behalf the claims were filed, because, he argued, the legal struggle could not serve both.

Naturally, I am not claiming to have the same stature as Derrick Bell, but my intention is similar. It is to open up the taboos of the child rights discourse as we, people engaged with that discourse, have as a movement reached a level of maturity and security to allow us to address any weaknesses in ways we previously could not have done without putting the whole child rights project at risk. I believe, however, that we have now reached an academic and social level of maturity – and have wide enough support – for us to be able to afford a self-critical examination of how we represent child rights theory and advocacy, especially how we are to navigate democracy's loss of its hegemonic position. In addition, I find that there is an absolute urgency to make this self-critical examination in the light of the declining popular support of liberal democracy as the given system of governance put on display with the Swedish election in 2022, and with the election of Trump in the United States that the election of Biden did not cure. Child rights theory and advocacy cannot be understood in isolation from the democratic decline taking place across the world. When the society in which child rights are to be understood is becoming less democratic and more authoritarian, this places a heightened burden upon child rights theorists and advocates to also examine the authoritarian impulses of the child rights regime itself.

The reluctance to examine the use of age as the constituting element of the child needs to be addressed – does this serve the child rights movement more than children? For a movement that has been so questioned and, initially, ridiculed, it was necessary to demonstrate assertiveness as a sign of strength, turning nuance and the possibility of doubt into signs of weakness. However, today, the field of child rights within academia is an established and respected discipline, and the child rights movement is now a fully established concept. I am confident that both child rights as an academic discipline and a social movement are strong enough to meet and evolve on the basis of self-reflection and self-critique.

The organization of this volume is as follows. Chapter 1 examines the first of the aspects mentioned earlier: What are the overarching values of child rights? Are they part of the universality of human rights, or do child rights constitute their own universality for children?

The second chapter critically examines the making of the child-rights identity as a monist construction, separating child rights from all other forms of identity-based rights. This is both the weakness and the strength of the child rights regime – that its constitution is only dependent on age, and that the body and the mind of the rights holder are without meaning for its construction.

Chapter 3 develops the monist identity construction of the child by challenging the way children are visualized through a set of Google search images based on keywords. The mystification of age as what constitutes the child is challenged and analyzed from what this book calls a perspective of complex intersectionality, referring to how the monist child-rights identity intersects with the social construction of race and gender while at the same time rejecting the possibility of social construction itself.

Chapter 4 draws on Gayatri Spivak's question: When we say that the child has a right to be heard, does that also mean that the child can speak? In other words, will what the child says be given the respect and recognition needed for this to become speech?

Chapter 5 addresses what it means to be a monist identity construction not dependent on group consciousness, even though, as an identity, it clearly refers to a group of persons. Where is the child within the child rights movement, and what is the child rights movement without children?

The book in Chapter 6 moves from the vantage point of the child-rights identity to a legal systemic view where law becomes the focus, addressing the example of Sweden's incorporation of the CRC into Swedish law. The incorporation was done by insisting that all levels of the public authorities, from individual social workers, to police, to supreme court justices, all had equal authority to interpret and apply individual articles of the Convention without any higher level of norms and without any guidelines for what legal meaning was to be deduced from each article of the CRC. This led to what Giorgio Agamben has defined as a perpetual State of Exception.

Chapter 7 examines the example of the CRC as a monist pull of universal positivism when the distinctions between internal democratic processes and an international communal child rights regime implode and make democratic deliberation impossible from within the child rights regime itself.

Chapter 8 returns to the main theoretical argument of the book: The monist construction of the child-rights identity is a means to create certainty where there is none to be found. This monism is exemplified by the child-rights identity, but it also holds a general attraction for sensibilities that are uncomfortable with the ambiguities and the uncertainty that comes with democratic deliberation. On this issue, Sweden serves as a place through which one can examine strong waves of this neo-authoritarianism – in both its benevolent and malevolent forms.

This uncertainty, or the ethics of ambiguity, that one thing might also be its opposite, is what authoritarianism tries to replace with monism, not necessarily in bad faith, but, when it comes to child rights, at times in good faith. Still, I argue, we should instead embrace the split in identity and law that allows for doubt and forces deliberation as part of a democratic, open society, where self-doubt is to be seen as a guaranty for a democratic society and not as a weakness of advocacy because at the core of democracy rest ambiguity and uncertainty, the risk that the opposing side of the argument might be correct.

The CRC and the child-right-identity it constructs do not hold the internal contradiction that is embedded within other forms of identity construction, between the formalism of law and the substance of social construction, the monism of age replaces the function of ambiguity in the identity of the child. Monism should not dissuade child rights theorists and advocates from reassessing one's own role through questioning and exercising a self-critique that will hopefully open a split within the monism of child-rights identity to allow in the light of democratic deliberation.

1

The Child and Human Rights

The Birth of the Child Rights Regime

Children are not given rights. Instead, adults should stop withholding those rights that children already have. This distinction, between giving and withholding rights, underscores a curious contradiction within the language of rights. Once you argue that rights belong to all individuals because they are human beings, you place yourself in the position of fighting against the withholding of those rights, rather than having to ask for something the other must grant you anyway. You are no longer fighting for your rights to be given to you, even though oddly enough, the struggle is still often described in this way. In the case of child rights, international law should hold adults accountable for withholding already existing rights from children, instead of placing the burden on children to fight for their rights as if adults have the option to not give them what is already theirs.

There is some unclarity at the core of the child rights regime: What is the source of its authority? Does the UN Convention on the Rights of the Child (CRC) create rights for children, or do children already have universal rights that are being withheld from them? In the early years of the development of child rights, the issue of whether rights were guaranteed to children by virtue of the fact that they are human beings – and thus covered by the universal rights that all humans have – or whether children's rights constituted their own separate universal rights regime was not fully addressed. The issue remains unsettled to this day.

One serious consequence of not being able to settle the source of the authority of the child rights regime is that the question of who has the legitimacy to decide how it should be interpreted and applied remains unanswered. Even more importantly – considering that it is a human rights treaty and as such often needs to be used to challenge the social and legal consensus that gives rise to international treaties – where will the legitimacy come from to question not only its interpretation and application but also its foundational construction? To date, the legitimacy to question an instrument that has been put in place on behalf of a group has, in large part, been the privilege of that very same group. The group that is the subject of the treaty is seen to have the authority to ask: Is this working for us? Does this set of rights in our name do the work we would like it to do, and if not, what should be changed or rectified? In the context of human rights in the form of child rights, however, to this day, a large question mark remains about the legitimacy of the child as an interpreter of her own rights. I will argue throughout this book that, for this reason, we need to seriously examine the legal theoretical foundations of child rights as they are constructed through the CRC.

This book was written through a particular historical lens. I began thinking about child rights long before I began studying the topic. The issue touched my life first as a child, later as a young woman, and then as the mother of a daughter. This is not a book about me but about the development of a child rights regime as I have seen it evolve. I believe that when we attach child rights to a concrete place and time, we can evaluate their strength and their value and – most importantly – their possible biases. It is too easy to embrace the concept of child rights at a distance; people seldom evaluate the topic in the context of a specific place and time. By many random coincidences, however, my personal history has coincided with the history of child rights at a few crucial moments.

My first engagement with child rights happened in 1988, one year before the UN General Assembly adopted the CRC, the treaty that would be the most quickly and widely ratified human rights treaty in the history of the UN. I was a sixteen-year-old high school student living close to the Arctic Circle in a small town in Sweden called Piteå. I was completely unaware of rights in general, and it had never crossed my mind to think about whether children had rights or not. But I was soon to be witness to the process of the final drafting of a new international treaty on child rights where Save the Children Sweden held a significant role through the work of Simone Ek. Even more importantly, I witnessed how to apply this process to the real lives of children in Sweden and around the world. Later, I was part of the Save the Children team that worked closely with the first post apartheid government as it drafted the child rights chapter of the South African Constitution. It was a privilege as a young person still in law school to be able to attend meetings in both Sweden and South Africa and hear debates about all the pros and cons of the language of child rights in the new constitution.

I learned a great deal as a person, as a lawyer, and as a child rights activist from these meetings and from conversations with Minister of Justice Dullah

Omar, who was also a law professor. He was the person who opened my eyes to what would later become a critique of human rights as inherently biased toward Western values within Third World approaches to international law (TWAIL). I learned from him that I did not need to accept the whole package of human rights even if I approved of their foundation but could continue questioning them from the perspective of what might not be said or seen, or what the very rights a treaty or constitution granted might obscure from vision.

This is what Professor Omar explained to me when I tried to understand the choice by South African framers to include social and economic rights in their constitution. For him, it was by including both social and economic rights, and child rights, in the new constitution that South Africa could recognize the long struggle of black and colored people against apartheid. By "colored people" I refer to the American tradition of abolitonist, antiracist and anticolonial work, first coined by Frederick Douglass and later used by W. E. B. Du Bois in his famous line: "the problem of the twentieth century is the problem of the color line."[1] When I asked Professor Omar about the inclusion of this, often called second generation of rights in the constitution – a radical move at the time – he pointed toward one of our bodyguards and told me that this man had fought apartheid at the risk of his life. How was Professor Omar going to justify anything less than a progressive constitution to him? This conversation changed my whole view on international law and human rights. I watched Professor Omar ferociously fight to include child rights in the constitution, even though he was fully aware of their weaknesses and the need over time to reform them.

It is no coincidence that the CRC reads like a Swedish welfare state directive of the 1980s. The Swedish branch of Save the Children, the largest child advocacy organization in the world at the time, was the lead agency for the drafting of the CRC in the Open NGO Working Group in Geneva. That group was headed by Senior Advisor to the NGO network Simone Ek, who was the director for international relations at Save the Children Sweden in Geneva.[2] She is to be credited for a large part of what was to become a unique treaty, the first UN human rights treaty to have an active NGO element

[1] Fredrick Douglass, "The Color Line," *North American Review* 132, no. 295 (1881): 567–577; W. E. B. Du Bois, *The Souls of Black Folk* (New York: Oxford University Press, 2007 [1903]). For more recent work using the term to signal an antiracist position, see the work of Katrina Quisumbing King, "The Global Color Line and White Supremacy: W. E. B. Du Bois as a Grand Theorist of Race," in Aldon D. Morris et. al (eds.), *The Oxford Handbook of* W. E. *B. Du Bois* (Oxford: Oxford University Press, 2022).

[2] Ek's work in the drafting of the CRC can be found in the collection of preparatory works, Simone Ek on behalf of the Office of the United Nations High Commissioner for Human Rights, "Legislative History of the Convention on the Rights of the Child," vols. 1 and 2 (2007).

involved in the drafting process itself. She came to the drafting of the CRC with lengthy experience in child rights advocacy. She had previously worked for Save the Children Sweden in promoting the Swedish antispanking law in the international arena. The Swedish antispanking law was the first such law in the world, adopted in 1979 and placed within the Swedish Parental Code.[3] Another example of the influence of the Swedish welfare state can be found in the wording of the CRC's article 12, which is an almost verbatim copy of the provision in the Swedish Parental Code that established the right of the child to be heard.[4] The transfer of this legal principal from Swedish domestic law to the CRC moved the scope of international standards from the private relationship between parents and children to the public relationship between the child and the State.[5]

Simone Ek was not the only Swedish member of Save the Children who was heavily involved in the creation and implementation of the CRC. Thomas Hammarberg, the secretary-general of Save the Children Sweden, was to become the first chair of the UN Committee of the Rights of the Child that monitored the implementation of the CRC. Karin Söder, the Swedish minister of foreign affairs who was also the president of Save the Children Sweden, had supported the UN to develop a legally binding child rights convention in her capacity as minister of foreign affairs, building on the Polish initiative. Poland initiated the idea in 1979 – the Year of the Child – to create a legally binding convention on the rights of children. These three people, Simone, Karin and Thomas, were highly influential in developing and setting the tone for what was to become the first legally binding child rights treaty and then monitoring its implementation. They were aware that Save the Children did not have children within its organization, but, even though it is a private entity and as such not legally bound by the convention, it is understood from within the organization that as a child rights advocate there is a moral obligation to fulfill article 12. To address the shortfall of child participation, Save the Children decided to create a child and youth movement in accordance with the CRC and article 12, in anticipation of the UN's adoption of the CRC the following year.

That is how I was recruited to Save the Children in 1988 as part of what is probably the first attempt in the world to fulfill article 12 of the CRC. I began

3 SFS 1978:853, entry into force July 1, 1979.

4 *Föräldrabalk* [Parental Code] (1949:381). An up-to-date Swedish version of the act can be found on the Swedish Parliament's website at www.riksdagen.se/sv/dokument-lagar/dokument/svensk-forfattningssamling/foraldrabalk-1949381_sfs-1949-381. The introduction of the spanking prohibition was by the Act on Amending the Parental Code, SFS 1983:47 with respect to paragraph 6.1 of the Parental Code.

5 The legal amendment is done through Lag (1983:47); Chapter 6, Section 6.1.

as a member of the first Youth Committee under the CRC under the direct guidance of Thomas Hammarberg and Karin Söder. Later, I joined the National Board of Save the Children. It was from that position that I came to learn about child rights and the CRC in more detail. I watched the effects of the ratification and implementation of the CRC during the early and very dynamic years of the new child rights regime in the late 1980s and 1990s. The treaty, ratified in record speed by the largest group of states to date (the United States remaining the only non-member of the treaty), captures the spirit and the sentiments of the early post–Cold War years and made a significant impact on the international human rights agenda.[6]

1.1 UNIVERSAL HUMAN RIGHTS OR UNIVERSAL CHILD RIGHTS?

One basic question is whether child rights should guarantee a universal right of children to human rights or whether it is instead a regime based on universal rights that each child has by virtue of being a child. In other words, did the CRC give me child rights for the *first* time, or was it the case that the whole time I had been deprived of already existing rights that the CRC now helped emphasize? Is the universal claim of child rights based on the fact that all children are humans and therefore all children are covered under the universality of human rights, or are those claims based on the fact that all humans are, or have been, children and that therefore child rights are universal in and of themselves? Or are child rights their own universal regime because the CRC is almost universally ratified? (Only the United States has remained outside the treaty; it has signed but not ratified it.)

These are important questions because the answers determine the role of the international child rights regime in advocating for children's rights and not necessarily limited to the rights of the convention. With an expansion of the claim the child rights movement will have to make choices between both different rights and different regimes, as well as different groups of children. If child rights are part of securing the universality of human rights, a large part of the regime's function would be to eliminate, and compensate for, social and legal practices that stand in the way of children being able to enjoy the universality of human rights to their fullest. If child rights are what is universal, their function would be to develop universal standards and definitions for

6 Initially, members of Save the Children used the term "youth movement" rather than "child rights movement" in the context of its fulfilling the provision of article 12. The CRC's legal definition of the child as everyone under the age of eighteen was different from the social and cultural understanding at that time, namely that a child was someone who was younger than a teenager and a youth was a teenager.

child rights regulations. If universality is achieved through the almost universal ratification of the CRC, then it is a treaty that should be understood in the context of treaty law, and the focus would be on pushing for universal ratification. That is the strategy Save the Children originally pursued in all of its development aid work.

The origins of the unclarity regarding which rights regime children's rights belong to can be seen in the human rights treaties that predated the CRC. For example, article 16 of the International Covenant on Civil and Political Rights (ICCPR) seems to indicate that child rights are part of the universality of human rights: "Everyone shall have the right to recognition everywhere as a person before the law."[7] However, within the same document, article 24 seems to say that child rights originate within the family, in society, and in the State (probably in that order): "the right to such measures of protection as are required by his status as a minor, on the part of his family, society and the State."[8] Child rights cannot be both at the same time since there cannot be partial universality.

This makes the identity of the child different from other forms of identity, particularly in the question of emancipation. For example, it is arguably possible to eliminate practices that discriminate against women and thus include women fully in the universality of human rights. But it is not so easy to do that for children without doing significant harm to them. Children need adults to care for and provide for them. This is different from the situation of women, covered in another important UN convention that preceded the CRC: Women do not need men to care and provide for them as a biological fact; women's dependency on men is socially constructed.[9] Children are not autonomous beings to the same extent that women would be if discrimination against them was eliminated. Children – at least young children – need assistance in order to survive. So it is all well and good to talk about the absolute rights of children, but those rights will almost always be granted through adults who have clear ideas about how they want to use the rights and how they want to shape the child. Those goals may infringe on universal rights that children supposedly have by virtue of universal human rights.

7 Article 16, "International Covenant on Civil and Political Rights" (hereafter ICCPR), adopted December 16, 1966, entry into force March 23, 1976, UN General Assembly, Resolution 2200A

8 Article 24, ICCPR.

9 Convention on the Elimination of All Forms of Discrimination against Women, adopted December 18, 1979, entry into force March 3, 1981, UN General Assembly, Resolution 34/180.

To me, child rights mean something more than the absence of child discrimination. This distinguishes child rights from the way most people view women's and minority rights as originating from the foundation of equality. For example, for women, an equality approach in the workplace involves removing barriers to equality. But that does not work for children. Child labor regulations are founded on the principle of protection from harm, not on the principle of equality. Labor is considered to be a harm when it is performed by children under the same conditions as adults. At a minimum, children must have shorter workdays, access to education, and parental care, and a large group of child rights advocates will argue that children should not work at all.[10] In other words, child rights are something more than – if not entirely different from – a protection against discrimination. In fact, not even the CRC protects the child from being discriminated against for being a child: the antidiscrimination protected categories are race, color, language, religion, political or other opinion, nationality, ethnicity, social origin, property, disability, birth or other status.

However, a strand of child rights analysis has recently turned toward the antidiscrimination framework. Elisabeth Young-Bruehl was one of the first authors to attempt to bridge the gap between child rights and universal human rights by labeling the particularity of discrimination against children as childism.[11] Simon Flacks makes a direct link between child rights and the equality principle in his comparative study of child rights and disability rights in light of the UK Equality Act of 2010.[12] Reifa Kaya further develops the equality principle in her exploration of the effects of the climate crisis on children. She advances an antidiscrimination argument based on age, rather than the child- rights identity, arguing that we should rely on the protection against age discrimination, rather than the child-rights identity the CRC has

[10] For an in-depth study of child rights for the working child, see Edward van Daalen, "Could It Be That They Do Not Want to Hear What We Have to Say? Organised Working Children and the International Politics and Representation of Child Labour," in *The Politics of Children's Rights and Representation*, ed. Bengt Sandin, Jonathan Josefsson, Karl Hanson, and Sara Balagopalan (London: Palgrave Macmillan, 2022). See also Seamus Byrne advocating for a more expanded use of socioeconomic rights in child rights, Seamus Byrne, "Reclaiming Progressive Realisation: A Children's Rights Analysis," *The International Journal of Children's Rights* 28 (2020): 748–777.

[11] Elisabeth Young-Bruehl, *Childism: Confronting Prejudice against Children* (New Haven, CT: Yale University Press, 2012). For more recent work see, Gerald L. Neuman & Abadir M. Ibrahim, When is Age Discrimination a Human Rights Violation?, 36 Harvard Human Rights Journal, 223 (2023).

[12] Simon Flacks, "Is Childhood a 'Disability'? Exploring the Exclusion of Children from Age Discrimination Provisions in the Equality Act 2010," *Child and Family Law Quarterly* 26 (2014): 421.

constructed.[13] In this way, one could argue that child rights have finally "come home" to join the other identities international law has constructed – those of women, racialized groups, and ethnic groups that are discriminated against. Seen through the lens of the age discrimination argument, child rights, like the rights of other groups, emerged from the recognition that children are subjugated in ways that cause them harm.

The CRC managed this paradox in a pragmatic way by granting children both sets of rights – one set that derives from the principle of equality founded in the principle of universality and another that derives from the specific status of the child – without explaining whether we should understand child rights as part of the universality of human rights or whether we should regard child rights as having their own universality. The preamble of the CRC does both. Its provision of protecting children against discrimination upholds the principle of equality and emphasizes the universality of human rights: "Everyone is entitled to all the rights and freedoms set forth therein, without distinction of any kind." But that language is followed by a statement that can be understood as support for a separate regime: "Childhood is entitled to special care and assistance." Even though the preamble of the CRC neither excludes the universal human rights understanding of child rights nor clarifies whether childhood is the basis for a separate rights regime, it was always clear to me as a child that we could not just borrow the feminist strategies of liberation and equality – that children were different from the other UN treaty constructed identities. It is not only discrimination and subjugation that create and shape the child identity. Children need adults to advocate for them and to interpret some of the rights of children on their behalf, and this places an extra responsibility on adults and on legal theory to address the construction of the child identity derived from the CRC. How should this responsibility be understood from a legal theoretical perspective when the human rights legal regime leaves us with the choice between two forms of universalities, one of humanity and the other of childhood?

This tension between the universality of human rights in general and the particular rights of specific identities was discussed, but was not developed into any form of resolution in the early years surrounding the adoption of the CRC. However, since then, that debate has mostly fallen silent. In 1990, David Balton, arguing that children are included in the universality of human rights, pointed out the risk that the CRC would weaken the existing inalienable

[13] Reifa Kaya, "Environmental Vulnerability, Age and the Promises of Anti-Age Discrimination Law," *Review of European, Comparative, and International Environmental Law* 28, no. 2 (2019): 162–174.

rights children possess by virtue of the fact that they are humans.[14] He gave the example of article 14 of the convention:

> 1. States Parties shall respect the right of the child to freedom of thought, conscience and religion.
> 2. States Parties shall respect the rights and duties of the parents and, when applicable, legal guardians, to provide direction to the child in the exercise of his or her right in a manner consistent with the evolving capacities of the child.[15]

Article 14.1 states that children already have the right to freedom of thought, conscience, and religion, but 14.2 immediately derogates this right by giving parents the right to shape those rights. Thus, the child's right to freedom of religion, for example, is far weaker than the same right for adults.

The drafters of the convention could not reach a consensus about whether the CRC should codify the provision that had already been established in article 18 of the ICCPR ("Everyone shall have the right to freedom of thought, conscience and religion").[16] Thus, it is arguable that the specialized convention gives weaker protection than the universal protection because it allows the child to be excluded from access to the full universality of human rights. Balton raises the obvious question: How should one understand the meaning of the concept of the universal rights of the child when it is clear in the language of the CRC that the states intended to infringe upon a universal right in the case of children?[17]

In contrast to the other specialty UN conventions, which focus on eliminating the barriers to equal enjoyment of universal rights, the CRC is open to the interpretation that it articulates a different set of rights, rather than a qualification of existing universal rights. This position is strengthened by the writings of Jamie Sergio Cerda, who pointed out that the convention set out entirely new rights specifically for children: for example, the right to an identity and the rights related to adoption.[18] Geraldine Van Bueren proposes a legal methodological solution to the dilemma of the universality of human rights and the role of child rights: place child rights within the universality of human rights and negotiate the equality principle through the best-interest principle. That is, allow affirmative actions in favor of children only when they

[14] David A. Balton, "The Convention on the Rights of the Child: Prospects for International Enforcement," *Human Rights Quarterly* 12, no. 1 (1990): 124.
[15] Article 14, CRC.
[16] Article 18, ICCPR.
[17] Balton, "The Convention on the Rights of the Child," 124.
[18] Jaime Sergio Cerda, "The Draft Convention on the Rights of the Child: New Rights," *Human Rights Quarterly* 12, no. 1 (1990): 117.

can be justified as being in the best interest of the child.[19] Van Bueren argues that this practice would counter the risk that the differential treatment of children would reflect social and cultural beliefs about children and not be in their best interest.[20] David Archard and John Tobin seem to break with the universal human rights approach and instead treat child rights as their own regime when they point out that the CRC might mean that some rights that are uniquely for children are denied to people who are not children.[21]

In 1990, Thomas Hammarberg's reflections supported the position that child rights constitute a regime of their own. He emphasized the additional vulnerability of children in times of war (he gave the example of the war between Iran and Iraq) and the effects of debt crises.[22] He moved the child rights agenda closer to being its own regime by noting the conflicting interests of children and their parents.[23] The argument that the child has separate and conflicting interests from her parents is still one of the major fault lines within child rights. The clearest clash between two scholars on this issue is the one between Michael Freeman and Martin Guggenheim.[24] The question is whether children are an interdependent part of the adult community around them (as Guggenheim argues) or whether children are to be seen as autonomous actors just as their parents are by virtue of their human rights (as Freeman advocates).

The argument that child rights might be universal but not primarily part of the universality of human rights can be taken one step further by following the reasoning of Joel Oestreich in his evaluation of the first decade of the CRC. He changes the focus from trying to fit child rights within the universality of human rights to instead regarding child rights as universal by virtue of their

[19] Geraldine Van Bueren, *The International Law on the Rights of the Child* (Dordrecht: Martinus Nijhoff, 1995), 38.

[20] Ibid.

[21] David Archard and John Tobin, "Article 1: The Definition of a Child," in *The UN Convention on the Rights of the Child: A Commentary*, ed. John Tobin (Oxford: Oxford University Press, 2019).

[22] Thomas Hammarberg, "The UN Convention on the Rights of the Child – And How to Make It Work," *Human Rights Quarterly* 12, no. 1 (1990): 98. A more contemporary reflection from a Swedish perspective can be found in the work of Bengt Sandin. He connects a universal approach to an expended development of a State responsivity to guarantee the rights of the child. See Bengt Sandin, "Recognizing Children's Rights: From Child Protection to Children's Human Rights – The 1979 Swedish Ban on Corporal Punishment in Perspective" in *The Politics of Children's Rights and Representation*, ed. Bengt Sandin, Jonathan Josefsson, Karl Hanson, and Sara Balagopalan) (London: Palgrave Macmillan, 2022).

[23] Hammarberg, "The UN Convention on the Rights of the Child," 99.

[24] Martin Guggenheim, *What's Wrong with Children's Rights* (Cambridge, MA: Harvard University Press, 2007); Michael Freeman, "What's Right with Rights for Children" (review essay), *International Journal of Law in Context* 2 (2006): 89.

almost universal support from ratifying States.[25] Joel Oestreich mentions an aspect of the CRC that is often overlooked: In its original form, it lacked any enforcement mechanism. In this respect, the CRC differs from the other specialized human rights treaties that precede it. Both the International Convention on the Elimination of All Forms of Racial Discrimination (CERD), at article 22 and the Convention on the Elimination of All Forms of Discrimination against Women (CEDAW), at article 29 contain provisions for adjudication between States parties to the treaty.[26] In 2011, the General Assembly adopted a Third Optional Protocol for the CRC that brought it closer in line with CEDAW by allowing for individual communications by children or organizations on their behalf at moments of disputed rights infringements and violations. But the protocol does not provide a mechanism for legally binding decisions in the case of disputes.[27] Instead of directly acknowledging that the committee that drafted the CRC deliberately chose to not model it on CERD and CEDAW,[28] analysts more often describe the lack of an enforcement mechanism as a general weakness of enforcement of human rights, which can be cured by creating enforcement mechanisms. This is partly correct; it is not the dispute settlement mechanism in CERD or CEDAW that gives them their authority necessarily but it does send a different signal to the States parties in comparison with the CRC that in its totality lacks a dispute settlement mechanism, giving the impression of having been intended to being more of a moral than a legal treaty.

1.2 THE EQUALITY PRINCIPLE AND PROTECTION AGAINST DISCRIMINATION

There is an embedded tension between the idea that every person has equal value with every other person and the protections against discrimination that

25 Joel E. Oestreich, "UNICEF and the Implementation of the Convention on the Rights of the Child," *Global Governance* 4, no. 2 (1998): 184.

26 Ibid.

27 Optional Protocol to the Convention on the Rights of the Child on a Communications Procedure, adopted December 19, 2011, entry into force April 14, 2014, UN General Assembly, Resolution A/Res/66/138.

28 Articles in CEDAW and CERD provide mechanisms for legally binding dispute resolution. Article 29, Convention on the Elimination of All Forms of Discrimination against Women (hereafter CEDAW), adopted December 18, 1979, entry into force September 3, 1981, UN General Assembly Resolution 34/180; article 22, International Convention on the Elimination of All Forms of Racial Discrimination" (hereafter CERD), adopted December 21, 1965, entry into force January 4, 1969, UN General Assembly, Resolution 2106 (XX). See, for example, Abhinaya Ramesh, "UN Convention on the Rights of the Child: Inherent Weaknesses," *Economic and Political Weekly*, June 2, 2001.

equality calls for. The first premise is that human rights are distributed as "equal and inalienable rights of all members of the human family."[29] The second premise gives the first premise a twist because there are special rights for some people – women, racial minorities, children, to name a few – that complicate the claim of inalienable equality. If there is no essential inferiority because everyone is equal, then providing special protections to certain groups is discriminatory against other groups and a violation of the equality principle. Ultimately, the question is what to do with substantive difference in formal equality. What to do about it will depend on what one believes causes the difference. Where child rights fit within the overall human rights regime is the core of the child rights question.

Inalienable rights have connotations of natural law that can lead one to think of this view of human rights as being much older than it is. Actually, the concept did not break through in the context of rights language until after World War II. Before that time, the idea that everyone should be included in the concept of the universal was invariably met with a "but" – but not for men who do not own land, but not for women, but not for black people, but not for children. There are two routes to expanding the concept of universality. One path involves putting in place robust protections against discrimination, and the other involves expanding the original scope. If one does not use the age discrimination argument, the CRC cannot be seen as expanding universal human rights for children through the first route of offering protection against discrimination. However, it could be said that the CRC has used the second route by expanding the scope of the universal human rights to include children. The challenge to that argument is that the CRC infringes upon at least one established universal provision – the freedom of religion, as addressed earlier.

However, the equality principle and its expression in the form of prohibiting discrimination are relatively new in the realm of human rights documents. In April 1919, the Paris Peace Conference rejected a suggestion from the Japanese representative to include a provision in the Covenant of the League of Nations that stated that human rights were to cover all nations and their nationals equally.[30] In 1948, the United Nations adopted the Universal Declaration, which stated in the first principle of its preamble: "Whereas recognition of the inherent dignity and of the equal and inalienable rights

[29] Universal Declaration of Human Rights, adopted December 10, 1948, UN General Assembly, Resolution 217 A (III).

[30] John Humphrey, "The International Law of Human Rights in the Middle Twentieth Century," in *The Present State of International Law and Other Essays Written in Honour of the Centenary Celebration of the International Law Association, 1873–1973*, ed. Maarten Bos (Deventer: Kluwer, 1973), 75.

of all members of the human family is the foundation of freedom, justice and peace in the world," even though at the time, the United States still had Jim Crow laws on its books.

These examples illustrate that the strength of a core value of an international agreement is revealed only when it is seen in its real-world context. "Equality" to the nations that rejected Japan's request at the Paris Peace Conference included the concept of exclusion. To the United States in 1948, "equality" included legal racial discrimination. As this book will show, the strength or weakness of the principle of children's equality is revealed in the ways equality or rights are applied in concrete situations.

1.3 UNIVERSALITY AND THE EQUALITY PRINCIPLE

In the later part of the twentieth century, there was a clear move on the part of rights analysts to push both the UN and States parties to live up to the promises of that first principle of the preamble. Yoram Dinstein argues that the UN did not begin taking the equality of human rights seriously until the mid-1960s, when the General Assembly adopted CERD (in 1965) and the ICCPR and the International Covenant on Economic, Social and Cultural Rights (ICESCR)[31] (both in 1966).[32] The adoption of CERD kicked off a wave of new conventions that addressed the equal enjoyment of human rights. Both CEDAW and CERD constructed the subject of rights by starting with the equality principle for fulfilling the universality of human rights. CERD defines the target of the convention as the behavior of the States parties:

> In this Convention, the term "racial discrimination" shall mean any distinction, exclusion, restriction or preference based on race, colour, descent, or national or ethnic origin which has the purpose or effect of nullifying or impairing the recognition, enjoyment or exercise, on an equal footing, of human rights and fundamental freedoms in the political, economic, social, cultural or any other field of public life.[33]

CEDAW also described the behaviors it seeks to prohibit:

> For the purpose of the present Convention, the term "discrimination against women" shall mean any distinction, exclusion or restriction made on the

[31] International Covenant on Economic, Social and Cultural Rights, adopted December 16, 1966, entry into force January 3, 1976, UN General Assembly, Resolution 2200A (XXI).

[32] Yoram Dinstein, "Human Rights: Implementation through the UN System," *Proceedings of the Annual Meeting (American Society of International Law April 5–8, 1995)* 89, Structures of the World Order (1995): 242–247.

[33] Article 1(1), CERD.

> basis of sex which has the effect or purpose of impairing or nullifying the recognition, enjoyment or exercise by women, irrespective of their marital status, on a basis of equality of men and women, of human rights and fundamental freedoms in the political, economic, social, civil or any other field.[34]

Both conventions thus construct the subject of the rights by combining descriptions of discriminatory acts with prescriptive statements that such acts ought not to take place. The search for mechanisms to challenge the named wrongs gave rise to the rights-holding subject in both CERD and CEDAW.

These treaties began first and foremost as protections against discrimination, and logically, they uphold the universality of human rights because what they seek to guarantee is the full enjoyment of human rights through the elimination of discrimination standing in its way. As already mentioned, the CRC does not have an equivalent provision that constitutes the child as a subject through the prohibition of child discrimination. In other words, unlike CERD and CEDAW, the CRC is not founded on the principle of equality as part of the universality of human rights, and its prescriptive force does not stem from narrowing the distance between the description of society as it is (unequal) and the hope that society will become what it ought to be (equal). This seems to support the argument that child rights is its own regime, especially considering that article 2 of the CRC has a general prohibition against racial and gender discrimination, among other protected categories:

> States Parties shall respect and ensure the rights set forth in the present Convention to each child within their jurisdiction without discrimination of any kind, irrespective of the child's or his or her parent's or legal guardian's race, colour, sex, language, religion, political or other opinion, national, ethnic or social origin, property, disability, birth or other status.[35]

A more recent set of child rights is developing in line with intersectionality theory and seeing children in their social context. This might be more frequently done outside the field of law, for example, Michael Wyness, using a sociological approach, grounds his studies in the specific place where he encounters the child in his study.[36] In law, Nazia Yaqub gives a different perspective on child rights, through the lens of the Muslim community in the

[34] Article 1, CEDAW.

[35] Article 2, CRC. For an overview of the protection against discrimination provision in the CRC, see Marit Skivenes and Karl Harlad Søvig, eds., *Child Rights and International Discrimination Law: Implementing Article 2 of the United Nations Convention on the Rights of the Child* (New York: Routledge, 2019).

[36] Michael Wyness, *Childhood and Society*, 3rd ed. (London: Bloomsbury Publishing, 2019).

United Kingdom where children are seen by the courts to be at risk of being abducted to Islamic jurisdictions.[37] Catherine Smith addresses children living with same-sex parents as a group of children whose rights need to be understood in its social context.[38] Both Yaqub and Smith can rely on external legal frameworks outside child rights for their arguments. The question is whether child rights themselves are able to sustain this type of legal theoretical scrutiny; when child rights move from the general abstract to a place-specific context. The challenge is how to make that move within child rights as a legal regime. My argument in this book is that in order to move to where the specific social context of the child also becomes part of the identity formation of the child, we must begin to take child rights theoretically seriously by examining the very child-right-identity construction itself.

1.4 TEMPORAL UNIVERSALISM

The child-rights identity is temporary; everyone will outgrow this identity when entering adulthood. The child-rights identity is not made out of biological essentialism nor is it made out of its counterargument, social construction formed in subjugation. Instead, child rights are grounded in the universally shared status of being a child or having been a child. Child rights create a temporal universalism, having at one point covered every now living adult. Rather than a Hobbesian idea of possessive individualism founded in the notion of freedom, child rights universalism is transitional.[39] Everyone once had the identity of a child that they passed through on the way to adulthood. Because child rights have an expiration date, the child identity differs from other forms of identity that offer rights in perpetuity. Because of this, the child identity cannot be examined with the same methods analysts use to critique the essentialization of raced and gendered identities. Social definitions of the child can, of, course be critiqued as being constructed on

[37] Nazia Yaqub, *Parental Child Abduction to Islamic Law Countries: A Child Rights Analysis of the Legal Framework* (London: Bloomsbury Publishing, 2022).

[38] Catherine Smith, "Equal Protection for Children of Same-Sex Parents," *Washington University Law Review* 90 (2013): 1589–1642; See also Jameson Garland and Santa Slokenberga, "Protecting the Rights of Children with Intersex Conditions from Nonconsensual Gender Conforming Medical Interventions: The View from Europe," *Medical Law Review* 27 (2019): 482–508.

[39] For an introduction to Hobbes' freedom as motion, see Quentin Skinner, *Liberty before Liberalism* (Cambridge: Cambridge University Press, 1998), 9. And how this connects to the idea of ownership of one's body in motion see C. B. Macpherson, *The Political Theory of Possessive Individualism: Hobbes to Locke* (Oxford: Oxford University Press, paperback ed. 2010 [1962]).

the basis of essentializing social impulses, but the child-rights identity as specified in the CRC cannot be defined in that way. It has no essence because it does not come with any other content than the way it depends upon age. That shell, empty of content, does not say anything about the imagined qualities of a person. It does not connect attributes with identity.

The instrumentality and function of human rights have evolved over time and place. Richard A. Falk describes the evolution of human rights from a toothless instrument that had only moral authority to an important tool of the Cold War, when human rights were used to attack the opposing side.[40] He describes how human rights have come to serve as an important instrument for resistance movements that struggle for liberation and/or recognition from what is often the majority community in a State. For a community of Indigenous people or groups that are a minority in other ways, human rights have been a platform of last resort because they originate outside the direct control of the State from which the group is seeking its liberation.[41] Eric Posner articulates a more skeptical stance toward human rights: "Until recently, hardly anyone bothered to use rigorous scientific methods to test the effect of human rights treaties and institutions."[42] He points out that only limited scientific evidence supports the practice of forcing poor countries to submit to what he views as an abstract formulation of human rights in the Western imagination.[43] David Kennedy highlights the darker, unintended consequences of a human rights agenda in which bureaucrats running high on power are not accountable to anyone.[44] The postcolonial feminist theorist Ratna Kapur has made a serious critique of human rights. She demonstrates how human rights, and especially the desire of Western women to emancipate the women of the Global South, are reproducing colonial patterns and Western imaginations of savagery in the South.[45] A common theme among the critical legal schools is that the normative and prescriptive claims of human rights conflict with the way their goals function in the world and/or that the presumptions of human rights advocates about the subjects of human rights regimes are socially constructed reflections of bias. None of these

40 Richard A. Falk, *Human Rights Horizons* (New York: Routledge, 2000), 58–59.

41 Ibid.

42 Eric A. Posner, *The Twilight of Human Rights Law* (Oxford: Oxford University Press, 2014), 143.

43 Ibid., 147.

44 David Kennedy, *The Dark Sides of Virtue: Reassessing International Humanitarianism* (Princeton, NJ: Princeton University Press, 2005).

45 Ratna Kapur, "The Tragedy of Victimization Rhetoric: Resurrecting the 'Native' Subject in International/Post-Colonial Feminist Legal Politics," *Harvard Human Rights Journal* 15, no. 2 (2002): 1–38.

critical approaches are easily transferred to child rights because neither social inequality nor a clear common vision of society, of universal liberty, is the starting point of the CRC.[46]

As an almost universal legally binding rights instrument, the CRC has moved child rights from a regime based on social and cultural values to a formal rights-based regime of black-letter law. I will admit that I am conflicted over this move. As a legal scholar who has studied the theory of rights within the field of critical legal studies on the one hand and on the other hand having been a child rights activist most of my life I find myself in a similar position as Patricia Williams and most scholars in critical race theory when confronted by the internal contradiction of the person believing in the efficacy of rights while at the same time fighting their shortcomings.[47] In what is now an iconic argument, Williams explained how even though she and Peter Gabel were both law professors, his position as a white male and her position as a black woman, both in America, made their relationships to formal versus substantive law inherently different. For him, throwing formalism overboard is a progressive act, symbolizing a rejection of conservativism, while for her, rights are what give her a formal claim to equal treatment and the possibility of a legal claim against discrimination.[48] For Duncan Kennedy, my supervisor and academic role model, and the founder of critical legal studies, the idea of human rights is a theoretical fantasy.[49] Why would the State as the maker of rights create any tool powerful enough to threaten its continued existence and operation in a serious way? Critical race theory cannot easily answer this question. If it is argued that the State, or at least the operation of the State, is inherently racist and sexist because racism and sexism are structural in society, then rights become nothing but window dressing.

46 In previous work, I have addressed the postcolonial bias of those who police the CRC's implementation but not such a bias in the content of the treaty. See Maria Grahn-Farley, "Neutral Law and Eurocentric Lawmaking: A Postcolonial Analysis of the UN Convention on the Rights of the Child," *Brooklyn Journal of International Law* 34, no. 1 (2008): 1–32. For an important postcolonial contribution, see Elizabeth A. Faulkner and Conrad Nyamutata, "The Decolonisation of Children's Rights and the Colonial Contours of the Convention on the Rights of the Child," *International Journal of Children's Rights* 28 (2020): 66–88.

47 See Duncan Kennedy, "The Critique of Rights in Critical Legal Studies," in *Left Legalism/Left Critique*, ed. Wendy Brown and Janet E. Halley (Durham, NC: Duke University Press, 2002); and Patricia Williams, *The Alchemy of Race and Rights* (Cambridge, MA: Harvard University Press, 1992).

48 Patricia J. Williams, "Alchemical Notes: Reconstructing Ideals from Deconstructed Rights," *Harvard Civil Rights–Civil Liberties Law Review* 401 (1987): 80–90.

49 Duncan Kennedy, "Legal Education and the Reproduction of Hierarchy," *Journal of Legal Education* 32, no. 4 (1982): 591–615.

Still, having been a child who participated in ushering in the child rights era, I cannot deny that child rights empowered me vis-à-vis adults and has come in very real ways to shape my life and I have at first hand observed the power of child rights as an instrument making other children's lives better than they would be without rights. This is where I can say that formalism has value, even though it is not a magic bullet against subjugation and even if it is vulnerable to being used against its original purpose by virtue of its open-endedness. This is where I end up with Williams and other critical race theory scholars. It is not that we do not understand the weakness of rights, but our lived experience also tells us that our lives would have been worse without the formal identity-based rights now available in law. At some points in life, form over substance has its own value, even if more often than not we see and experience the shallowness of formal rights.

Before 1989, human rights regimes defined the child only within the context of socioeconomic and cultural values. The CRC made an absolute switch to defining the child only through the legal construction of age without the possibility of any other influences on how that definition is constructed. In its first article, the CRC legally defines the identity of the child as "every human being under the age of eighteen years."[50] This definition of the child is delinked from the body and the mind of both children and adults. It is delinked from the body and the mind of children because there is no room within this identity construction for the rights-holding subject to shape its definition, and it is delinked from the mind and body of any adults because whatever their perception of what a child is, it will not affect the legal definition.

The use of age as the identity-constituting element for the child-rights identity, and the almost universal ratification of the CRC, comes close to what Pierre Schlag describes as "a coherent global model of law."[51] However, Schlag doubts that a comprehensive global model of law is possible.[52] He delivers an equally devastating critique of realism, stating that the fact that "realism is both partial and merely an approach means that it is not in charge of its own destiny."[53] In other words, law does not apply itself. It is people embedded in social structures and shaped by the social context in which they live who apply the law. This critique can be leveled against the hyperconcrete child-rights identity the CRC creates. As critical theory has shown, even though the identities of women and minorities are often presented as

50 Article 1, CRC.

51 Pierre Schlag, "Formalism and Realism in Ruins (Mapping the Logics of Collapse)," *Comparative Law Review* 4, no. 1 (2013): 22.

52 Ibid., 23.

53 Ibid.

unchanging and fixed, in fact, they are fluid and change over time and space. That change is what opens law up for critique and sparks ways to imagine another future, ways that the law helps bring into being, instead of serving as an obstacle. In contrast, the child identity of the CRC is fixed, and what changes is not the meaning of the identity but the person holding the identity – by growing up. In comparison with, for example, civil rights claims, differently constructed rights claims will demand a different form of critical analysis from that which critical theory has developed when it comes to gender and race.

1.5 MONISM IN CHILD RIGHTS

When I refer to the child-rights identity as monist, I do not use the term to mean that international law and the laws of States form a unity as monism is typically used in international law.[54] I use it to refer to the fact that the CRC has created a definition of a child-rights identity that has only one meaning. That identity is free of subjectivity and beyond the possibility of social construction because it is connected to one single data point – a person's age outside the reach of the social. It lacks the interplay between the social and the legal to be found in other forms of identity constructions. The consequence of this is that any argument based on how child rights operate in the world is either pushed outside the realm of law and into the realm of subjectivity and opinion, or it is completely contained within the formalism of law, unable to connect to the effects of its application. This means that if one wants to use child rights as an argument on behalf of an actual child, one must either work outside the realm of law completely or rely in totality on a hyperformal legal construction of a child, unable to take into account the actual child in its social context. The argument becomes one that relies either on the pure strength of its persuasiveness or on the pure force of formalism. It is not able to take into account the interconnectedness between the descriptive and prescriptive elements of law, to describe society as it is while also pointing society toward what it ought be. Instead of child rights being able to serve as a critique of society and provide an alternative imaginary, they get stuck in the static question of compliance and violation.

One issue that illustrates the distance between the hyperformalized child-rights identity and what is actually taking place is child sex trafficking. Pantea Javidan describes how this practice pushes the child outside the sphere of

[54] For a contemporary address on monism in international law see Paul Gragl, *Legal Monism: Law, Philosophy, and Politics (International Law and Domestic Legal Orders)* (New York: Oxford University Press, 2018).

child rights and into the sphere of criminal law.[55] Her analysis demonstrates that sex work theory is unable to deal with the identity of the child as constructed by law because it relies on the adult/child binary and assigns the capacities of adults to children, even though children are clearly in a much weaker position than even socially weak adults.[56] I am not arguing that law is not also part of socially constructing the child; what I am arguing is that the child-rights identity is not open to social factors. Barbara Bennett Woodhouse is a scholar who has developed the understanding of the social construction of the child with the help of law. Her work looks at how legal concepts of minority status reflect social views of children as incapable of being rational persons and in need of adult supervision.[57] But this form of valuable social critique is difficult to squeeze into the CRC's construction of the child-rights identity since the social construction of children is foreclosed to the child-rights identity. Since the child as the subject of rights pre-exists any act taken by a State party, it is constructed by the law and not by actions in the social realm. This makes the child subject look deceptively like the *a priori* constructed human rights subject that Hersch Lauterpacht imagines. That would be an argument for the claim that child rights are inherent and fall within the realm of universal human rights. But it would be a mistake to draw the conclusion that child rights have finally realized the *a priori* universality Lauterpacht dreams of – the subject who has liberated herself from social constructions.[58] This is because what creates that *a priori* is not connected to the human condition but to the way we orbit the Sun, creating years on Earth.

Despite all the differences in how the child has been socially constructed compared to its identity construction through law, the topic has been under-examined in law. The child-rights identity is the only identity international law has created that is not tethered to the societies in which it operates.

1.6 SUBJECTHOOD AND CHILD RIGHTS

The social aspect of subjecthood is central to the law. Anne Peters examines the relationship between the prescriptive and descriptive characters of law in

55 Pantea Javidan, "American Legal Discourse on Child Trafficking: The Re/Production of Inequalities and Persistence of Child Criminalization" (PhD diss., London School of Economics and Political Science, London, 2017), 53.

56 Ibid., 296.

57 Barbara Bennett Woodhouse, "Re-Visioning Rights for Children," in *Rethinking Childhood*, ed. Peter B. Pufall and Richard P. Unsworth (Rutgers, NJ: Rutgers University Press, 2003), 229.

58 Hersch Lauterpacht, *An International Bill of the Rights of Man* (repr., 2013 [1945], Oxford: Oxford University Press, 2013), 3–4.

the context of the individual as a subject in international law.[59] She questions the view that sanctions are necessary when constructing individual subjecthood within international law.[60] Neil MacCormick deals with the duality of what he calls personhood through time. He sees personhood in law as being constituted of both passive and active factors, noting that persons commit acts that others passively receive.[61] The critique of this argument is that it presumes that the ability to cause harm is evenly distributed and correlates to the distribution of those who are the passive recipients of harmful acts. Personal identity as MacCormick defines it draws on the idea of sameness, the view that a person is the same over time and space and that power is evenly divided among persons.[62] Critical legal theory takes this assumption to task. In critical legal theory, power and harm are distributed through social hierarchies, the same hierarchies that force persons into identities through subjugating force.[63]

The question of subjecthood is of significance to child rights in practice. Subjecthood cannot be disregarded when examining how law, and particularly rights, construct identity, but identity and subjecthood are not overlapping concepts. Peters notes that "the child is a holder of (human) rights irrespective of the child's capacity to act, i.e., the capacity to exercise those rights."[64] Identity, in contrast, is not centered on the relationship between substantive and procedural rights. However, neither is it wholly delinked from this relationship because law and the possibility of claiming one's rights contribute to the understanding of the "I" as seen through the eyes of the "Other." From a political theory position, Francis Fukuyama has reopened the discussion of how recognition of one's identity plays into a sense of dignity and self-worth.[65] The part that law plays in the process when social subjugation also creates identities is well documented by legal scholars who address

59 Anne Peters, *Beyond Human Rights: The Legal Status of the Individual in International Law* (Cambridge: Cambridge University Press, 2000), 35.

60 Ibid., 47–48.

61 Neil MacCormick, *Institutions of Law: An Essay in Legal Theory* (Oxford: Oxford University Press, 2007), 78.

62 Ibid.

63 See, for example, Scott Veitch's argument on the construction of debt and the distribution of obligations; Scott Veitch, "The Sense of Obligation," *Jurisprudence: An International Journal of Legal and Political Thought* 8, no. 3 (2017): 415–434.

64 Peters, *Beyond Human Rights*, 48–56, referring to Inter-American Court of Human Rights, "Judicial Condition and Human Rights of the Child," Advisory Opinion No. 17, August 28, 2002.

65 Francis Fukuyama, *Identity: The Demand for Dignity and the Politics of Resentment* (New York: Farrar, Straus and Giroux, 2018).

intersectionality and multiple consciousness.[66] In those analyses, both law and society construct identities that force women of color, for example, to choose either race or gender as their manifested identity while feeling that they belong to both and do not fit into either. Both intersectionality and multiple consciousness theory have at the center the element of harm to one's dignity when one's identity is not recognized. Children cannot demand recognition of their identity or express indignation of it being misinterpreted because the child-rights identity does not depend on recognition, and its construction is not an expression of society in flux.

1.7 CONCLUSION

It is difficult to make the argument that child rights are part of the universal human rights regime in the form of a set of rights that seeks to make the universal enjoyment of human rights accessible. That is because there is no substantial link between the universal human rights regime and the child rights regime in the form of protection against discrimination. However, on an ethical level, children are, of course, humans. In that sense, there is a gap between the child rights regime and the universal human rights regime, a gap that has not yet been fully bridged. (It is not even clear if that is the aim of the child rights regime.) At the same time, it might serve children well to have their own universal regime.

One of the crucial steps for retaining the significance of child rights is developing a plurality of child rights approaches and schools that can both challenge each other and catalyze new forms of theoretical and legal arguments that are positioned to take on the challenges of a society that is very different from the one I knew as a child. I grew up when democracy was on the rise, but my daughter is becoming an adult during the largest decline in democracy since World War II. It is important for children to experience the recognition of their identity, as Fukuyama notes. But he also points out that the failure to recognize one's identity can be linked to a failure in granting that recognition to others. Our appreciation for an inclusive democracy rests on our ability to see each other and to be accepted for what we are.

[66] Angela P. Harris, "Race and Essentialism in Feminist Legal Theory," *Stanford Law Review* 42, no. 3 (1990): 581–616; Kimberlé Crenshaw, "Demarginalizing the Intersection of Race and Sex: A Black Feminist Critique of Antidiscrimination Doctrine, Feminist Theory and Antiracist Politics," *University of Chicago Legal Forum* 140 (1989): 139–167; Adrien Katherine Wing, "Violence and State Accountability: Critical Race Feminism," *Georgia Journal of Gender and Law* 1 (1999–2000): 95–114.

Why does this quite theoretical understanding of identity construction matter when it comes to child rights? It matters because this construction also becomes the limiting factor in how society and laws other than the CRC talk about children. This understanding shapes how people imagine that children operate, and most importantly, it is the law that protects, controls, helps, or liberates the child. All of these factors are connected to how people understand the child-rights identity. Until we can resolve and deliver a credible definition of what constitutes the authority of child rights, to go beyond merely interpreting and applying child rights (which today remain unspecified), the impact of the child rights regime in advancing and – more importantly – protecting an open, inclusive democratic society for coming generations will be weaker than it should be. Today's children are the adults of the future, and if the child-rights identity fails to include the possibility of recognition, how then will children come to want to preserve that possibility for others?

Most importantly, who has the legitimacy to question and reconstruct the identity the CRC created? Do children have the legitimacy to analyze whether the given identity works for them? Before we critically examine if this is even a possibility, it will also be a challenge to motivate young people to preserve and protect the values of democracy and inclusion in the service of social justice and change. Those values are worth more than the so much easier and more direct ways of addressing change that we see in the authoritarian wave currently sweeping across the previous centers of stable democracies, shifting the conditions for critically engaging in social change and justice through ideas of inclusion and recognition.

2

The Monist Construction of the Child

Without Mind or Body

The use of age as the sole element to define the identity of the child, making the definition incapable of taking social and lived experiences or realities into account, results in a monist construction of a child identity. As a child, I did not think about myself as not existing or being less than a full person because I did not know that I had rights. Learning about child rights did not make me feel more of a person. However, I have encountered people who want to save children but do not think that children should have rights. So clearly rights are important not only for the people who have them but also to others not directly affected by children having rights. Evidently, a person does not need rights to exist, even though rights are often connected to personhood. Rights and personhood have historically been strongly connected to civil rights. The example that comes first to mind is the civil rights struggle in the American South, sprung out of a history of slavery. There law and society were equated, through law, individuals were legally turned into objects of property through enslavement, and consequently, socially, they no longer existed, as if they had socially died.[1] This view in later years has been challenged, for example, by literature professor Saidiya Hartman, who distinguishes between how others understand your agency, and what that agency might mean to yourself and your own understanding of who you are.[2]

A coined phrase in child rights is that the CRC turned children into subjects of rights instead of objects of care. This can be debated in ways similar to the idea that civil rights are what created personhood among

[1] The concept of social death was made infamous by Orlando Patterson with his book, Orlando Patterson, *Slavery and Social Death: A Comparative Study* (Cambridge, MA: Harvard University Press, 1982).

[2] Saidya Hartman, *Scenes of Subjection: Terror, Slavery, and Self-Making in Nineteenth Century America* (Oxford: Oxford University Press, 1997).

formerly enslaved persons in the American South. Enslaved people were, of course, persons, even though others did not recognize their civil rights, in the same way as children were persons before the CRC. Children do not become thinking beings with agency because they have rights, but rights rather prescribe that people surrounding the child must recognize the agency and personhood of the child, not that a child is incapable of having agency without adult permission.

That children have rights was not widely accepted at the time of the adoption of the CRC among human rights activists, not even within Save the Children itself. The switch from a child caring paradigm to a child rights paradigm was controversial among grassroots organizations. Works by scholars such as Michael Freeman center around the battle for children to be seen as active subjects of rights that force adults to take children's agency seriously.[3] Freeman's position at the time of the adoption of the CRC was controversial and radical, and not necessarily accepted even among child-promoting groups. Over time, his work has helped normalize the view of children as social actors with individual will and rights. Possibly because of the resistance that scholars like Freeman met in the early child rights days, further nuances of child rights were lost as the resistance against seeing children as full subjects of rights was so strong. The debate over whether a child should and could have rights risked overshadowing the more nuanced debate as to how these rights should be constructed as well as the resulting consequences dependent on the construction assigned to the child in the early days of child rights.

Whether child rights are part of the universality of human rights, or in themselves universal, raises not only the question of systemic coherency, as addressed in the previous chapter where we examined whether child rights are a regime to guarantee the full enjoyment of universal human rights, or if child rights create their own systemic universalism. To understand child rights and their relation to universal human rights, one must also examine the construction of these rights. This construction has two components, the child and the right itself. We begin here by examining the child as constructed through the CRC, followed by the right itself.

2.1 SOCIAL CONSTRUCTION AND AGE

The CRC constructs the child through law in a manner that disconnects the process of creating the identity from social variations. Article 1 of the CRC

3 A position reinforced in his later work, Michael Freeman, A *Magna Carta for Children?: Rethinking Children's Rights* (Cambridge: Cambridge University Press, 2020).

defines a child as “every human being below the age of eighteen years unless under the law applicable to the child, majority is attained earlier.” The need to address the construction of child rights had previously not been palpable until the adoption of the CRC. Even though there is room for modification in the second part of the article, the convention maintains the same focus on age as being the subject creator. The two previous declarations, which were not legally binding, did not provide any definition or construction of a child. The Geneva Declaration on the Rights of the Child from 1924 leaves it to each State party to define what constitutes a child for the purposes of the declaration.[4] The UN Declaration on the Rights of the Child from 1959 provides a social and biological construction through negation in relationship to adults, in the preamble by declaring that “the child, by reason of his physical and mental immaturity, needs special safeguards,” indicating that to be a child is to be immature, and that it is this immaturity that gives rise to the rights in the declaration.[5] Still, the exact definition of who is a child is left to each State party to define.

The strength of the child identity construction in the CRC is also its weakness. The strength of the CRC by not using social construction avoids the entanglement with perpetuating abusive subordination, which is the weakness of socially constructed identities when the subjugation process (the creation of the subject) often takes place through subordination.[6] Or where they are constructed out of privilege in a child rights framework the equivalent would be to initiate a field of “adulthood studies”; even when a field comes out of a position of privilege, it comes out of someone else’s subordination, as with whiteness studies in critical race theory. Whiteness studies, in the exploration of subject construction out of privilege, has turned the process of subjugation against itself in illustrative manners that might also inform child rights studies.[7] It is therefore not necessarily a negative thing that the child identity in the CRC is not a social construction. It is a clear benefit that social inequalities and prejudices are not carried over to the child identity even when it makes it more difficult to take into account social realities of the particular children. However, there is also a weakness in placing the child

4 League of Nations, Geneva Declaration of the Rights of the Child, adopted September 26, 1924.

5 UN Declaration of the Rights of the Child, adopted November 20, 1959, General Assembly, Resolution 1386 (XIV).

6 For a comprehensive study of social construction and intersectionality see Adrien Katherine Wing, *Global Critical Race Feminism* (New York: New York University Press, 2000).

7 For an example of a study on whiteness in the educational setting see, Angelina E. Castagno, “Multicultural Education and the Protection of Whiteness,” *American Journal of Education* 120 (2013): 101–128.

identity outside the reach of social construction as it cannot then be adjusted or made to reflect social change that might be positive. It cannot reflect local conditions and particular circumstances, and it has a clear deficit in the sense that the child herself cannot participate in her own identity creation, which is a basic condition for other identity constructions. If child rights are constructed out of age, it should be possible to develop a "back-up" approach when the strict application of age in specific situations becomes impossible to apply or clearly unjust to enforce.

2.2 DENATURALIZING AGE

The child-rights identity in the CRC is not a case of law attempting to describe a child and failing to do so, but instead, it is an attempt to construct a child out of an unconnected fact, the orbiting of the Earth around the Sun, through the force of law. Questioning presumed links between causes and effects is done in many forms. For example, Alf Ross, in his (in)famous Scandinavian realist article, Tû Tû, describes how Tû Tû gains mystical meaning founded in what he describes as "a state of darkest superstition,"[8] on the South Pacific island of Noît-cif, when one expression gains both prescriptive and descriptive force.[9] Denaturalization is another example of questioning the presumed link between cause and effect, this time from a critical approach. The classic example of this is Judith Butler's denaturalization of gender. She writes, "Just as bodily surfaces are enacted as the natural, so these surfaces can become the site of a dissonant and denaturalized performance that reveals the performative status of the natural itself."[10]

In its technicality, age is the most primal of relationships, the one between the Earth and the Sun. Only that which can change is open to critique, and the orbiting of the Earth around the Sun will not change before the Sun burns out. The site of denaturalization here becomes the nexus between the elements of Earth's orbiting of the Sun and the CRC's reliability on age for the construction of the child subject. Age, as a conceptualization of how many times the Earth has circled the Sun, is the Tû Tû of child rights. That which we must do is denaturalize the "superstitious" linking between identity and the assumption that the Sun generates substantive knowledge about an individual person. The insistence that a person must prove her identity by proving her exact age to the

[8] Alf Ross, "Tû Tû," *Harvard Law Review* 79 (1957): 812.

[9] Ibid., 813.

[10] Judith Butler, *Gender Trouble: Feminism and the Subversion of Identity* (New York: Routledge, 2007 [1990]), 244.

day must be open to question. This Tû Tû, in some instances, holds the power to determine the individual outcome between life and death.

2.3 THE YEAR OF THE REFUGEE CRISIS

A good place to start this investigation of the monist child identity forged out of age, free from the need of a factual connection to the individual person or the place of the person, can be found in the year 2015, which is often described as the year of the European refugee crisis.[11] Even though the war in Syria was the impetus for most of the migrants arriving in Europe that year, the situation was slightly different when it came to unaccompanied minors – they were mostly males from Afghanistan and not Syria.[12] In the EU, there was a drastic increase in persons claiming unaccompanied minor status seeking asylum between the years 2013 and 2015, with such applications increasing from just above 10,000 persons in 2013 to almost 90,000 in 2015.[13] According to Eurostat, the statistical office of the European Union, Sweden was the EU Member State that received and registered the highest number of these children.[14] The EU connects its definition of the unaccompanied minor to the definition of the child in the CRC, using the age below eighteen as the definition of a minor.[15]

These Afghani males were classified as either children or adults, depending on which side of the eighteen-year-old line they could prove they belonged.[16] Unaccompanied minors make up a category of individuals that is a reminder

[11] BBC called it the migrant crisis, see BBC, "Migrant Crisis: Migration to Europe Explained in Seven Charts," March 4, 2016, www.bbc.com/news/world-europe-34131911, last accessed June 23, 2022.

[12] Eurostat, Press Release, 87/2016 – May 2, 2016.

[13] Ibid.

[14] Ibid.

[15] The EU applies the definition of the CRC for what constitute a child when it uses the terminology "minor." See, for example, Anja Radjenovic, "Vulnerability of Unaccompanied and Separated Child Migrants, Briefing," European Parliament, EPRS, PE 690.575, April 2021, p. 2. For a nuanced examination of the distinction between trafficked and migrated, and adult and children, see Julia O'Connell Davidson, "Moving Children? Child Trafficking, Child Migration, and Child Rights," *Critical Social Policy* 31 (2011): 454–477. Davidson brings to light how the distinction between trafficked and moved is dependent on whether a person if defined as a child or not. For an adult the distinction rests on consent, while for children it is enough to have been exploited, regardless of whether the child has given consent.

[16] Jonathan Josefsson addresses how the limitations of treaty and domestic law constructed interest groups' ability to serve as places of representation – he instead argues that representation should be understood as lived experiences of children. See, Jonathan Josefsson, "Children's Representation in Times of Inequalities and Injustice," in *The Politics of Children's Rights and Representation*, ed. Bengt Sandin, Jonathan Josefsson, Karl Hanson, and Sara Balagopalan (London: Palgrave Macmillan, 2022).

of the failure of the CRC to resolve whether children have rights that go beyond the rights of adults, or simply have rights that put them on an even par with adults. David Archard and John Tobin articulate internal and external boundaries of the child rights regime by explaining that some rights of children also entail the denial of the same rights to nonchildren.[17] One argument that child rights should be seen as a separate regime from universal human rights is that the 1959 declaration was meant to be both distinct from an adult human rights agenda and yet still intimately linked to the Universal Declaration of Human Rights (UNDHR).[18] The drafting of the child rights declaration ran as a parallel process to the development of the International Covenant on Civil and Political Rights (ICCPR)[19] and the International Covenant on Economic, Social and Cultural Rights (ICESCR).[20] The UN Social Commission expressed its intention to develop a child rights document that would establish a broad set of principles toward which the world should strive.[21]

Refugee law is one of the clearest examples of where the very fact of being a child grants additional rights and protections that go beyond the regular rights of adults. This is also why this has been such a contested debate in the aftermath of the 2015 refugee crisis. The distinction between being classified as a child or as an adult in a refugee process results in significantly different available recourses. While those who are eighteen or seventeen-and-a-half behave socially in a similar way and might see themselves as the same cohort, regardless of the eighteen-year-old divide, their new lives are radically different, for example, in Sweden for an Afghani male, depending on whether the taxation authority classifies him as seventeen or eighteen years old. As a child, he will have free housing, free education, and free food and live in a family house–like setting with staff around the clock tasked to care for his needs. If he is classified as an adult, he will most likely have to rely on the provision of social services for people without financial means, with no automatic rights to housing or food or care.

17 David Archard and John Tobin, "Article 1: The Definition of the Child," in *The UN Convention on the Rights of the Child: A Commentary*, ed. John Tobin (Oxford: Oxford University Press, 2019).

18 An International Bill of Human Rights, Universal Declaration of Human Rights, adopted December 10, 1948, UN General Assembly, Resolution 217 A (III); for the decision to develop a parallel child rights instrument, see E/CN.5/L.96.

19 International Covenant on Civil and Political Rights, adopted December 16, 1966, entry into force March 23, 1978, UN General Assembly, Resolution 2200A (XXI).

20 International Covenant on Economic, Social and Cultural Rights, adopted December 16, 1966, entry into force January 3, 1976, UN General Assembly, Resolution 2200A (XXI).

21 E/CN.5/L.96.

2.4 THE SOCIETY IT TAKES TO DETERMINE AGE

Not only has the Tû Tû of child rights in the form of age overwhelming power over the destiny of individual persons, the issue of age also requires us to examine the challenges for societies to build and maintain an administration capable of producing reliable data for establishing an identity dependent on the correctly documented date of birth. Our foster daughter has a sister still remaining in the home country with a small child. When the child was born I kept insisting on the importance of her sister registering the birth. I felt I was not really getting anywhere with my reminders of how important this was. Finally our foster daughter just stated it plainly to me, there is no place where her sister lives to register the birth of a child. For the CRC to invoke age as the sole thing constructing the child-rights identity, we have not only limited the security of child rights to this marker, but this marker of age, based on evidence of the exact date of birth, as gathered by societies valuing and having certain functionalities, reduces the availability of such proof of age to a narrow span of societies. In addition, this also effectively risks excluding places where child rights can be invoked as the exact recording of a person's birth date in a large part of the world is not bureaucratically possible or that highly valued. This means that child rights that are designed to protect exceptionally vulnerable children who come from places of war or who are displaced because of war will be ineffective, as those children will not have access to formal registration at birth. Not all states have the bureaucracies – required by this CRC definition – with the capacity to track and document every single birth within its domain and to maintain accurate records of the individual person until the age of eighteen. Nor are all bureaucracies formed by a universal appreciation of keeping track on each person by using the birth date as an identifier. It is true that in some parts of the world, societal systems and cultures identify individuals through birth dates, but there are many societies that do not. There are still many places where individuals are born into the world without their individual identity being constructed by their date of birth. The reality is that the coverage of the administrative state varies from place to place, and even if there is a right to be registered at birth in the CRC, this is far from a universal reality.

Age as the construction of a child-rights identity is not only an ontological challenge but also a highly practical and concrete concern. The level of public administration needed for the maintenance of birth records of each and every born child cannot be taken for granted. For example, children born at home in many countries are not part of systematic records of birth on the level that maternity wards have in place.

Some of the unaccompanied minors I met in 2015 withheld their administrative age deliberately, while others had a genuine question about this issue. This is the year my family met Lisa (her real name is different). She had just arrived in Sweden when we met. She was an exception in more ways than one: She was a girl, with females making up just 9 percent of those who arrived in 2015 and she was not from Afghanistan but from a country located on the African continent. She was younger than seventeen and possibly even younger than thirteen. No one really knows, including Lisa herself.

Lisa, my daughter Astrid, and I met at an ice rink where she was learning how to skate. In Sweden, children learn how to skate around four years of age, and this girl was clearly older than that. She seemed to be at least eleven, the age she had been assigned by the taxation authorities upon her arrival in Sweden, which also happened to be the age of my own daughter, a figure skater at the time and the basic reason why I volunteered to give figure-skating lessons on Sunday mornings at the figure-skating club. Lisa had been lucky to be placed in a well-functioning house together with other unaccompanied minors. She was the only girl there among mostly Afghani males. One of the persons working in the house taking care of the children had decided that Lisa should learn how to skate so that she could be able to participate in physical education at school. Lisa came to the ice rink with a note in Swedish saying that she should learn how to skate. This is how we met, and over the years, both my daughter and I have grown close to Lisa, who is now an important part of our family.

This is also how I realized that my own birthday was probably not so precise and not so certain as I had always thought but I had arrived to Sweden in the time when we still celebrated name days. We had known Lisa for only a few months, and we were taking her out for lunch, together with one of the staff from the home where she lived. During lunch, the caregiver told me that it would soon be Lisa's birthday. I told her that it would also be my birthday before long. It turned out that it was, in fact, the same day! When we had figured out that it was the same day, Lisa first looked excited but soon got a sad look upon her face. I asked her why she looked sad. It turned out that it was not her actual birthday but the day that she had been given when she came to Sweden. It then struck me for the first time in my whole life that, living in Sweden as an adopted person, it was probably not my real birthday either, that it was a date I also had been given when I arrived in Sweden in the early seventies as an adoptee from South Korea. I had always presumed that my birth date on record was also my factual birthday. I now realized that it of course was not, and that it was an administrative date of birth. The reason why I had never questioned this distinction between an administrative date of birth and a factual birthday was because this had not been of importance in the

Sweden I grew up in. When the public sector was still public and not as now a privatized voucher system the billing system was not formalized. Today, each "user," as we are now called, must be correctly documented for the private provider to be able to bill the State for the cost of each service rendered to an individual. Age and identity all of a sudden becomes very important for accessing the basic welfare services previously provided for by the State but now in the hands of a myriad of private for-profit actors billing the State for its services.

Regardless of the authenticity of the date, we have celebrated our birthdays together since that time. On our first birthday together, we went to an outdoor museum in Stockholm and had ice cream and cake, all in all a very good day. In the car on the way back Lisa told me that it had previously made her sad to celebrate the date of birth allocated to her. The fact that she did not know her real birthday was a constant reminder that she did not have any living parents. Her parents had been killed in the war that had torn her country apart, within just a week of one another. Since then, she had lived with different extended family members until she was sent to Sweden as an unaccompanied minor. On the way home, Lisa asked me if I thought that if her mother had been alive, she would have known Lisa's birthday because were not birthdays something that mothers knew about and would keep track of for their children? I told her I was not sure as I had just myself realized that I did not know my own birthday and that it was not until I met her that I had realized that the taxation authority handed out the same day to many people without a proven birthday. By coincidence a few weeks ago, I found myself next to a group of young lawyers with family origins from the same country as Lisa. I told them about Lisa and the issue with the birthday. They all started laughing and asked me to tell her that their mothers, though very much alive, did not know their daughters' birthdays either. Birthdays were just not significant where their mothers originated from.

As shown so poignantly in Lisa's case, many people can genuinely not know their age or birthday, which can be a source of pain that makes someone feel abandoned. Or it may be, in fact, that a birth date is just an administrative decision that sometimes is deliberately withheld as information because of the wish to apply for asylum as an unaccompanied minor. The point is that in any case, it may not be possible for the State to establish the authentic birth date, and in many cases, the person and the State will have to be satisfied with just accepting the administrative date. The problem, of course, is when more than a birthday cake depends on this date, when the very identity of being a child and the rights that come with that are based on it. There is an important aspect to knowing about birth dates that one might not think about when the administrative date and the authentic date coincide: that is, where there is no need to untangle any uncertainty. However, when these dates do not coincide and when your ability to get free housing and food upon seeking asylum depend on your birthday, the question is put in a significantly different light.

2.5 PROVING AGE: SOCIETY VS. CHILDREN

As mentioned, the group of unaccompanied minors arriving in 2015 was a particularly homogenous group. Even though the war in Syria generated the refugee wave to Europe, the largest refugee group consisted of unaccompanied minors who primarily came from Afghanistan and not Syria. According to Eurostat, 51 percent of the unaccompanied minors arriving in Europe in 2015 were from Afghanistan, with the second-largest group from Syria at 16 percent.[22] A little over 45,000 unaccompanied minors arrived in the EU from Afghanistan during this time. Four out of ten applied for asylum in Sweden, and in total, 23,400 Afghani were registered in Sweden as unaccompanied minors that year.[23] Sweden was the EU Member State that had accepted the most unaccompanied minors in all of the EU – 40 percent of all EU unaccompanied minors from the whole world, a total of 35,300, applied for asylum in Sweden.[24] By way of comparison, Germany was second, with 14 percent of all minors applying there for asylum, a total of 14,400 children, followed by Hungary with 10 percent – 8,800 minors – and Austria with 9 percent – 8,300 minors.[25] Ninety-one percent of unaccompanied minors were male, and over half were between sixteen and seventeen years old – 57 percent, 50,000 persons – and 29 percent were fourteen to fifteen years old– 25,800 persons – and only 13 percent were younger than fourteen years old.[26] To put these numbers into context, Sweden today has a total of 50,670 internationally adopted people: This includes every now-living internationally adopted person, from the end of the 1960s to today.[27] In just one year, 2015,

[22] Eurostat, Press Release, 87/2016 – May 2, 2016.
[23] Ibid.
[24] Ibid.
[25] Ibid.
[26] Ibid.
[27] Official statistics from the Swedish National Board of Health and Welfare, Socialstyrelsen, "Ny kartlaggning visar brister i stöd till adopterade" [A New Survey Shows Deficiencies in Support to Adopted Children], www.socialstyrelsen.se/om-socialstyrelsen/pressrum/press/ny-kartlaggning-visar-pa-brister-i-stod-till-adopterade/, last accessed January 4, 2023. For a general overview on international adoption in Sweden see Cecilia Lindgren, *Internationell adoption i Sverige: Politik och praktik från sextiotal till nittiotal* [Adoption in Sweden: Policy and Practice from the 1960s to the 1990s] (Stockholm: Myndigheten för Internationella Adoptionsfrågor, 2010).

Sweden received 35,300 unaccompanied minors, more than half of the total number of internationally adopted children from the 1960s until today.

When I asked one of the unaccompanied minors I met why so many of them came to Sweden, the answer was that they believed that Sweden had advertised for people to send their children to them. This seemed to be a common view among these children that Sweden had asked them to come, and most of them had parents in the sender countries, but for one reason or another, it had been decided to send them to Sweden. On one of my journeys between Leeds and Manchester in the United Kingdom, the taxi driver, who himself had been an unaccompanied minor from Somalia in 2015, told me that he had friends who arrived in Sweden at the same time. I asked him about his choice to come to the UK, while his friends went to Sweden. He explained that he had come to the UK by chance and that his friends went to Sweden because, at the time, it was generally believed that it was best to go to Sweden as it was seen as the best gateway into Europe and people followed the general trend of movement.

It might often be just the luck of a draw that determines on which side of eighteen years dividing line an unaccompanied minor ends up. Furthermore, it has been shown to be an administrative impossibility to distinguish, with any degree of certainty, between seventeen- and eighteen-year-olds within these groups without the support of official public documentation, which, in many cases, is withheld or cannot be obtained, or when obtained, is not believed.[28] The use of age as the essential element of the rights-based identity of the child was adopted to avoid the debates about the influences of biology, society, and culture on legal rights that have plagued the identities of other groups, particularly women and minorities. Yet we find that we have ended up with another conundrum, one now without a vocabulary. This absence of a vocabulary to describe the discrepancy between the rights-based child identity in the CRC and its sociocultural counterpart becomes manifestly apparent when unaccompanied minors knock at the door of our borders.

In the abstract, unaccompanied minors are one of our most vulnerable groups of children and therefore in need of a specialized immigration system adjusted to children. In the words of José Noronha Rodrigues, unaccompanied children are "by their very nature, children, defenseless, sensitive and,

[28] The uncertainty of medical age tests and the call for mandatory medical age tests is now almost a forgotten debate but for a reminder of this debate, see Ned Stafford, "German Doctor's Leader Condemns Support for Refugee Age Tests," *MBJ: British Medical Journal* 360 (2018): 70.

unable to manage their person and/or assets because of their age."[29] When they show up at our borders, however, they are not necessarily as easy to identify as Rodrigues envisions, even though the regulations concerning unaccompanied minors and child rights were written for them. What happens when the person arriving at the border does not necessarily meet this acquired image of vulnerability, sadness, and victimhood but looks like an adult, and has lived socially and culturally as an adult in Afghanistan or Iran before arriving in Europe?

2.6 THE MONIST CONSTRUCTION

The child in the CRC is not a socially constructed identity but a monist construction – not dependent on a physical child or its society for its making, as the child is constructed simply by age. This process of being constituted as a subject of legal rights by years – not through experiences and mental growth, or the changing of the body – does not tell us much about children as a social identity, or about any particular child in a specific child rights application. Instead, age becomes the stand-in for the assessment of the actual child. An example of this is a Swedish Supreme Court decision concerning a female from Russia adopted in Sweden.[30] No official records of her birth in Russia existed; instead, there were two medical tests conducted at the time of adoption in 2008, one in Russia and one in Sweden; both tests concluded that she was five years old and was born in 2003. She was therefore registered by the Swedish taxation authorities as being born on November 3, 2003. This is how she socially – and legally – lived her life until 2016. She and a male person, also a child, both living in the custody and care of the State in special housing, began a sexual relation. The male was later prosecuted and convicted of statutory rape of a child because in accordance with the records of the taxation authority, she was under the age of fifteen. The case was appealed all the way to the Supreme Court. The question was whether she really was under the age of fifteen, as the taxation authority's records stated and as she had lived her life until this point. The Supreme Court reasoned, "The expression 'under the age of fifteen' must against the backdrop of the case be presumed to define a group of underage persons, that typically does not have the mental maturity required for sexual consent. In the light of this, it

[29] José Noronha Rodrigues, "Refugee and Migrant Children in Europe," in *The Rights of Unaccompanied Minors: Perspectives and Case Studies on Migrant Children*, ed. Yvonne Vissing and Sofia Leitão (New York: Springer, 2021), 87–129, at 124.

[30] Högsta domstolens dom B 5057–18, April 29, 2019.

appears obvious that the expression in all the legal sections aims at the victim's factual lived age."[31] The Court equates the number of Earth orbits around the Sun with the capability of a specific child to consent and exercise sexual autonomy. Instead of investigating her actual mental capacity, the court concluded that it is the actual days on the Earth that will determine this person's sexual maturity, and not her individual capacity. Of course, determining her factual birthday is an impossibility in this case, and therefore, she cannot be found to be beyond any reasonable doubt under the age of fifteen as the taxation records state, and the taxation records are put aside by the Court. In addition, even though the Earth and the Sun have nothing to do with an individual person's sexual capacity, the Court treats the number of days under the Sun to determine whether a person has the capacity to consent to sex. The child rights–constructed identity is wholly dependent on the documentation of birth and it is remarkable that there is no possibility of a backup plan when such knowledge is not available. The elements that go into "making" age have nothing to do with children, even though a full regime of rights is attached to the outcome of that process. This is both a symbol of modernity as it takes a fully developed and organized state administration to produce the records needed for the child-rights identity, while, at the same time, it is primordial – a most pagan practice, placed all in the power of the movement around the Sun to construct identity.

Taking up this disconnect with respect to the identity of the child is not an attempt to undo the child-rights construction itself. Rather, it is an effort to examine the consequences of what for human rights is a unique monist identity construction and it could be useful to draw inspiration from legal theories developed for bifocal or binary forms of identity constructions. Race, sexual orientation and gender are examples of how social, cultural, and biological beliefs have been and continue to be codified in law as if these are naturally appearing in society, creating a legal status that, in turn, affects and reshapes social, cultural and biological beliefs, which, in turn, affect man-made laws with the consequence that the biological belief comes to look natural.[32] To use age in different forms of legislation or social practices is not new. For example, age is a recognized form of discrimination within the European Convention of Human Rights, even though it is not an identity-constituting category.[33] What is new with the CRC is the constituting of an

[31] Ibid., para. 14.

[32] In Swedish Erik Mägi and Lina-leas Zimmerman have written about the child within the rainbow family, see, Stjärnfamiljejuridik (Falkenberg: Gleerup, 2015).

[33] Age under the European Convention on Human Rights has been found to be a protected "other status" for the purpose of discrimination protection, See for example, *Schwizgebel v. Switzerland*, Application No. 25762/07, June 10, 2010, first section.

identity that brings with it the applicability of a complete rights regime that otherwise is not applicable, instead of the regulation of a particular situation.

Where the social child as an identity differs is in its absence of a relation with its legal status. The child-rights identity is a pure legal construction. The function of law itself when it comes to other forms of legal identity constructions normally serves a masking or a reinforcing role of already socially construed identities. Compare the function of law when it comes to the child-rights identity of gender, sexual orientation, and race, which are constructed through an interplay between law and social context. Both political goals and critical legal scholarship have focused on deconstructing how statuses based on gender, sexual orientation, and race are constructed out of subordination and not nature. This demonstrates how society has either created differences where there are none or has emphasized differences by codification of discriminatory social and cultural practices. When biological beliefs provide a thin veneer of acceptability for bigotry, law in these instances help masks the subjugating social practice in making an identity by using the power of the State through law to enforce social practice with legal precision, thus making the social practice seem like a social order upheld by nature. When it comes to the use of age to define the legal status of the child, it is the negation of that status that is used to define it – the age of majority, when a person is no longer a child but an adult – and this is also how we know that someone is not a child. It is important to note that the capacity of the person under the age of eighteen years is legally constructed through age and not through a factual capacity or through social context. The child identity should be distinguished from the social condition of childhood. This distinction between child identity and childhood can be illustrated by Neil MacCormick's use of childhood to illustrate the varied capacities that evolve over the period of childhood.[34] This is a different set of statuses compared to the child-rights identity itself, which is characterized by precisely the omission of a gradation in capacity and status. The legal use of different ages within the rights identity of the child (below the age of majority) does not affect the identity construction per se, for in the identity construction, it is only the age of majority that matters for the constitution of the child-rights identity. Allowing driving at the age of sixteen years does not change the fact that the age of eighteen years constitutes the child-rights identity per se. Returning back to the Swedish supreme court case concerning the Russian adopted girl

[34] For a developed exploration of the use of age in law – within the child identity itself, see Neil MacCormick, *Institutions of Law: An Essay in Legal Theory* (Oxford: Oxford University Press, 2007), 96.

illustrates the general factual difficulty of using age in law even when it does not constitute a complete identity.

2.7 THE RETURN TO BIOLOGY AS IDENTITY CONSTRUCTION

The reality of society seeps back into the child-rights identity, despite attempts to keep it out. The use of age has failed to disconnect the child from social inequalities. Instead of drawing its constructions from the inequalities of the social in the same way as the identities of class, race, and gender are directly linked to social subordination, age primarily redirects the focus to place and biology – not as a construction but as a proxy to and a consequence of age. Place and biology come to create an uncomfortable alliance that, if happening in other contexts, would trigger our memories of more uncomfortable times of identities constructed out of nationality and race. Age draws its construction to place through its reliance on a comprehensive and interconnected administration and bureaucracy, and it draws on the biological in the form of medical tests for age, in search of a perfect melting together of the administrative age constructing the child and the factual days lived under the Sun. This mission is doomed to fail, but still these efforts seem to have no end in sight.

The importance of place, and a place that risks becoming nationalist, is evident in several of the UN communications submitted to the UN Committee on the Rights of the Child, as well as Swedish case law (in the example of the Russian adoption). An example of how nationalism is a close partner, not consciously and deliberately, but as an uncomfortable consequence of supremacy of national place, is the process of assigning an age to someone born in another country, not in the context of "We and Them," but in the idea of national supremacy, not supremacy of people but of place and the location of administration.

The first example here of this intertwining of place and nationalism concerns a communication submitted to the UN Committee of the Rights of the Child authored by A.D. from Mali seeking asylum as an unaccompanied minor in Spain.[35] The Spanish authorities refused to recognize the validity of the identity documentation he presented to the authorities, stating that he was a minor according to documents issued by the Embassy of Mali. The Spanish authorities, however, did not accept A.D.'s documents as genuine.[36] In the

[35] Decision, The Committee on the Rights of the Child, "Views Adopted by the Committee under the Optional Protocol to the Convention on the Rights of the Child on a Communications Procedure, Concerning Communication," No. 21/2017. CRC/C/83/D/21/2017, March 10, 2020.

[36] Ibid., para. 2.4.

complaint communication submitted by A.D., he explains that the Spanish refusal to recognize as genuine his documents issued in Mali contributed to his being classified as an adult and as such being without child protection from the Spanish State during his time in Spain.[37] The reliance on age and the melting together of the administrative age as reflecting the actual birthday, and a belief that this can be measured with precision through biology create a reliance on State administration and bureaucracy that is all-encompassing and unavoidable. The cracks that unknowingly exist in any such administration are replaced with a belief in one's own national administration as supreme, for example, in this case, the supremacy of Spain over Mali.

Another example of the significance of place and age in asylum cases is the communication submitted by K.L. from Algeria against Spain to the UN Committee on the Rights of the Child. In this communication, K.L. was able to obtain two letters of safe conduct issued by the Algerian Consulate in Barcelona confirming that K.L. was an Algerian minor deported from Spain.[38] By July 15, 2020, the legal representative of K.L. confirmed having lost all contact with K.L. since his deportation.[39] The perceived supremacy of national administrative place not only operates in the designation of child identity but also in its implementation. This is also seen in the Russian adoption case addressed earlier.[40] The age of the female adopted from Russia had been agreed upon both in Russia and later on confirmed in Sweden and had remained so for several years. The ultimate factor in the end when determining the age of the female was that her exact birth date in Russia could not be confirmed. Assigning an identity in the movement between places, as when establishing the age upon arrival of unaccompanied minors seeking asylum as children in Europe, or including persons living in one place with an age already permanently assigned but with an uncertain identity, as with the Russian adopted girl, is a quite radical consequence of the belief in national administrative supremacy. A person can live for a significant number of years with one day as her assigned birthday, only for this to be questioned and changed because the original exact birthday is impossible to establish with absolute certainty.

37 Ibid., para. 3.1.

38 Decision, The Committee on the Rights of the Child, "Views Adopted by the Committee under the Optional Protocol to the Convention on the Rights of the Child on a Communications Procedure, Concerning Communication," No. 29/2017. CRC/C/85/D/29/2017, November 11, 2020, pp. 3–4.

39 Ibid., p. 6.

40 Högsta domstolens dom B 5057–18, April 29, 2019.

There is no way of creating a factual absolute link between the Earth's orbit and that going on in the body and mind of an individual child. Still, this is what is being attempted through medical age tests. These tests cannot provide answers with any higher accuracy than within one year of the birthdate age, in other words, no more precise than the already claimed administrative age in most instances.[41] For example, the medical age test of A.D. stated, "According to the medical report dated 10 March 2017, the author had a bone age of between eighteen and 19 years."[42] … "On the same day – that is, 10 March 2017 – Almería Court of Investigation No. 6 ordered the removal of the author to his country of origin."[43] Also, in the Russian adoption case, the medical age test was introduced not just once or twice but three times, but never for the purpose of determining the factual age for the legal capacity to consent to sex. With the Russian adoption example – one medical age test conducted in Russia at the time of adoption and one medical age test conducted in Sweden when the female arrived in Sweden – both medical age tests concluded that the girl was five years old, and this is how she was designated as being born on November 3, 2003.[44] When the girl turned eight years, she was showing signs of entering into puberty, and another medical age test was conducted – not with the purpose of determining her age but to exclude the possibility of premature puberty. The conclusion was that her skeletal age was about ten years and one month.[45] According to Swedish medical expertise, this did not give a clear answer as to her real age. It was still not possible to determine whether she was a child who had entered into premature puberty, or whether she was a child who had been misclassified by as much as two years in the first two medical age tests, that is, both in Russia and in Sweden.[46] This was the situation at the time of the trial. The conclusion therefore was that it was not possible to confirm her age beyond reasonable doubt, resulting in her administrative age no longer determining her age, but without being replaced with some other form of determination of her true age.

2.8 THE CONNECTION BETWEEN PLACE AND BIOLOGY

One of the unintended consequences of using age as the method to construct identity is the renewed link between place of national origin and biology to

[41] Stafford, "German Doctor's Leader Condemns Support for Refugee Age Tests."
[42] Decision, The Committee on the Rights of the Child, "Views Adopted by the Committee under the Optional Protocol," No. 21/2017, para. 2.1.
[43] Ibid., para. 2.2.
[44] Högsta domstolens dom B 5057–18, April 29, 2019.
[45] Ibid., para. 27.
[46] Ibid.

determine identity, this time not in the form of race but in the form of national administrative supremacy and medical science. The medical age tests are only actualized when a person's origin is connected to another national place. What is asked from the medical age test is something that the test cannot provide: an absolute birth date. This is how place and biology are linked again in the name of science, a validation that can only be confirmed through a belief in national place and the ability of medical practices to interpret the body of someone to give a true answer about identity. The supremacy of one national place is what triggers the medical age test, and the biological outcome overrules the administrative evidence from the other national places.

One more example of a link between national place and biology can be found in the child rights communication, M. A. B. against Spain. According to his documentation, M. A. B., who was from Guinea, was fourteen years old when he arrived in Spain seeking asylum as an unaccompanied minor.[47] He was denied the status as a minor due to a medical age test that had found him older then eighteen years of age:

> On 8 February 2018, the author obtained a copy of his birth certificate through the Red Cross, which he submitted to the public prosecution service with a request to be recognized as a minor. The request was denied the same day on the grounds that the validity of the document could not be confirmed and that the medical test had already determined that he was of legal age.[48]

The return of the link between national place and biology is ethically troublesome, first because it cannot determine age with the precision it is asked to provide. Second, to revive the relationship between place, biology and identity is historically troublesome.

2.9 THE CONVENTION AND SUBJECTHOOD

The reason why the CRC does not define the beginning of childhood and only defines its end is for the Convention to keep the door open for an abortion ban. This was a deliberate choice by the drafters as a compromise between nations in favor of legal abortion and nations that find life to begin at conception and uphold the prohibition of abortions.[49] Throughout the

47 Decision, The Committee on the Rights of the Child, "Views Adopted by the Committee under the Optional Protocol to the Convention on the Rights of the Child on a Communications Procedure, Concerning Communication No. 41/2018. CRC/C/89/D/41/2018," March 10, 2022.

48 Ibid., p. 2.

49 "Discussion and Adoption by the Working Group," 1980, E/CN.4/L.1542, paras. 5–22.

drafting of the CRC, there was a struggle between those countries who wanted to keep abortion legal and those who wanted to maintain an abortion ban. The compromise was to place the abortion prohibition in the preamble in the phrase: "the child, by reason of his physical and mental immaturity, needs special safeguards and care, including appropriate legal protection, *before as well as after birth*."[50] The Vatican clarified the meaning of this compromise to mean that the CRC would cover the "child" from the moment of conception and that the CRC should be read through its preamble via article 31 of the Vienna Convention on the Law of Treaties.[51]

What the CRC brought to child rights was civil and political rights. Previous declarations had only contained social, economic, and cultural rights. With the CRC's inclusion of civil and political rights, child rights moved into something akin to a liberal framework with roots in the protection of fundamental freedoms without fully transitioning from a regime based on child saving to a child rights regime founded on liberty and equality. The civil and political rights are based on the concept that individuals are in possession of their own freedom, in this way making a connection between the idea of freedom and the person holding this freedom. One foundational idea in making the individual the possessor of rights is that the right is embedded in the body of the person, and it is exercised with the help or free will of the rational mind of that body. Instead of persons needing rights to exist, rights generally need persons for their existence. To illustrate this point, we can look to the first line of the first article of the UNDHR, which states: "All human beings are born free and equal." The universal rights of the UNDHR begin with the birth of a person. The universal rights depend on a person being born. The CRC challenges this presumption that rights need a body to reside within. They are not dependent on the child being born. Instead of beginning with the birth of the child, they remain silent on the point in time when the child as a rights-bearing subject begins. Not only do human rights need a person with a body, but human rights also require a rational mind to control

[50] Emphasis added.

[51] Declaration made by the Holy See at ratification of the CRC:

> The Holy See recognizes that the Convention represents an enactment of principles previously adopted by the United Nations, and once effective as a ratified instrument, will safeguard the rights of the child before as well as after birth, as expressly affirmed in the "Declaration of the Rights of the Child" [Res. 136 (XIV)] and restated in the ninth preambular paragraph of the Convention. The Holy See remains confident that the ninth preambular paragraph will serve as the perspective through which the rest of the Convention will be interpreted, in conformity with article 31 of the Vienna Convention on the Law of Treaties of 23 May 1969.

that body to not infringe upon the equal freedom of others. An example of this can be found in the second part of the first article of the UNDHR, making the connection between rights and reason: "They are endowed with reason and conscience and should act towards one another in a spirit of brotherhood." That the exercise of rights is expressed through the body's actions but controlled by the rational and conscious mind – and its limitation is the intrusion upon another body or mind – is what connects human rights with the ideas of a freedom and equality. Since the CRC is constructed to be applicable on the subject of rights from the moment of conception (dependent on national and religious contexts), the child as a subject challenges the premise of the body being necessary for the existence of rights. It is not clear that for child rights to exist, there needs to be a body though which to be expressed. This is a unique human rights construction that is not found in any other of the UN human rights treaties.

As established, the CRC does not necessarily need a body for its subject; neither does it need a rational mind to direct the actions and will of this body. This, of course, does not mean that children cannot be rational. Instead, it means that a rational mind is not a condition for the rights framework of child rights. That children will not have to be in possession of rational minds is taken into consideration by the CRC itself, when, for example, its article 12 states that "the view of the child should be given due weight in accordance with age and maturity." This is the only human rights treaty where the substance of the right is dependent on the qualifications of the individual rights holder. Normally, all human rights are focused on the elimination of individual concrete qualifications as a measurement for the scope of a right; irrespective of the concrete capacity of the person, the scope of that person's right is the same as any other person's rights in the same situation. This the basic principle of legal security that law is generally applicable. In addition, for infringements of this principle of law, the derogation must be established by law. This sets the whole notion of possessive individualism into play, which, from a child rights perspective, can be seen as a controversial idea of human rights.[52] In summary, adult human rights rely on formal equality in their application, while child rights are founded on individual concrete assessments of each child's maturity to determine the substance of each right to be enjoyed by the individual child.

Not only might there not be a body for the mind to inhabit, but it might also be unclear what type of mind exists from the moment of conception. In other

52 See Quintin Skinner for a clear explanation of the construction of personal liberty. Quentin Skinner, *Liberty before Liberalism* (Cambridge: Cambridge University Press, 2012 [1997]).

words, the subjecthood of the child is not based on its body or the mind's ability to be rational and therefore free. This form of identity construction calls into question the notion that the CRC has turned children from being objects of care to becoming the subjects of rights because it is not completely easy to point to a required subjecthood for there to be both a child and rights in the Convention. If there is not a need for a body or a rational mind – how is this a subject of rights, in the sense that some form of agency is possible? This does not mean that children should not have rights; what it means is that we must look to the specific child-rights construction and understand both its strength and its weakness, and how the possible disadvantages to children that come with this construction can be addressed.

2.10 THE SOCIAL CONSTRUCTION OF THE APPLICATION OF RIGHTS

The monism of the child identity is not only monist in its position of the self and others, but it is also not affected by either. The consequence, as addressed earlier, is that the child-rights identity remains monist in relation to society. A comparison of this foreclosure of social critique by children themselves of the child identity can be made with how W. E. B. Du Bois used "double-consciousness" in describing the formation of a black identity. Du Bois uses double-consciousness to challenge the one-dimensionality of blackness constructed by the legacy of slavery and Jim Crow. It is through double-consciousness that Du Bois makes possible the individual agency of the person constructed by racism and thus able to challenge the subjecthood constructed through racism with an identity shaped by the self.[53] Du Bois moves from the understanding of identity as something that begins with the thinking "I", which connects the mind to the body, a body judged by society as something that is not aligned with the self-understanding of black persons in America. This means that black identity in the United States, but also globally, since for Du Bois, the color line is not limited to the US experience, is an identity born out of subjugation. This identity inhabits a body that is labeled and marked but also possible to challenge through the thinking self. He writes: "It is a peculiar sensation, this double-consciousness, this sense of always looking at oneself through the eyes of others."[54]

[53] W. E. B. Du Bois , *The Souls of Black Folk* (New York: Oxford World's Classics, 2008 [1903]), 8; see further pp. 136–137.

[54] Ibid., 8.

The question is what would the *Du Boisian question* – how does it feel to be a problem? – sound like if posed to a child?[55] The answer is that we would not understand the question as the child would not be capable of voicing it as a child under the CRC. There is no doubleness for such a question to spring out of the CRC. Not because the interpreter has taken the place of the child but because there is no place to occupy, either by the child or by the Spivakian speaker.[56] This necessity to know both the I as understood by others and the self gives identity a bifocal characteristic holding both an externality through which one can understand how one is seen through the eyes of others and its discrepancy from how one knows oneself from within.[57] For subjugation to not singularly be the extension of suppression, one must have the body through which to voice one's conscious mind in a community of recognition.

It is in this split that Du Bois creates the space for resistance. If the child identity needs neither the body or mind – and it is an identity completely independent of society – where is resistance to be placed? From where can the child generate a discomfort through the eyes of the observers enough for the identity construction itself to shift? To beg the question that all might not be as it is believed to be, to make space for this sense of suspicion? The child-rights identity is monist in contrast to what I term a bifocal identity construction following the understanding of the identity construction held by Gilles-Gaston Granger, from whom Paul Ricoeur borrowed the idea of annunciation and anchoring as an expression of the relation between the thought and the matter.[58] There is no knowing involved in the rights identity of the child under the CRC because the child's identity is not itself embodied. In short, the rights identity has not been constructed out of a theory with a thinking child in mind or being placed within an active body. Instead, the child-rights identity has theoretically made provisions for the protection of life but is itself located outside social and biological life.

The location of suspicion constituted in the split between annunciation and the named is not simply an ambiguity of matter but also of thought within

55 Ibid., 7.

56 Esteania Peñafiel Loaiza and Gayatri Chakravorty Spivak, *Can the Subaltern Speak?: Two Works* (London: Afterall Books, 2021).

57 Judith Butler has taken us through the subjugation process of gender, in Judith Butler, *The Psychic Life of Power* (Stanford, CA: Stanford University Press, 1997).

58 Gilles-Gaston Granger, "Les conditions proto-logiques des languages naturelles," *Philosophiques* 16, no. 2 (Fall 1989): 253; Paul Ricoeur, "Philosophical Anthropology," in *Writings and Lectures*, vol. 3, ed. Johan Michel and Jérôme Porée, trans. David Pellauer (Oxford: Polity, 2016 [2013]), 218.

matter.[59] Ricoeur's suspicion is located within the wedge between describing what is and its annunciation. This will itself threaten the nonsubjective position of itself as the general and with the risk of falling into particularity. This reading – approaching an ethics of ambiguity with a fundamental embedded suspicion – is asserted by Gadamer to be the position of the radical and to, at the same time, relate both to a given sign's objectivity and to its intelligibility, while fundamentally questioning the possibility of objectivity itself.[60] Regardless of whether a radical position of the "totality of double-meaning expressions"[61] is in place, the rights identity of the child is objective without being possible to challenge it through subjectivity. In this way the child-rights identity is immune or resistant to suspicion because a monist rights identity can only be true or false, or right or wrong since it is about age, and the only form of age permitted is where the administrative records are indivisible from the birthday of the child – where any form of suspicion is made impossible. In the moment the child identity allows itself to become ambiguous it is no longer an identity constructed out of age but a bifocality of either the body and mind, or the self and others, and has undone the very child-rights identity construction upon which the whole regime rests.

2.11 CONTESTATION OF IDENTITY

Legal identities reflect the choices posed through law and, thus, they are presented as either binary or fragmented. To understand how legal identity theory follows this pattern, we can look to Kimberlé Crenshaw[62] and Angela Harris.[63] Crenshaw argues that women of color are confronted with a binary choice: to describe themselves as either "women" discriminated for not being a man, or as "persons of color," discriminated for not being white. For Crenshaw, the law forces them to choose one binary over the other, either a binary of gender or a binary of race to define themselves. In contrast, Angela

59 This location between the identity that speaks and the identity who is spoken about when the I announces itself. See, Ricoeur, "Philosophical Anthropology," 218.

60 Hans-George Gadamer, "The Hermeneutics of Suspicion," in *Phenomenology and the Human Science*, ed. J. N. Mohanty (reprinted from *Man and the World* 17, nos. 3/4, 1984) (Amsterdam: Kluwer, 1985), 317.

61 Paul Ricoeur, *Freud & Philosophy: An Essay on Interpretation*, trans. Denis Savage (New Haven, CT: Yale University Press, 1970), 7–9.

62 Kimberle Crenshaw, "Demarginalizing the Intersection of Race and Sex: A Black Feminist Critique of Antidiscrimination Doctrine, Feminist Theory and Antiracist Politics," *University of Chicago Legal Forum* 140 (1989): 139–167.

63 Angela P. Harris, "Race and Essentialism in Feminist Legal Theory," *Stanford Law Review* 42, no. 3 (1990): 581–616.

Harris sees race and gender as fragmentations of a person's identity, having to maintain both an identity as a "woman" and another identity as "person of color." Devon Carbado and Cheryl Harris have addressed the division between these two schools of thought by revisiting MacKinnon's dominance theory through the lens of the particularity of race and gender.[64] The constraints of law are further challenged by Wing's critical race feminism, which takes a realist approach to identity as being multiple in its application but also painful in its singularity.[65] The school that presents the strongest rejection of law's binary constraints is LatCrit, which is based on a norm of inclusion and respect for the self-announcing identity.[66] Jessica Clarke challenges the binary construction of law by considering transgender identity.[67] Recent scholarship in ClassCrit makes connections between a deregulated market and the idea of the individual as autonomous.[68] This last school is close to Martha Fineman's theory of vulnerabilities, which asserts that vulnerabilities are both produced and maintained through law and that the role of the State is to actively mitigate the vulnerabilities produced upon different persons in a postidentity society.[69]

It is not a bad thing in itself that the child-rights identity has left the binary identity construction of "child" as simply meaning "not adult." Alice Hearst, in a thoughtful reflection on the law's part in producing a child-rights identity out of a binary relationship to adults writes, "Laws defining a child's relationships of dependence take effect immediately at birth and continue to place the child in relation to various adults throughout the child's dependence."[70] This binary of child and adult is rendered irrelevant in the identity construction of the child in the CRC because the question is not whether a person is a child

64 Devon Carbado and Cheryl Harris, "Intersectionality at 30: Mapping the Margins of Anti-Essentialism, Intersectionality, and Dominance Theory," *Harvard Law Review* 132 (2019): 2193–2239.

65 Adrien Katherine Wing, *Critical Race Feminism*, 2nd ed. (New York: New York University Press, 2003); Adrien Katherine Wing, "Violence and State Accountability: Critical Race Feminism," *Georgia Journal of Gender and Law* 1 (1999): 95–114.

66 Francisco Valdes, "Under Construction: LatCrit Consciousness, Community, and Theory," *California Law Review* 85 (1997): 1087–1142; See also Josephine Ross, "The Sexualization of Difference: A Comparison of Mixed-Race and Same-Gender Marriage," *Harvard Civil Rights – Civil Liberties Law Review* 37 (2002): 255.

67 Jessica E. Clarke, "They, Them, and Theirs," *Harvard Law Review* 132, no. 3 (2019): 894.

68 Martha T. McCluskey, "Efficiency and Social Citizenship: Challenging the Neoliberal Attack on the Welfare State," *Indiana Law Journal* 78 (2003): 783.

69 Martha Albertson Fineman, "The Vulnerable Subject: Anchoring Equality in the Human Condition," *Yale Journal of Law and Feminism* 20(2008): 1.

70 Alice Hearst, "Recognizing the Roots: Children's Identity Rights," in *Rethinking Childhood*, ed. Peter B. Pufall and Richard P. Unsworth (Rutgers: Rutgers University Press, 2003), 248.

or an adult, but whether the person is over or under the age of eighteen years. The relation is not with others but with the Sun. Just because the binary does not play a part in constituting the child-rights identity, it does not take away the binary's significance in almost every part of the life of children and in the making of childhood.

In the words of Gilles Deleuze, "There is cruelty, even monstrosity, on both sides of this struggle against an elusive adversary, in which the distinguished opposes something which cannot distinguish itself from but continues to espouse that which divorces it."[71] This approach of creating identity through a person's lack is questioned by both gender and race scholars as being excluding and hurtful.[72] The binary, that children are understood through their lack of adulthood, affects children's lives because the binary, even if it does not construct the child-rights identity, determines, in large part, how and what type of rights should be connected to a specific child and how to address a specific understanding of childhood. As Woodhouse writes, "justice for children requires that we revise rights to fit children's unique situation."[73] Michael Wyness has made the argument that a binary approach is in itself not a very good fit for a theoretical analysis of children. He makes the observation that the child as an independent holder of rights challenges other forms of binaries such as private/public and the State/family.[74] He writes of the child as not placed completely in the public or the private but existing between the two, he breaks the binary into three, first as the political child and as an independent subject not absorbed by the family unit altogether and also not completely in the hands of the State. The child therefore falls within both and is also its own subject.[75] This argument has similarities with the one made by Jessica Clarke on a non-binary identity for "They," where she recommends a strategic approach to at times deploy a binary approach and at other times a non-binary understanding of identity, dependent on the situation.[76]

None of the identity theories just discussed is applicable to the rights identity of the child as constructed through the CRC because of the use of age as the constituting element. This, of course, does not eliminate adult-generated harm to children. It just fails to permit the tools of critique through

71 Gilles Deleuze, *Difference and Repetition* (London: Bloomsbury, 1968), 37.

72 See for example, Clarke, "They, Them, and Theirs."

73 Barbara Bennett Woodhouse, "Re-Visioning Rights for Children," in *Rethinking Childhood*, ed. Peter B. Pufall and Richard P. Unsworth (Rutgers: Rutgers University Press, 2003), 230.

74 Michael Wyness, "Children, Family and the States: Revisiting Public and Private Realms," *Sociology* 48, no. 1 (2014): 60.

75 Ibid., 67, 65.

76 Clarke, "They, Them, and Theirs."

critical legal theory's anti-essentialist method of deconstruction. One of the consequences when administrative age becomes the only constituting element is that being a child becomes an administrative binary that presumes a narrow span of society, where the birth of a person is recorded to the hour and where records are kept, maintained, and made accessible in ways that meet the standard of every encounter with the State.

2.12 A CASE FOR A MONIST CONSTRUCTION

Even if the link between national place and biology may seem dangerously close to earlier European history of territorial supremacy, a monist identity construction still has value that might be worth preserving while we work hard on mediating its risks. The monist construction in itself once acknowledged can be separated from what often leads to unacceptable connection between nation and biology in determining a particular person's child identity. Instead of abandoning the monism of the child identity, might we not instead develop methodologies and critical theories that take the monism of identity constructions into account? For example, when it comes to medical age tests, they could be abandoned as a methodology of establishing child identity; and instead the administrative age a person has been given should be treated as their factual age. In situations where the birthday of a child is impossible to establish there must be an acceptable alternative way of granting child-rights identity. In Swedish, there is a saying, which roughly translates as "My child and others' kids." This refers to a distinction and a kinship connected to the concept of the child. This socially constructed understanding of the child also comes with a special feeling of love and responsibility that is connected to parenting. Andrea Rigg and Jan Pryor's discovery – in a study where children themselves were asked about their perception of family – shows that children and youth regardless of age and their own family structures or culture connected "love and support as essential features of a family."[77] The German delegation at the drafting of the CRC brought forth a concern for what they called "natural" children, referring to what the final version called "out-of-wedlock" children. There was a concern that these "natural" children would not automatically be included in the CRC's definition of a "child," and the delegation wanted to make it clear that they would also be included.[78] Germany pointed to the wording of certain articles in the draft version of

[77] Andrea Rigg and Jan Pryor, "Children's Perceptions of Families: What Do They Really Think?," *Children & Society* 21 (2007): 17–30.

[78] Germany, E/CN.4/1324, para. 8.

the CRC that stated that primary responsibility for the child rests "with his parents." This led the delegation to request a modification since "natural" children are most often brought up by the family of the mother and not by both parents as a couple.[79] Malawi raised similar questions, asking for clarification on whether the CRC was to cover the so-called illegitimate children in its definition of the child.[80] Concerns were also raised regarding children living with foster parents.[81]

It is understandable and even commendable to strive to break free from the tradition of cruelty connected to the understanding of what socially constitutes a child, especially when the social connotations are so connected to the feelings of love for one's own children and often indifference toward others' children. Indeed, the children who are most vulnerable – and therefore in most need of the legal protection that a child rights regime can provide – may be children without parents or other adults to care for them.[82] Considering the social and cultural history and context of the socially constructed child subject, the CRC cannot be criticized too hard for wanting to find an alternative approach to socially constructed identities for the purposes of the CRC. The problem, however, is that the consequences of this departure from bifocal or binary socially constructed identities are that the field of child rights as it is today is in need of a thorough analysis, but we lack a critical language for addressing this form of monist identity construction.

2.13 THE CONSEQUENCE OF MONISM

The CRC as a treaty is its own subject prescribing compliance with its provisions. It is a treaty where the legitimacy of the people set in charge to enforce and interpret as well as evolve its interpretation never have been made clear. At the same time it is a treaty often invoked in support of various policy and legal decisions or critiques of policy and legislation. On what grounds are some adults better judges of what is good for children then other adults, and how can a whole treaty concerning a group of people not need the representation of this group of people in the process of interpretation, enforcement and evolution for its legitimacy? It is therefore necessary to clarify who has the legitimacy to argue on behalf of the children holding the rights in the treaty.

79 Ibid.

80 Malawi, E/CN.4/1324/Add. 4.

81 Germany, E/CN.4/1324, para. 10.

82 Pantea Javidan, "American Legal Discourse on Child Trafficking: The Re/Production of Inequalities and Persistence of Child Criminalization" (PhD diss., London School of Economics and Political Science, London, 2017), 296.

The challenge with the CRC is that its rights-holding subject is not a legal subject similar to that of the citizen because the child of the CRC can never master the CRC in the way that a citizen is a legislator or litigator with respect to the law that also governs her. With law within a democracy, it is ultimately the legal subject that is also the master of the law it creates, the same law out of which it springs. Through law a child is constructed as an identity and holder of rights, but to what extent a child is also a legal subject in the traditional meaning of the word is less clear. Mattias Kumm has described the subject constructed through the "We the people" moment as the constituent power.[83] This is not the case with the child, who will never be the master of the legal regime designed for her protection because at the very moment the child is able to formally affect her legal construction she is no longer a child because, by definition, she has then reached the age of majority.

The CRC is a legal instrument with the power to create legal life, but it is also completely free of masters because if the child rights subject is not its master, who can claim the power to interpret the convention on behalf of children? In fact, one of the most serious weaknesses of the CRC is the absence of an understanding of the source of the authority to represent the CRC and its agenda. The convention is never subordinated by its subjects because the child can never be its creator or master, or even a full agent under law or within the politics of democracy. Neither is there any other legitimate constituent of the "We the people" character to control or challenge the evolution of the treaty. Once the CRC was adopted, it became its own master.

The adoption of the CRC in 1989 meant that the child for the first time was constructed as a monist rights identity and given legal life. This was a construction through only law itself, free from the oppressive social, cultural, and biological contexts that have often been used to justify child abuse. Practices committed against children that would be criminal, or even seen as torture if directed toward adults, are too often naturalized and justified with references to tradition when these practices concern children. Spanking and circumcision are two examples of practices often justified by social and cultural arguments, as well as biological and medical beliefs in support of actions that are illegal and criminal if done to adults. The capabilities and characteristics of children as a group are often described in ways that are no longer seen as acceptable when they are applied to other group identities. For example, it would be unthinkable today to talk about women or minorities as holding specific characteristics that are not the result of social subordination

83 Mattias Kumm, "Constituent Power, Cosmopolitan Constitutionalism, and Post-positivist Law," *I*CON* 14, no. 3 (2016): 697–711.

and legal constructions, but this is precisely how many people still talk about children as a group. For example, to presume that a whole group is immature would be unacceptable in connection with any other group identity. Of course, children are immature in relation to many adults, but not all adults, and a seventeen-year-old will by and large be difficult to distinguish from a nineteen-year-old when it comes to maturity.

The vulnerability of essentialism is central to critical theory, regardless of whether the critique takes place within the social, cultural, or biological arena. Simone de Beauvoir made the classical anti-essentialist feminist critique against the impact of biology in *The Second Sex* when she deconstructed the biological claim that women are biological identities and therefore by nature subordinate to men. Beauvoir demonstrates how female subordination to men is socially constructed. She simply points out that women give birth to both women and men and that men give birth to neither women nor men.[84] Similarly, a person who is a child at one moment is no longer a child at the moment of the person's eighteenth birthday. Even if the child-rights identity is not biologically essentialist, but holds similar traits to the biological construction of identities, it is rather fundamental and unambiguous as it is a rights construction void of its body and mind and instead a construction made up by law alone. Its application can be ambiguous and critiqued, but not its construction. This is what places the child apart from other identities because it is impossible to assimilate the rights-based child into the universal of human rights. It is the ultimate nonsubjectivity, a unit free from subjectivity in its composition.

There is little doubt that the strategy to anchor the CRC's construction of the child outside the child itself was well motivated, based on the factual treatment of children. However, the enormous success with which the convention was able to change the paradigm of child advocacy, not only for children but also for law, presents great challenges. The absence of a location in which to anchor a critique of the regime of child rights is a key weakness. For any discipline or regime that is to survive, develop and grow over time, the possibility of an internal critique is a necessity.

84 See, for example, Simone de Beauvoir in discussing motherhood, Simone de Beauvoir, *The Second Sex*, trans. Constance Borde and Sheila Malovany-Chevallier (New York: Vintage, 2009 [1949]), 551.

3

The Complex Intersectionality of the Child

Growing up in the Arctic, adopted from an Asian country living in a majority Caucasian society, on stolen land from the indigenous population of the Sámi, race is inevitably interconnected with gender, and when childhood is added to this equation, we have a highly complex intersectionality for society to both understand and emotionally come to terms with. Unlike the child-rights identity, childhood is a social construction, even though limited by an age span since it ends when the person is no longer under the age of 18. As Karen Wells points out, there are both place-specific elements and universal commonality due to being, for example, a small child.[1] Most adopted children in Sweden are girls, and this was especially the case for my generation of Korean adoptees in the 1970s. This was seen as a perfect match, boys were favored in Korea and more likely to be kept, while girls were favored in Sweden because to be Asian was already to be seen as feminine, and it was believed that it would be easier for Swedish people to accept an Asian girl, rather than an Asian boy. This chapter examines the split between images of the child and the child-rights identity of the CRC, as seen through the complex intersectionality of child-identity, race, and gender. The gap between law in books and law in action normally challenges either law or society to adjust to fit each other and to reconcile the split and move closer to each other. The elasticity that comes with bifocal constructions is missing in the monist child-rights identity of the CRC. The split here between law and society is definitive when the CRC is immune to the social for its child-rights identity construction. The social connection to bifocal law is not only a one-way street – where society shapes law, the shaping also goes the other way – the efficacy of law also shapes society, but for either to be possible, there

[1] Karen Wells, *Childhood in a Global Perspective* (Cambridge: Polity, 2021), 2.

must be a link between the two, and this link is cut off when it comes to the child-rights identity.

When we give children a legally monist definition based on age, it becomes in certain ways a childwashing of reality. One need only look at images of children, for example, on the Internet, to realize that they are supercharged by gender and race in two ways; images of children make first the structure of race and gender extreme, and second an overemphasized connection between innocence and childhood as the only moment when race and gender have not shaped a person. The image of the child reinforces race and gender structures while at the same time in other places suppresses both race and gender, presenting the child as innocent, free from the realities of race and gender. This role of the image of the child, to preexist the social structure of racism is described by W.E.B. Du Bois. For him, childhood is the time of innocence before awareness of the color line. He describes the innocence of childhood in two sections of his book, first when retelling his own coming to consciousness of the color line, and the second time, in the death of his first-born son. First describing his own childhood in New England and the discovery of the color line while in school when the new girl does not accept his card: "It is in the early days of rollicking boyhood that the revelation first burst upon one, all in a day, as it were. I remember well when the shadow swept across me."[2] The interlinking between childhood innocence and pain caused by racism is laid bare in the section when Du Bois describes the death of his son:

> All that day and all that night there sat an awful gladness in my heart, – and my soul whispers ever to me, saying, "Not dead, not dead, but escaped; not bond, but free. No bitter meanness now shall sicken his baby heart till it is a living death, no taunt shall madden his happy boyhood." Fool that I was to think or wish that this little soul should grow choked and deformed within the Veil.[3]

It is not only Du Bois who is looking toward the child in order to imagine a different society, one that is free from engrained conflict and inequalities. The idea that children are their own group and should stand above the conflicts and destruction of adults is exemplified in the very first international child rights agreement, the non–legally binding Geneva principles adopted by the League of Nations in 1924. Their preamble clearly states this intention:

> Men and women of all nations, recognizing that mankind owes to the Child the best that it has to give, declare and accept it as their duty that, beyond and above all considerations of race, nationality or creed.

[2] W. E. B. Du Bois, *The Souls of Black Folk* (New York: Oxford World's Classics, 2008 [1903]), chapter 1, 7–8.

[3] Ibid., chapter 11, pp. 143–144.

This has been the ethos of the child rights movement until the present day. The idea that children constitute their own universality bringing with it its own form of obligations, not only between nations but also for adults regardless of nationality, race or creed, goes back to the origin of this declaration. What this chapter will demonstrate is that the image of the child is complex because both race and gender are superenforced when it comes to the image of the child but also because the child is its own unit outside race and gender.

A shadow of Du Bois' reflections of the pain of racism in connection with childhood is present in the conversations parents belonging to ethnic minority groups have among ourselves today. I have had these conversations with parents in Sweden, the United Kingdom and the United States. These conversations circle around two questions: First, when is the appropriate time to introduce your child to the reality of racism, and second, when that time comes, how much should you tell your child about racism? As a parent I only hoped that the time to tell my child about the racism she will meet in her life, a racism that will never go away, would fall to me to pick and that the moment would not be chosen by the racist. That it will not be a racist slur thrown my way in front of my child that will determine the moment to talk with her – I was hoping that I would be able to choose the moment to talk with my girl when she was old enough to have a sense of self without racism being an embedded part of her. Trying to find the balance between making sure your child knows about the racism she will encounter in life, in order to minimize its harm by preparing her so that she will not get blind-sided by a racist act, while at the same time, wanting her to live if possible still innocent, unaware of the oppression and hurt of racism, to not let racism form her self-image while still teaching her to be proud of her heritage. Strangely enough, parents, in my experience, do not have similar conversations about gender. I find that in my experience there is more parental agency in determining the gender views under which to raise your child than race seems to allow. This will, of course, be different in a society with more formally segregated gender structures then in Sweden and the United States, as well as where within these countries one is living most of one's life. When it came to gender, I felt as if I was able to raise my daughter to make her own choices, while when it came to race, I had to prepare her for the attacks to come, both how to limit their damage upon her personhood but also how to navigate them, and make her feel able to embrace this part of her identity that will also be connected to most of the obstacles she will need to work around in her life. Racism is not a thing that can be squashed or overcome – or at least that is my experience; it can only be worked around. Racism will be with us as long as people are benefitting from it. This does not mean that racism is necessarily more severe than sexism; it means that the nature of subordination and the responses to subordination are different between the two, at least in Sweden and the United States where I have encountered both racism and sexism aimed at myself and my daughter. It is incredibly painful as a new mother to realize that you will have very little ability to control or protect your child from what you know will be the cause of most of her limitations in her life, the barriers to her life dreams that she must learn how to find ways around in order to survive and thrive.

3.1 SOCIAL IMAGES OF A CHILD

One aspect of the child-rights identity, due to its rigidity, is that what is seen or unseen by using only legal age as the construction cannot be adjusted to societal shifts or make alternatives possible when the records of birth are missing or are not trusted. To identify societal images of children, I have used the Google search tool to conduct two sets of Internet (or Web) searches on Google with the following keywords: “children”; “cute children”; “happy children”; “vulnerable children”; “violent children”; “sad children”; “abused children”; and “help children.”[4] These keywords were chosen because they are often part of defining the adult relationship as to children: the children of tender care during the time of innocence, on the one hand, and the children affected by society, on the other hand. The Web searches were done in two different places and times: in 2017 in Uppsala, Sweden, and in 2022 in Cambridge, MA, USA. The search words in the two searches were the same, and to a surprisingly large extent, the structure of the images brought up were also similar. Unlike Roland Barthes’ photos in *Camera Lucida*, the pictures were not selected because they spoke to me or triggered a specific interest.[5] The results of the searches are the outcome of Google algorithms and demonstrate that the social image of the child is highly contextual – often in ways that directly contradict the monist generic identity construction of the CRC even when not selected by a specific subject but the result of algorithmic programing.

To conduct a Google search is by no means a “neutral” act, in that the results returned are not produced randomly, nor do they objectively reflect some truth about children. Greg Lastowka argues that Google results are the outcome of the combined user experience and commercial interest.[6]

4 I Googled the images of the eight different search subjects (not using quotation marks around the terms when searching) on April 11, 2017 and on June 17, 2022.

5 Roland Barthes, *Camera Lucida*, trans. Richard Howard (New York: Vintage Classics, 2000 [1980]).

6 Greg Lastowka, “Google’s Law,” *Brooklyn Law Review* 73 (2008): 1410.

However, Safiya Noble has shown that the same social structures and hierarchies that exist in our everyday social lives are often reproduced through Google searches because the algorithms and inputs are constructed by people and are therefore unable to escape gender and racial biases in society.[7] Noble used the term "algorithmic oppression" to refer to this reproduction of racism and sexism in algorithmically driven data.[8] Jasmine Bains similarly encourages librarians to become more aware of the fact that search engines are not neutral: There are risks of racial and sexist biases built into the seemingly objective design of every search engine. She emphasizes this point by reasoning that even when people are racist and sexist, they might not behave in a racist and/or sexist manner 100 percent of the time, while an algorithm will return racist and/or sexist results 100 percent of the time until the code is altered in some way.[9] These considerations inform the way that the Google searches are being understood in this chapter as a reflection of social structures when it comes to children in Sweden and the United States in 2017 and in 2022, respectively, as seen through a very narrow lens of both history and place.

To this end, I have followed a methodology similar to Noble's attention to "algorithmic oppression," but with a different purpose. My purpose in my use of Google in this chapter is simply limited to analyzing the search results themselves. There is no attempt to explain how codes and algorithms are made. In turn, the Google results I analyze are not used as if they are reflections of what a child is, but rather to give an appreciation of what images are commonly communicated when different child-related keywords are used.[10] As such, the chapter does not make an ethnographic claim that images tell us what children are or what kind of life they live.[11] In other words, I am not trying to obtain ethnographic knowledge about childhood.[12] Even though I am borrowing from visual ethnography by relating to the interconnectedness between the search words and the images as simple forms of hypertext and by referencing connections between images and keywords plugged into the

7 Safiya Umoja Noble, *Algorithms of Oppression: How Search Engines Reinforce Racism* (New York: New York University Press, 2018).

8 Ibid., 4.

9 Jasmine Bains, "Search Engines and Algorithms Are Biased: Here's Why That Matters," *Information Outlook* 24, no. 1 (January/February 2020): 21.

10 Today, to Google something is an integral part of everyday life – but it took until 1989 for the first search engine to appear. The beginning of a Google search engine was to come about by 1997. See Lastowka, "Google's Law," 1332–1333, 1335.

11 For an explanation of the method and the concept of visual research see Sara Pink, *Doing Visual Ethnography* (London: Sage, 2013 [2001]), 7.

12 Pink, *Doing Visual Ethnography*, 7.

search engine, this chapter is not conducting a study within the field of visual ethnography; it is rather inspired by it but makes no claims in departing from the area of legal theory. In addition to borrowing the term "hypertext," I am taking advantage of the ways in which images communicate information that words cannot. I consistently use the term "children," the plural form of "child." Even when the searches generated only images of individual children, I used the keyword "children" in each of the categories.

One limitation of this study is that Google automatically affixes a Google region, such as google.se when conducting searches from within the Swedish territory and google.com when doing searches from a location within the United States.[13] The results, in other words, are place-specific, or rather specific to the Google domain. There is still an overlap in both images and structure between the two results, which is even more remarkable considering the time span between the two searches. There is an important distinction – between making a claim that the identity of children is connected to place and claiming that the search result from Google is place-specific. This chapter makes the latter claim. To examine how children's places also affect their identities falls outside the scope of this text since the searches have no way of identifying the place where the pictures were made.[14]

I first Googled each keyword and took a screenshot of the images that appeared as search results. I have only included complete pictures in the count of the study; when an image is cut off, I have not included that image in the count. I have described in detail each screenshot.

I subsequently tallied each Google search result into responses to seventeen different questions divided into five main sets: The *first* set of questions looks at the structure of the screenshot:

(1) How many images in total are returned by the search?
(2) How many persons in total are depicted in the images when taken together?
(3) How many of the images returned depict groups of people?
(4) How many images showing individual persons are returned?

[13] See "The Rights to Be Forgotten" judgment of May 13, 2014, *Google Spain SL & Google Inc. v. Agencia Espanola de Protection de Dator (AEPD) and Maio Costeja Gonzalez*, C-131/12. ECLI:EU:C:2014:317; see also Directive 95/46/EC-Articles 2, 4, 12, 14.

[14] For two informative texts addressing children and place from an anthropological, or a psycho/sociological understanding, see, for example, Jonathan Scourfield, Bella Dicks, Mark Drakeford, and Andrew Davies, *Children, Place and Identity: Nation and Locality in Middle Childhood* (London: Routledge, 2006); and Liv Helga Dommasnes and Melanie Wrigglesworth (eds.), *Children, Identity and the Past* (Cambridge: Cambridge Scholars Publishing, 2008).

(5) How many images show pairs of people?
(6) How many images showing adults with children are returned?

The *second* set of questions relates to ethnicity represented in the images:

(7) How many of the children are ethnically ambiguous?
(8) How many of the children are black?
(9) How many are Asian?
(10) How many are Latino?
(11) How many are Caucasian?

The *third* set of questions relates to gender:

(12) How many of the children are male?
(13) How many are female?
(14) How many are gender ambiguous?

The *fourth* set, comprising just one question, relates to age:

(15) What age do the children in the image seem to be?

The *fifth* set relates to whether or not the children in the images are depicted in a specific context:

(16) How many of the images are context specific?
(17) How many of the images are noncontext specific?

The problem with studying identity, and especially race and gender, by looking at images, as done in this study, is that stereotypical notions of ethnicity and gender are presumed for classification to be made possible. I was running into the similar dilemma as Ashburn-Nardo describes as the constant bind between the tendency toward stereotyping in the literature and clinical research on the inefficacy of stereotypes.[15] My way of mediating this risk is by trying as carefully as possible to provide as much detail as possible about the pictures returned by each search term.

One point of the present study, however, is that stereotypical notions of race and gender are constantly communicated through images of children, even though we might not notice this, because we presume that children, for legal purposes, are race and gender neutral since they are measured by age and not a socially constructed identity. The social construction is pushed out of the field of child rights altogether and can only be addressed outside law, despite

[15] Leslie Ashburn-Nardo, "Fairly Representing the Stereotyping Literature?," *Industrial and Organizational Psychology* 1 (2008): 412–414.

the fact that these factors determine legal considerations in the application of rights and the choice between the variety of rights of the CRC. Within child rights, there is something unseemly in acknowledging race and gender in children, yet I argue that we nonetheless do, even where our best aspirations are not to do so. Although these Google searches partly validate the idea that ambiguities about gender and race remain when it comes to images of children and that there is something of a moment for the child-rights identity outside gender and race; nevertheless, this moment is fleeting.

When it comes to children, the ambiguity of race and gender seems to affirm that the child as an identity is sometimes a glitch between the two intersecting binaries of gender and race, to a certain extent, indicating that there might be something like a child identity standing on its own. This suggests that the social child identity might, at moments, occupy the place of its own forms of identity constructions to a larger and more effective extent than possible for an adult. The adult image is almost never race and gender free – while there seem to be moments when especially very young children can be free from gender and race designations, which would validate the idea that there is a moment, however brief, before socially constructed identities of race and gender have taken hold.

3.2 WHAT WE SEE IN CHILDREN

In this section we describe the images returned in this study of the eight search terms: "children"; "cute children"; "happy children"; "vulnerable children"; "violent children"; "sad children"; "abused children"; and "help children," first the 2017 and then the 2022 results. The search results are presented first, followed by a theoretical analysis in Section 3.3.

3.2.1 *Keyword:* Children

3.2.1.1 2017 Results, Uppsala, Sweden

Of the fifteen images returned for the keyword "children," all but one group image represent a clear majority of Caucasian children. Of approximately ninety children, ten are black and two are possibly Latino. This distribution means that about 13 percent of the children represented are children of color. When it is possible to identify based on impressions, the gender distribution is roughly even, consisting of twenty-seven boys and twenty-three girls; however, as many as forty children are gender ambiguous. We can compare gender ambiguity with ethnic ambiguity, where only ten children are difficult to assign to an ethnic association. What is significant for these images is the narrow age span of the children represented: All are depicted as of elementary school age. Four of the images show children with school bags, which suggest an elementary school context. The children are also dressed in primary colors and appear in large groups. Interestingly, despite the fact that they are in groups, none of the children appears to interact with one another. Instead, their attention is consistently directed toward the camera, rather than toward each other. This idea of children as directing their attention forward, toward the observer, in their individuality despite appearing in a group, stands in stark contrast to the idea of other group-constructed identities where group consciousness is central to what constitutes the group itself.[16]

3.2.1.2 2022 Results, Cambridge, USA

Of the fifteen images returned for the keyword "children," sixty-two children in total, thirty-eight of the children could be read as black and fifteen as Caucasian. Seven of the children are possibly Latino and possibly one Asian. This is a radical difference in comparison with the reading of the same keywords from Sweden 2017, almost a reversal of the numbers. Where it is possible to identify gender based on impression, the distribution is roughly even, consisting of twenty-nine boys and twenty-seven girls. We can compare gender ambiguity with ethnic ambiguity, where nine children are difficult to assign to an ethnic association. Even though gender is more similar to the readings from 2017, the difference is that the images of 2022 had almost no gender ambiguity, while in 2017, a large proportion of the children did not exhibit clear gender identifiers. What is significant for these images is the narrow age span of the children represented: All are depicted as of elementary school age around four to nine years of age. Four of the images show children with school bags, which suggest an elementary school context. The children are also dressed in primary colors and appear in large groups. The children in this search result are interacting to a higher degree than in the 2017 Swedish return, even if the focus in all but one image is still on the camera's gaze – there are three images where children appear to hold hands or to hold each other and one where the child is surrounded by what seem like caring adults. The clearest difference is the return of children of color as being in the clear majority as a result to the word "children" in the 2022 search.

[16] For a historical overview of the construction of women's group identities, see Nancy F. Cott, *The Bonds of Womanhood* (New Haven, CT: Yale University Press, 1997), 202.

How do these images of children from both 2017 and 2022 hold up against the UN-defined legal construction of the child? Even if the 2022 search produced a majority of black children, one striking discovery is that there are no children in any of the searches that easily read as coming from Afghanistan or Syria, where most unaccompanied minors of the refugee crisis of 2015 are from. It almost goes without saying that the age of the children under the search term "children" are all much younger than the males who arrived in the EU in 2015. The gender and ethnic affiliation are almost uniformly coherent and clear among the group of 2015, a stark contrast to the ethnic heterogeneity displayed in the pictures of both 2017 and 2022.

3.2.2 *Keywords:* Cute Children

3.2.2.1 2017 Results, Uppsala, Sweden

In conducting a Google search with the keywords "cute children," fourteen images were returned. All of the children depicted seem to be Caucasian, with one little boy possibly being Asian. Nine of the children are clearly girls, one is clearly a boy, and four are difficult to assign to a gender. Judging by the results, the "cute child" seems to be a Caucasian girl, or a gender-ambiguous child. This Google search generated the most baby images of all the searches, and all the children appeared alone in the picture.

3.2.2.2 2022 Results, Cambridge, USA

When it comes to cute children, there were nineteen pictures in total, and, with only one exception, all the children appeared alone. That one picture showed a child and an adult, and there were no groups of children at all. Unlike the 2017 search, where only one of the pictures read as racially ambiguous, the level of ethnic ambiguity was high in the 2022 result: Almost half of all the children, nine, read as ethnically not possible to specify. Four out of these children can be read as black and two possibly as Asian. The results this time are more diverse than the results from 2017, but they are still overwhelmingly Caucasian. None of the babies read as explicitly male, and eleven read as female based on gender-signaling attributes, bows, skirts or dresses; the other eight children read as gender ambiguous. The 2022 group is significantly larger than the 2017 group. One thing that is similar between the two results is that the children are young, babies to toddler age, and all but two are pictured outside a clear context. Of these two children, one is taking a bath in the tub and the other is playing in the ocean. One more thing that is similar between the results is that the children are alone in all but one picture. To be cute reads as gendered and is the keyword that returned the youngest children and in age the furthest away from the seventeen-year-old males constituting the 2015 refugee wave of unaccompanied minors.

3.2.3 *Keywords:* Happy Children

3.2.3.1 2017 Results, Uppsala, Sweden

For this search, nine images were returned, all showing children in groups. I excluded the partly cut-off image of children running in a field. (There is a bar of alternative subject images above the search results, including the modifiers “Day,” “Playing,” “Indian,” and “School,” which are not included in this analysis.) Of the nine images in total, four include a child or children of color. In total, there are seven black children and two Asian children out of fifty children represented. However, eleven of the children are ethnically ambiguous and might be children of color, while there are in total thirty Caucasian children represented. Judging again by appearance, there are more girls than boys, with twenty-four girls, nineteen boys, and seven who are gender-ambiguous. High numbers of both ethnic ambiguity and gender ambiguity were found in this search. Notably, some of the images that are returned under “happy children” also appear when searching for “children.” The structure and composition of these images are similar to what appears when searching with the keyword “children.” Here, all the images show groups and, as with the group images of “children,” there is no interaction between individual members of the group.

3.2.3.2 2022 Results, Cambridge, USA

The result returned sixteen pictures with sixty-two people in total: twelve of the pictures were of children in groups, and two of the pictures included child interactions with adults, one with a man who seems like a father and one with a woman who seems like a mother. Just as children can read as gender ambiguous they can also read as ethnically ambiguous. In these results as many as nine children cannot easily be read as belonging to a specific group; twelve children read as black and six as Asian or Latinas or Latinos, while twenty-seven read as Caucasian. Twenty-four of the children read as male, while thirty as female, judging by hair and clothing, and eight of the children read as gender ambiguous. The children are indoors in all the pictures, except for one, where they are in a forest, outside a specific context. The clearest difference between the results from 2017 and 2022 is that there are adults appearing in the images and that there is a larger diversity of children in the pictures from 2022. What remains the same is that the first of the pictures is a photo of children holding balloons. Another similarity is that the children when appearing with other children in groups remain focused on the camera and not on each other. This absence of an interactive gaze between the children themselves contradicts the whole notion of children with an identity that is constructed from a group consciousness.

3.2.4 *Keywords:* Vulnerable Children

3.2.4.1 2017 Results, Uppsala, Sweden

For this search, we have fourteen complete images. In these results, there are a total of sixteen children depicted, nine of whom are black, one is Latino or Asian, and six are Caucasian. There are six girls and five boys, while five of the children cannot be assigned a gender. There is one image of a pair of children: two young children on what looks to be a makeshift bed.

The most misplaced image in this collection is one of a group of seemingly happy schoolchildren who have their hands raised in the air as if they are excited about school and about learning. These children do not look sad like the children in the other images but they are clearly identifiable as black. The only group image in the fourteen results is the image of engaged school children. Each of the other images depicts a lone individual child or the two children without a proper bed. The children represented are very young, with the exception of two images depicting teenage girls.

3.2.4.2 2022 Results, Cambridge, USA

There are in total sixteen images and fifty-four persons in the pictures. Six of the pictures are of groups (more than three people). While nine of the pictures are of individual persons, one is of a pair of children holding each other while walking down a road. There is one picture of a child together with two adults. Two of the children read as ethnically ambiguous, while twenty-two of the children read as black, and twenty-one as Asian, and none as Latino/a and only nine as Caucasian. When it comes to gender, thirty-one read as male and only eight as female, and as many as eleven as gender ambiguous. The children read as early elementary school age. Only two pictures read within a context, the child with the adults on the street and the lone boy sitting on a swing.

Thus, the keywords "vulnerable children" result in unaccompanied children or children who are subjected to structural discrimination and oppression as the most important signifiers. A stark contrast to the real situation of the refugee wave in 2015 is that the vulnerable child is so overwhelmingly depicted as single and alone, while the unaccompanied children of 2015 came and moved in groups. This means that the clearest signifier of vulnerability is singularity and loneliness, when unaccompanied children and structurally disadvantaged children often come in groups. For vulnerable people, banding together should be expected, while the pictures send a different message of singularity and loneliness.

3.2.5 *Keywords:* Violent Children

3.2.5.1 2017 Results, Uppsala, Sweden

Here, we have sixteen images representing a total of twenty-three people, including one adult woman. Five of these images depict more than one child. The images with more than one child show aggressive behavior directed from one child toward another. These results are quite different from the images returned by searches for "happy children" and "children," which depict groups of children who do not interact with one another. One of the images in this search shows two boys mimicking the execution of another boy. There are no gender ambiguities in this particular search: In each image, it is clear who is a girl and who is a boy. Only one of the images returned a clearly identified girl as the active party. The absence of ambiguity in this search differs from the other searches, which present a significant number of images of gender-ambiguous children. The only possible person of color who appears in this search is in an image depicting a black adult woman, and it is possible that the image is intended to reflect a challenging family situation. Taken together, the "violent children" and "cute children" keywords are the only two searches that so predominantly returned white children. In this respect, it might be interesting to address how both "violent children" and "cute children" exhibit the same type of race structure.

3.2.5.2 2022 Results, Cambridge, USA

Two of the pictures returned are the same in both searches: a boy screaming and a boy hitting a girl. There are in total fifteen pictures and twenty-three persons. Only one picture covers a group of people, and there are seven pictures of only one person but six of pairs, where one party reads as the aggressor and the other the recipient of the aggression. One picture has one adult – an adult seemingly hitting the child with a rod. The majority of the children in the pictures read as Caucasian – fourteen, and only three as black.

None of the black children is depicted as the aggressor; two of the pictures depict black girls, in both sitting in contemplation and in one seemingly quite content, and it is difficult to read any violence in either picture. A third image depicts a black girl seemingly being hit with a rod from a woman (at least a person wearing a skirt). The only picture of children with guns are of two either Asian or Latino boys. One of the Caucasian boys seem to be the victim of violence – with the word STOP written on the palm of his hand, which is turned toward the camera. The aggressors appear in all but one of the pictures to be Caucasian children, and in all the pictures but one, a male is the aggressor. One thing to note is that four of the pictures may not necessarily display aggressive behavior, but rather children who are upset over something. The children are of primary school age. Only one girl is clearly depicted as an aggressor – pulling another girl's hair. The pictures do not provide much context, one of them is possibly taking place on a school bus, and another shows a child playing computer games.

If "cute" was gendered for girls, "violent" is gendered for boys. "Violent" is the opposite image of "cute" in almost every way. The keywords – "violent children" – mostly returned images of boys by themselves in both the 2017 and the 2022 search. These images clearly connect aggression with maleness.

3.2.6 *Keywords:* Sad Children

3.2.6.1 2017 Results, Uppsala, Sweden

There are sixteen images in the search results for "sad children," and each image depicts a sole child. Five images represent black children, eight represent Caucasian children, and three present children of ambiguous ethnic identities. Four of the images depict girls, seven depict boys, and five of the children presented in these images are gender ambiguous. When compared to the other seven searches, this search had the highest percentage of black children represented. Like most of the previous searches, the images in this search lack context and, with one exception, present close-ups, which seem rather intrusive, considering that the person in the image appears to be sad. A normal reaction when someone is sad is to recognize the person's need for comfort or, alternatively, need for privacy. An interesting pattern exists in these close-ups: With only one exception, the child's body does not appear. Another pattern observed is the absence of adults in each of the images to comfort the sad child and the high frequency of black-and-white photos.

3.2.6.2 2022 Results, Cambridge, USA

Two of the pictures are the same in 2017 and 2022. There are in total twenty persons depicted in the pictures. None of the pictures shows a group of people, but four pictures show a pair, three of these in a child–adult interaction. In two of the pictures, it seems as if the adult is comforting the child – in only one does the adult's hand appear. The children read as mostly Caucasian with twelve children, and three black and two Asian children. There are only two toddlers depicted; the rest are early school-age children. Six of the children read as males and ten as female. The only picture that provides a context is the one taking place within a kitchen. Vulnerable and sad children produce almost the same form of pictures in the search results.

3.2.7 *Keywords:* Abused Children

3.2.7.1 2017 Results, Uppsala, Sweden

This search yields sixteen images in total, and as in the previous search – sad children – each image depicts an individual child. The only child who is not alone is one small child holding the hand of an adult, and in this image, only the adult's hand is visible. This image of the child holding the adult's hand is one of only three other images depicting an adult presence across the keyword searches; the others were returned in searches for "help children" and "violent children." The percentage of black children in this search – four black children, with one Asian child, ten Caucasian children and one who is ambiguous – is almost as high as it is for "sad children," which depicted five black children. Again, much like the images returned for sad children, what is remarkable about the image results for "abused children" is the consistent use of intrusive close-ups. Each image depicts a cruel situation, often with taped-over mouths and visible bruises. In two of the images, the text on the tape over the child's closed mouth reads "IF YOU TELL ANYONE." Notably, the inclusion of accompanying text to explain the image only appears in this search and the search for "help children." Additionally, this search presents a noticeable imbalance in the representation of gender, with five girls, only two boys, and eleven gender-ambiguous children in the images. This search presents an imbalance quite similar to the results for "cute children," where there were more girls than boys depicted in the images.

3.2.7.2 2022 Results, Cambridge, USA

There are sixteen pictures and twenty people in total in these pictures. Two of the pictures are recurring, one of the pictures also appears in the 2017 search, and one shows up under "sad children." There are no group pictures, but there are five of pairs where it seems as if the child is being threatened by an adult. None of the pictures shows an adult protecting the child; fifteen of the children are Caucasian and only one is black. There are four males and eleven females, and only one gender-ambiguous, where the face is covered. There is only one toddler among the children. The children seem to be from five to nine years old, and all the pictures lack context. Even though pictures of sad children depict older children than cute children, it is remarkable how young the children in these pictures are and how narrow the age span is.

3.2.8 *Keywords:* Help Children

3.2.8.1 2017 Results, Uppsala, Sweden

"Help children" yielded thirteen images, depicting approximately forty-nine children in total. There are seven photos of children, three images of drawings of children, and three images that do not represent children at all. Within these results, there are two images depicting an adult–child interaction: One image represents a child's hand touching an adult's hand, while the other represents a doctor listening to the heartbeat of a baby with a stethoscope, perhaps the only adult–child interaction in the keyword results (or any interaction, for that matter) that seems joyous. In these results, there is only one image depicting an individual child: A girl in pigtails holding a sign addressed to adults that reads HOW YOU CAN HELP. Seven of the images represent groups of children. Only one child in these images, the black baby visiting the doctor, is depicted within a wider context. The other images could have been taken anywhere. What separates this keyword search from the other searches is that several of the images returned do not depict children (or entire children) at all: the image of a heart, the image of a cup filled with pens, the image depicting a child's hand reaching for crayons, and the image of a child's hand holding an adult's hand. Here again, the images depicting a group of children do not show the children in the group interacting with one another.

3.2.8.2 2022 Results, Cambridge, USA

There are fifteen pictures returned and forty-four persons (including several pairs of hands). Seven of the pictures depict groups and three pairs, and no picture depicts a lone child. Six of the persons are ethnically ambiguous – four of the silhouettes are paper cutouts. Seven of the children read as males and twelve as female, and four are ambiguous in gender. Ages range from toddler to early teen. This is the set of pictures that generate the most examples of context; several of the pictures seem to be taken in a school or in some other educational environment; there is one image in a living room and one in the garden. This is the only picture in all of the searches where two children are actively working together on a task.

3.2.9 *Gender*

Gender appeared in these searches in three significant ways. First, several image results presented children in a way that made it difficult to determine their gender identity. This pattern might indicate that the image of the child follows its own construction, one that is distinct and removed from the influence of the clear gender binary. The images on the keywords "cute children" together with "violent children" were the two most gendered keywords, cute for girls and violent for boys, a highly polarized and supercharged gender stereotype. This result correlates with the argument that Dowd brought forward. Her argument is that there has been an ability to understand child culture through a feminist analysis but that masculinity studies have been absent when understanding boys. She identifies one such area to be the juvenile justice system, where the majority of children are boys, and still, the system is not understood as gendered.[17] Williams makes a similar observation when it comes to education; girls are understood as being socially constructed, while boys are as nature made them.[18] If following the "traditional" feminist line of reasoning, it would mean that children are male as a norm because there is no need to define the gender except when as an exception, and according to this view of feminism, the female if not challenged becomes the exceptional gender. However, the research by Dowd and Williams seems to indicate that when it comes to children, there is a possibility to shape and to construct the person as a primary value over nature. This will fall in line with the very notion of child rearing, which builds on the presumption that children are to be shaped into their adult future. Michael Wyness has named the idea of the child on her way into adulthood: "The Child as a Proto-Individual."[19] The keyword search for "violent children" was the only search that did not introduce any images in which gender identity was ambiguous. For "violent children," a related gender pattern can be observed for the images: When there are multiple children represented in an image, boys are depicted attacking girls, who are passive recipients of their

[17] Nancy E. Dowd, "Boys, Masculinities and Juvenile Justice," *Korean Law* 8 (2008): 115.

[18] Juliet A. Williams, "Girls Can Be Anything: But Boys Will Be Boys: Discourses of Sex Difference in Education Reform Debates," *Nevada Law Journal* 13 (2013): 533.

[19] Michael Wyness, *Childhood and Society*, 3rd ed. (London: Bloomsbury Publishing, 2019), 29.

aggression. To sum it up, girls are cute and boys are violent according to the hypertexts in the Google searches.

3.2.10 *Race*

The role of race in understanding these images of children is telling. The majority of the children in the 2017 results from Uppsala, Sweden represented in the keyword search for "children" are Caucasian. Similarly, the keywords "happy children" present images predominantly depicting Caucasian children. This is different in the 2022 Cambridge, USA search, where the numbers have been turned almost upside down; under the search word "children," the majority of children are black, while "cute" children are mostly Caucasian in 2017 but of diversity in 2022. Accordingly, keywords indicating more troubled aspects ("sad," "help," "vulnerable") associated with children result in images with dark compositions and that represent children of color. For example, in the hypertext for "vulnerable children," in 2017, half of the images portray children of color. The hypertext for "cute children" with only Caucasian children and mostly girls in 2017 brings to mind footnote eleven in the American Constitutional Law Case, *Brown v. Board of Education*.[20] Where black children in Dr. K. B. Clark's doll study, "Effect of Prejudice and Discrimination on Personal Development,"[21] showed, if given the option to choose a doll, either black or white, they chose the white doll over the black one.[22] This was interpreted by the Warren Court as a sign of how school segregation "may affect their hearts and minds in a way unlikely ever to be undone."[23] It should be noted that both the Clark study and the wording of the Warren Court stem from the White House Children Conferences, where the study was presented and the conference adopted the mental health approach to racial segregation.[24] Robin Bernstein, sixty years later, provides a different interpretation of the results of the Clark study, not as a sign of mental damage and self-hatred among black children, but

[20] *Brown v. Bd. of Educ.*, 347 U.S. 483, 494 (1954).

[21] See Maria Grahn-Farley, "How Children Got Rights" (Doctoral thesis, Harvard Law School, 2013), 119.

[22] For a general discussion on the role of interdisciplinary approaches to adjudication and footnote 11 in *Brown*, see Michael Heise, "*Brown v. Board of Education*, Footnote 11, and Multidisciplinarity," *Cornell Law Review* 90, no. 2 (2005): 676.

[23] *Brown v. Bd. of Educ.*, 347 U.S. 483, 494 (1954).

[24] Midcentury White House Conference 1950, see Grahn-Farley, "How Children Got Rights," 119.

rather as an expression of the prevailing image of blackness projected and taught to children dating back to the civil war era.[25]

3.3 COMPLEX INTERSECTIONALITY

This chapter is not claiming a prescriptive connection between the Google results and the social construction of children; the chapter simply claims that the Google results reflect an image of children of this time period between 2017 and 2022 in Sweden and the United States. Regardless of whether one follows the interpretation of the doll tests as the White House conferences did in 1950, or as Bernstein did in 2011, cuteness still seems to possess a large amount of whiteness and biologically constructed femininity as the norm. These search results also support the critique of scholars such as Bridget Hiedemann and Jutta Joesch, who in their study found that Asian, Hispanic, and Native American children were all but absent from the field of child studies.[26] Of particular interest in the images returned for "vulnerable children" from the 2017 result is a depiction of a group of seemingly happy black children in a classroom setting. Similar unexplainable results appear in the 2022 search under vulnerability, where a group of clearly happy children from possibly Asia or Latin America is part of the result, as is a painting of black children standing in a group.

This association of race and setting might suggest that ethnicity is itself treated as a form of vulnerability, or at least it would seem to be within Google's image search algorithm. Hiedmann and Joesch show that gender performed differently dependent on race. In their literature study on children and gender, they found, for example, that Caucasian families in the United States more often rely on relatives for the care of their son than for their daughter, while Hispanic families do the opposite.[27] Overall, they found that the literature mostly focused on Caucasian and black families, with few studies of Asian American and Hispanic families and no studies on Native

[25] Robin Bernstein, "Children's Books, Dolls, and the Performance of Race; or, The Possibility of Children's Literature," *PMLA* 126 (2011): 160–169; see also references in Michael G. Proulx, "Professor Revisits Clark Doll Tests," *Harvard Crimson*, December 1, 2011.

[26] Bridget Hiedemann and Jutta M. Joesch, "Whose Sons and Daughters Are Treated Differently? (Re)Examining the Child Gender Literature through the Lens of Race and Ethnicity," *Seattle Journal for Social Justice* 4 (2005): 119, referencing, Joshua D. Angrist and William N . Evans, "Children and Their Parents' Labor Supply: Evidence from Exogenous Variations in Family Size," *American Economic Review* 88 (1998): 450.

[27] Hiedemann and Joesch, "Whose Sons and Daughters Are Treated Differently?" 119, referencing, Angrist and Evans, "Children and Their Parents' Labor Supply," 450.

American families at all.[28] Dorothy Roberts calls out the apartheid-like conditions of the US welfare system when she writes, "White children who are abused or neglected are twice as likely as black children to receive services in their own homes, avoiding the emotional damage and physical risks of foster care placement."[29] She continues, "Once removed from their homes, black children remain in foster care longer, are moved more often, receive fewer services, and are less likely to be either returned home or adopted than any other children."[30]

Again, the keyword "violent children" generated the most distinctive data, together with the keyword "cute." The children in the "violent" search results were overwhelmingly Caucasian, with the possibility of the exception of two children of color and a black woman in the forefront of one image. These results were surprising and in stark contrast to the literature on the conceptual link between blackness and violence, considering stereotypes of black people of both genders as being prone to violence. This stereotype of black male children as being violent subjects black boys to significant risk for their lives. Frank Cooper writes in defense of his maintaining race as an identity instead of replacing race with vulnerability as a category for identifying persons that more open categories such as vulnerabilities might risk making black boys even more vulnerable to the dangers of racism. It also obscured the precise risk that race adds to black boys' lives. He writes, "Was Trayvon Martin hunted and killed because he was 'vulnerable' in similar ways to many other people or because he had the identity of being young, black, and male?"[31] Curry adds a philosophical understanding of specific black-boy vulnerabilities as ethnicity interconnects with gender. He writes, "Our understanding of gender makes the disparities under which racial males suffer ultimately irrelevant to the theories that account for black maleness itself."[32] Rosemary Harris in her study of boy violence between ethnic groups in London finds that the largest problem was not the violence itself, which in its social effects was limited, according to Harris, but rather the problem was the reaction from the public that she argues was intensified because the violence took place between

[28] Hiedemann and Joesch, "Whose Sons and Daughters Are Treated Differently?," 119, referencing, Angrist and Evans, "Children and Their Parents' Labor Supply," 450, 136.

[29] Dorothy E. Roberts, "Child Welfare and Civil Rights," *UIII Law Review* 1 (2003): 172–173.

[30] Ibid., 173.

[31] Frank Rudy Cooper, "Uncomfortable Conversation: Vulnerabilities and Identities, Draft." The paper, as presented at Emory University School of Law, Atlanta, Georgia September 14–15, 2012, was called: "Experiencing Equality as Oppression: Why Vulnerabilities Cannot Replace Identities" (August 28, 2012).

[32] Tommy J. Curry, *The Man-Not: Race, Class, Genre, and the Dilemmas of Black Manhood* (Chicago: Temple University Press, 2017), 106.

ethnic groups.[33] However, in this study, the images of violent children mostly depicted Caucasian children and stand in quite stark contrast to the situation of children encountering violence in their lives as depicted in the literature.[34]

Race and gender are today accepted as socially constructed identities. The meeting point between gender and race as socially constructed identities has come to be called intersectionality. The child seems to both be a hypercharged expression of both race and gender constructions, while there are also clear indicators that the child is also a standalone identity, where race and gender are not possible to detect and the child-identity is not only dominant but also able to stand alone, free from the gender and race intersectionality.

3.3.1 *"The Child" or "Children"*

The CRC purposefully and explicitly addresses the rights identity of the *child*, that is, "child" in the singular. Yet children represented in the images studied here are clearly not the regular child, or the norm, imagined by the CRC. Many of the images returned for the keywords presented groups of children, and within these groups were images of children that resisted the norm. The keyword "cute children" presented an exception as each picture returned in the search represents a singular, happy child. Taken together, the images communicate the idea that the happy child is the norm of what it means to be a child without a specific gender but with a clearly Caucasian majority ethnicity in 2017 and a reverse view in 2022. As a result, we may conclude that the group aspect itself – which is observed as part of the child norm in the images – is in stark contrast to the singularity of the definition provided by the CRC. Furthermore, that each child within the group is not directly interacting with other children and only appears together among other children reinforces the sense of a collective without context or agency. In these images, attention is directed toward the observer, presumably an adult. This unmediated stare is particularly troubling as a norm: If we are treating children as possessing identities that can generate a child-rights agenda, then we should be able to examine the foundation of this agenda in a group consciousness – where children recognize each other in a way that constitutes a group identity. It is worth noting that the only search term that generated children interacting with other children was "violent children."

33 Rosemary Harris, "Interpreting Teenage Inter-Ethnic Violence," *International Journal on Minority and Group Rights* 4 (1996): 301–320.

34 For a substantial worldwide account on children, see Wyness, *Childhood and Society*.

3.3.2 *Adults*

Adults appear in only four images of all of the hypertexts from 2017 and sixteen pictures in total, whereas three of the pictures show adults representing abuse in 2022. One of these adults was returned for the keyword "vulnerable children" in 2017, which presented an image of a child holding the hand of an adult (only the hand is visible). Another adult in 2017 was depicted in the search for "violent children," where a mother seems to be at the forefront of an image of two fighting children. Two images in 2017 returned in the search for "help children" show adults: One image shows a child's hand holding an adult's hand, while the other image, as previously mentioned, shows a doctor examining a baby. In both 2017 and 2022, the "help children" search generated an image of an engaged, positive adult–child interaction.

3.4 CONCLUSION

The Google search results for "children" commonly returned children who reflected Eurocentrism and femininity as the model norm of the child. As more troubling modifiers were added, the more the images appeared to be children of color and, when violent, depicted as boys. Several of the searches generated images of children that displayed racial and gender ambiguities where it was impossible to distinguish the ethnicity or gender of the child in the picture. The results seem to give some support to the argument that the word "children" constitutes an identity that, to some extent, finds a location within the ambiguity of race and gender and outside its binary. Also, "help children" showed children in passive positions accompanied by images and symbols, such as hearts and crayons. The lack of adult interaction in the images returned for these searches was alarming, considering that children normally live within a family or adult context.

One aspect that stands out across the results is the noncontextual nature of the images of children, regardless of the keywords used. The children in the images are seldom placed in a meaningful context, even though it is very clear that the image of the child is highly context-dependent. Another issue is that the children are rarely depicted interacting with or displaying awareness of one another or their surrounding environment. Finally, the children in the images are very young: In almost every image, the children are elementary school age or younger, and considerably younger than the CRC's age limit definition of a child, which is under the age of eighteen years.

If my Google searches at all resemble our commonly held image of what a child is, the results of the Google search are a strong argument in support of the nonsocial context of the CRC construction of the child. If we followed common social conventions when defining who is a child, the children affected by structural and systemic violence would have difficulty in being included under the protection of the child rights established in the CRC. At the same time, the inability to challenge and debate the normalized definition of the child in the CRC also silences an important debate about the ways in which the individual situations of children are so clearly tainted by race and gender. This contrast between the pictures in the search and the CRC might help us critically question the ways society almost instinctively reacts to boys in groups when they are not Caucasian or of prepuberty age dressed in colorful T-shirts. Boys in groups of darker skin color are often disparaged and looked upon with adult fear. The idea that children join together in a situation of vulnerability is completely absent in the search results. If the 2015 Afghani groups of unaccompanied minors have taught us anything, it is that children when feeling vulnerable band together if possible. To instead understand children in groups as possible expressions of vulnerability would help us see the children in front of us, rather than the child of our imagination.

That boys were depicted as violent across the search results might be less of a surprise. However, the result that girls become more clearly defined when connected to violence – this time as victims – was not as expected. The fact that modifiers like "happy" returned either images of groups in contrast to a singular child in need of help in the other images is disturbing as both suggest that a child, whether in a bubble of other happy children or isolated in a bubble of loneliness, always remains in the exact same social context. Both options fail to show that a child – whether happy, vulnerable, or sad – moves in between groups and social contexts, while their vulnerabilities may remain the same.

This study shows major disparities between the rights-based identity of the child as established by the CRC and the representations of children returned by Google image searches, which also, in turn, differ from the world of particular children, for example the Afghani males arriving in Europe 2015. This gulf arose because there is no place within the rights-based identity to challenge the demarcation of the child identity according to age: Without a mediating understanding (or a socio-legal conceptual scheme) that can reconcile the disparity between the law and reality, the legal challenge can only find resolution outside of law. As Hearst notes about the identity of children, identification through belongingness to family, social and cultural groups matters for the law's operation: "conceptualizing identity rights for children requires envisioning children not simply as passive objects of legal categorization but as individuals taking an active role in shaping their identities."[35] The most important conclusion to take from this study is the notion that conceptions of childhood seem to reinforce inequality, rather than dampen it, that the complex intersectionality between race, gender and the child as an identity risks reinforcing already existing structures of race and gender inequality, while if theoretically developed might contribute to add agency and challenge set notions of race and gender as totalizing social constructions.

[35] Alice Hearst, "Recognizing the Roots: Children's Identity Rights," in *Rethinking Childhood*, ed. Peter B. Putfall and Richard P. Unsworth (Rutgers: Rutgers University Press, 2003), 245.

4

Heard but Unable to Speak

This chapter grapples with the disconnect between childhood as socially constructed and the child-rights identity as monist. More precisely, this chapter concerns the role of violence in creating childhood that the monist child-rights identity obscures since the social has no part in its construction. Childhood partly springs from a relationship between time, violence, and silencing, as well as love and care. The function of silencing in the making of childhood is present both when the child is being loved and cared for, and when there is violence and abandonment involved in the shaping of childhood. Ultimately, in both the loving and the abandoned child situations, silencing serves to maintain an adult-privileged position, allowing with impunity the reconceptualization of the use of violence against children, as either being done in the name of love or for the benefit of the child. The idea that harm and abuse are an act of love is a common misconception in the understanding of childhood, and silencing allows this misconception to remain unchallenged.

4.1 DENATURALIZING THE LINK BETWEEN VIOLENCE AND CHILDHOOD THROUGH SPEECH

To denaturalize the link between violence and childhood, one must go further than providing the opportunity for the child to be heard, and instead demand that the child to be able to speak. Far too much child rights advocacy stops at the right to be heard without taking the step into the freedom of speech; this is a significant blind spot in the advocacy of child rights. Even though the right to freedom of speech is established in the CRC, it is seldom invoked by child rights advocates, and it is not a guiding principle of the CRC. Instead of freedom of speech, it is the principle of the right to be heard that is the guiding principle of the CRC. The blind spot is connected to the way that the CRC constructs the child identity, as free from the social where violence has been diminished to the category of abuse, and an anomaly, instead of being understood as an intricate part of the construction of childhood itself.

Let us first begin with the distinction between the two provisions; the right to be heard on the one hand, and the freedom of speech on the other hand. There are two main provisions within the CRC addressing the possibility of agency through speech: article 12 on the right to be heard, and article 13 concerning freedom of expression. Article 12 is as already mentioned a guiding principle of the convention, meaning that each article of the CRC should be interpreted through the lens of article 12.[1] It reads, "States Parties shall assure to the child who is capable of forming his or her own views the right to express those views freely in all matters affecting the child, the views of the child being given due weight in accordance with the age and maturity of the child." The major weakness of article 12 as a justiciable right is that the scope of this right is dependent on the subjective assessment of someone other than the child and that there is no requirement that the derogation of this right should be established by law. Instead of the law regulating the meaning of the right in its concrete application, the scope is connected directly to another person's assessment of that child, without any qualifications establishing why and how this person has obtained this power of interpretation. For human rights in general, the child's right to be heard is an alien rights construction in that the scope of the right is dependent on not the right-holding person but on others' subjective assessment of the individual right holder's capacity. This is without any derogation being regulated through law and limited by objective criteria connected to the benefit of the society and community at large. The normal approach with rights is that they are the same for everyone within the same category regardless of any subjective individual assessment of the right holder's capacity. This is not the case with the child's right to be heard where the meaning is explicitly subjective and individual in its application.

Instead, as already addressed in Chapter 1, formal capacity is normally presumed, as expressed for example in the opening article of the Universal Declaration on Human Rights: "All human beings are born free and equal in dignity and rights. They are endowed with reason and conscience." The

[1] For an analysis of the limitation of article 12 to achieve social transformation see Afua Twum-Danso Imoh, "Adults in Charge: The Limits of Formal Child Participatory Processes for Societal Transformation," in *The Politics of Children's Rights and Representation*, ed. Bengt Sandin, Jonathan Josefsson, Karl Hanson and Sara Balagopalan (London: Palgrave Macmillan, 2022).

Universal Declaration does not limit the scope of the rights to the right holder's actual ability to reason, and whether that person, in fact, has a conscience as the article presumes. Instead the qualities are presumed to be present in every person, and it is this presumption that determines the scope of the right. With the CRC it is the opposite of how it works with the Universal Declaration: Instead of an abstract presumption of reason and conscience, the child's right to be heard is based on a concrete evaluation, an evaluation not guided by law. There is no regulation as to whom has the authority to make this evaluation about the scope of the right to be heard in the concrete situation. Further, there is no regulation as to how to evaluate the capacity and maturity of the individual child, or to determine to what extent the child's right to be heard should determine the outcome of concrete decisions concerning the individual child. It is this abstract presumption of both reason and conscience that creates the foundation for the fundamental freedoms at the core of all the UN human rights treaties apart from the CRC.

This is why child rights in comparison with general human rights are almost an upside-down regime. The subjective elements in child rights are not abstract formalized concepts but are to be understood as concrete individual qualities that determine the scope of the rights themselves for each individual child.

Article 13 is not a participatory right as article 12 is, but instead, as already mentioned, a traditionally constructed freedom of expression right. The purpose of article 13 is different from the purpose of article 12, and article 13 is constructed in line with the general norm for human rights on an abstract, objective ground. Its derogation must be made in law and must be necessary for a legitimate purpose: reputation of others, national security, public order, public health, or morals. It is therefore unclear how article 13 has become such an underused article in child rights advocacy when it, in several ways, is a much stronger right to rely on in the advocacy of children than article 12, which is deliberately subjective and does not require law for its derogation.

For a person to be able to exercise agency in one's own identity construction and expression is not only of ethical importance but also crucial for the life and health of children. I would say, especially children, because the social experience of violence against children is an intricate part of the childhood construction across cultures and regions. With violence comes silencing to prevent both exposure and to limit the resistance to the adult privilege of using violence against children. This is why it is important that children are not only heard but that they can speak, meaning that they are both free to say what they want and that what they express is to be understood as speech, and not only heard under adult discretion.

4.2 TIME AND VIOLENCE

This, the question of violence, time, and childhood, first came to my attention in the early 1990s when Sweden had received a wave of unaccompanied minors, younger boys from Iran escaping the war between Iran and Iraq. These boys had experiences of war not only as civilians but also as child soldiers. This was a new phenomenon in Sweden at the time. The Red Cross was already well established in working with mostly adult torture victim survivors from Chile and the atrocities committed by the Pinochet regime. When it came to children, at least in Sweden, knowledge and experience were lacking on how to rehabilitate children who were not only civilian victims of war but who also as child soldiers played a part in committing atrocities against civilians themselves. The victim–perpetrator lines had imploded and so had time itself.

As members of its national board, we would receive regular updates on developments concerning the Save the Children Sweden Clinic, the country's first clinic treating former child soldiers. The clinic was faced with several challenges, one being that these children had been through experiences so horrible that any regular Swedish adult therapist they encountered would have a difficult time envisioning the horrors at issue. This was an anticipated challenge, but what was less expected was the way in which time and the young ages of the children themselves affected the course of treatment. A child soldier's experiences and formation challenge the normal timeline for the formation and development of a child. In this way, they challenge the concept of age in and of itself. The children, in some aspects, were much less mature than their age would suggest and, in other aspects, had seen and done things that not even adults could imagine. For example, a child might have missed formal education altogether and not be able to read or write and, similarly, have been deprived of play as a way of developing as a person. In contrast, the same boy could expertly handle a rifle, and the killing of a person would not faze him at all. The clinic developed and came to use drawing and painting as part of its therapy method. But this was not the only challenge. Another challenge turned out to be that these children had no memory of a time before the war, which meant that there was no period of time they could remember before becoming child soldiers. The norm for them, consequently, was the reverse of that which the adults treating them were focused on, a trajectory back to normalcy. For these children, the normalcy was war and death, and this journey into "normalcy" in the meaning of peace and life was impossible to imagine for someone never having experienced it or having been old enough to remember it. Thus, the therapy did not then become a trajectory in the direction of a reconstruction of a past but toward an unknown future without a model to imitate. For the adult therapist, it was a focus on a return to normalcy, and for the child, it was a step into the unimaginable. In that sense, the therapist and the child moved in opposite directions as a consequence of time.

At that moment, I could understand the aspect of time and memory, but not, of course, the experience of war, since I myself was just around the age of leaving childhood and entering into adulthood. I was still existing at this stage when you experience adult conversation to center around memories, memories of past events, memories of past encounters with people no longer present. As one ages, I have discovered, conversations become more and more about connecting the present with a past as a way of context and connecting then to imagine the future. I also had come to meet some of these boys in school. I knew a girl who was dating a boy from Iran who had been a child soldier, and she told me about his nightmares and his agony, and how helpless she was in trying to comfort him. She also told me about his addiction to heroin with its origin in being a child soldier and being given heroin to cope with the violence given and taken. Heroin addiction at the time in Sweden was not a commonly occurring experience among schoolchildren, and it had gone undetected by the school and social workers treating this boy as if he was a regular boy from the Artic Circle going through teenage problems. I still remember how she in a quiet voice told me what he had experienced and how she tried to comfort him, unable to make it stop hurting. Now, as a mother of a daughter older than this girl and the boy she was dating, I understand that it was a task far too big for her to resolve. There was no place within Sweden at that time where what the girl in her quiet voice talked about could be understood by any of the adults in her already quite tarnished adult world. The violence of war and the violence in the aftermath of heroin addiction and the harm all this caused her were never understood by her adult surroundings because that could not be conceptualized as childhood, and her boyfriend was a child.

A similar but a far less dramatic example from the same period is the fear over what was called "video violence," and looking back at this today, it seems a naïve innocence to worry about this problem at that time. At about the same time as Save the Children developed its groundbreaking clinic for child soldiers, it also released a report on the harm of video violence on children. This is the late 1980s and early 90s when Sweden had only two television channels, both State-run, and broadcasting only started at 5 p.m. with the children's show, on for half-an-hour to free parents up just long enough to get dinner ready. Today, it is easy to forget that the TV right from its beginnings, at least in Sweden, was treated as a form of babysitter, but a safe one because the State controlled it, and the children's program only lasted thirty minutes. Then came video – allowing individuals and even children to freely control what they watched, when and for how long. Save the Children Sweden concluded that video violence was harmful because children – unlike adults – did not have enough life experience outside TV (at the time, there was still a large part of the population that had grown up as children without a TV at all). The study argued that people who had a life before and outside TV could compare that which one sees on the TV with reality – that is, one can subordinate the TV content to reality – while instead, children would turn the comparison around and compare their lives with the content on the TV, and find that it was their life that was wrong and not the TV depiction. Today, the reality TV genre streaming through platforms might be seen as proving this study correct with respect to the role time plays in imploding the hierarchy between fiction and reality.

These two examples from the late 1980s and early 1990s are not in several ways comparable, but both speak to the interconnectedness between the concepts of childhood, time, and violence. They are symptomatic of how violence and childhood are made invisible because violence is not to be understood as something that happens to children (but did happen to the former child soldier) or alarmist fears are expressed that children are too innocent to be exposed to violence (such as video violence). In both instances, it is the perception of the child as innocent and untouched by life that is distorting adults' ability to grapple with the actual violence in front of them; as with the child soldier where the violence in his life was made invisible to adults because the horror of the violence and the role of the child in producing that violence went beyond the adult imagination of what a child is. This while the video violence became hypervisible and exaggerated because it appealed to the idea of preservation of the child as innocent. The idea of the child both created an underreaction to violence and an overreaction to violence, and I will argue in almost exactly the opposite way as I would have thought was needed.

For child soldiers, the fact that they were children was also the reason why they were recruited and targeted into armed conflict because children can be made to do things that adults cannot because social norms have not yet taken root in children. Children both normalize the acts of violence and do not fully grasp their consequences. In comparison with the national panic over video violence as treated in the report, the idea that children because of less life experience are more impressionable to violence played a part in both the child soldier recruitment and video violence fear, in the child soldier case by making the violence invisible and in the video violence case making violence hypervisible.

To me, the only sure way to alter this formation of the child – through time and violence – is to give the child agency to not only be heard but also to speak, for the child to not only be the object of actions but to also be the subject acting. This means that adults must not place themselves in a position of never acknowledging being wrong – as long as it is the adult that determines the meaning of what the child says – the adults also controls when the adults is right and when the child is wrong, if there is a disagreements between the two, but without ever having to acknowledge that there is a judgment in giving meaning to what the child is saying through adult interpretation. This is why the child might have the right to be heard but for the child to be able to speak the interpreting of what the child says cannot only rest with the adult hearing it. The main difference between article 12 – the right to be heard – and article 13 – the right to freedom of expression – is that adults determine the concrete meaning of article 12 in the individual case, and the meaning of article 13 is determined in abstract manner by the law. The right to freedom of expression, on the other hand, means that adults must admit that they might not agree with what the child says – and this, of course, means that even the benevolent child rights advocate might have a different opinion from that of the child for whom she is advocating, but this is speech nevertheless and cannot be filed as immaturity and without weight as article 12 permits adults to do. The speaking child is what monism in child rights has such a hard time reconciling because there is no place for unmitigated agency in the child-rights identity construction. A speaking child will force open the monism of its identity construction because it takes away the power of adults to weigh the value of what is being said before it is being considered as a right. A speaking child will make it necessary for adults to deliberate with the child even when they do not agree with each other.[2]

The role of violence in shaping identity is recognized by feminist scholars and critical race theorists, and this understanding of how violence and the threat of violence shape identities of gender and race makes it possible not

[2] Edward van Daalen describes a situation from 2017 in Buenos Aires at the International Labour Organisation's IV Global Conference on the Sustained Eradication of Child Labour, when he argues that children were not only unable to participate but that there was an active will to not have them participate in the deliberation of the Congress. See Edward van Daalen, "Could It Be That They Do Not Want to Hear What We Have to Say? Organised Working Children and the International Politics and Representation of Child Labour," in *The Politics of Children's Rights and Representation*, ed. Bengt Sandin, Jonathan Josefsson, Karl Hanson and Sara Balagopalan (London: Palgrave Macmillan, 2022).

only to fight against the violence itself but to also alter its role in shaping identity. Violence is more than something that happens to children; it also shapes people for life. To be able to fight not only violence against children but also to resist the power of violence in shaping childhood, we first must recognize that violence is an integral part of the shaping of childhood, and I believe that the child's free and protected speech is one of the ways through which this challenge can begin.

4.3 THE HISTORY OF CHILD RIGHTS AND VIOLENCE

Children's rights and violence are not only theoretically linked, but they are also historically interlinked. The early laws in both Sweden and the United States regulating children were laws about protecting them from violent abuse: in the United States as early as 1874 and in Sweden in 1924.[3] Violence and children have always had a contradictory relationship. For instance, in many jurisdictions the law sees violence against children as a legitimate part of child-rearing. Often such violence is treated as a protected category for caregivers to use otherwise criminalized violence against children, for example, spanking, that if done to an adult, would be a crime of assault. Likewise, male circumcision if done to an adult, would be abuse and assault. On the other hand, child laws have primarily been focused on protecting children from violence while still turning a blind eye to specific types of child violence not entirely dissimilar to what we now term gendered or racialized violence.

Law when it comes to children and violence has been speaking with a forked tongue. Violence is sadly a part of many children's everyday life. Not only is violence in the form of abuse strongly linked to child regulations, but war itself has also been the catalyst for each of the major international child-rights agreements. The first international child declaration was adopted by the League of Nations in the aftermath of World War I. Eglantyne Jebb, founder of Save the Children, protested the victorious countries' treatment of German children. A set of principles for the protection of children was adopted by Save the Children in 1923 as a consequence of the war, to be adopted by the League of Nations the following year as the Geneva Declaration, the first

[3] It began in the United States with the case of Mary Ellen, a child being abused by her foster mother; see John E. B. Myers, "A Short History of Child Protection in America," *Family Law Quarterly* 42 (2008–2009): 449, 451; and in Sweden, it is the first welfare Act addressing childcare by the State; *Lag* (1924:361) *om samhällets barnvård* [The law 1924:361 on municipal childcare], entailing that every city had to install a childcare unit, a law that was in force until 1960.

international child-rights instrument.[4] The second major child-rights instrument, the UN Declaration on the Rights of the Child, was adopted in the aftermath of World War II.[5] The drafting of the Child Rights Declaration was to reflect its close relationship to the Universal Declaration of Human Rights (UNHDR) adopted in 1948 by the United Nations.[6] The CRC as the third major child-rights instrument was adopted just weeks after the end of the Cold War.[7] All these instruments address the failure by adults to fulfill the primary responsibility of any caregiver of children – to protect them from harm, violence, and destruction.

4.4 TIME AND SUBORDINATION

The monist CRC definition of the child is based on age and, consequently, time. As discussed in Chapter 2, age under the CRC is a legal concept of one sort of time – the time that is measured by Earth's orbits around the Sun – not the effects of time. The effects of time is a different thing and more in line with other identity constructions. The effects of time upon a person is away of explaining socially constructed identities. The child is made from time itself, instead of the effects of time. The time itself as measured by the Earth's orbits of the Sun, and not through the ways in which the events that take place with the passing of time upon Earth shape identity. The child-rights identity differs drastically from other identities that are socially constructed. The ways in which time affects the shaping of personhood is one of the most neglected consequences of the child-rights identity construction under the CRC. This is not only a theoretical concern but something that affects children and the treatment of children under the CRC in concrete ways. The effects of time are more powerful on children than on adults, and it is also the effects of lack of time that lead to the recruitment of children into very harmful situations but conversely trigger the strongest urge to protect children from adults. Still, we have an identity construction in the CRC that is unable to take this aspect of childhood into the understanding of the child identity. Jonathan Todres and

4 League of Nations, Geneva Declaration of the Rights of the Child, adopted September 26, 1924.

5 UN Declaration of the Rights of the Child, adopted November 20, 1959, adopted November 20, 1959, General Assembly, Resolution 1386 (XIV).

6 Draft Declaration of the Rights of the Child, The Economic and Social Council, Section C, E.Res.309(XI).EN (1950).

7 The Berlin Wall fell on November 9, 1989 and the CRC was adopted on November 20, that same year. It was not until *perestroika* and *glasnost* that proper negotiations could commence in 1986.

Shani King highlight how time itself affects the deprivation of specific rights during childhood and how it will have far more dramatic effects than during adulthood because of the way in which time is heightened in childhood.[8]

Freeing the child-rights identity from social construction is not to set the child free from the domination that can shape a person's life; it just places that domination outside its field of vision. The CRC child identity is deliberately based on an objective criterion in order to avoid the domination, stereotypes and biases prevalent in social constructions, even if domination is a shared experience for many children. In a similar manner, experiences of violence have shaped the child-rights regime but not the child-rights identity it created. Simply put, it is a question of how strongly one believes that the map can shape the landscape it is depicting. In legal terms, it is a question of how strongly one believes in the efficacy of law to bend and shape society and its structure and traditions.

4.5 TIME AND PLACE

Not only does time have its distinct role in the construction of the child-rights identity in years, but historicity takes on its own shape when it comes to the child, not as an identity but as a person affected by the shortness of time since birth. Time moves differently for a child than for an adult. We can all remember being young and how it was whole eternities between each birthday, and how the summer holiday lasted forever, while birthdays and summer vacations as adults seem to come at us and move by in a high-speed blur.

If you are very young, you might not be in a life situation where personal historicity will manifest as anything but nature, in the sense that you are being fed, put to bed, and bathed, but these will not be translated into a memory of events. When it comes to the wider context of time, in remembering non-routine events such as holidays and seasons of the year, time becomes part of one's understanding of social life, but even this might take a few cycles before maturing as a concept. These are, at all times, noted as uneventful routines, even if a meeting with grandparents is a nice event, it still takes place within a continuous time. When a person gets older, time as memories of the past and aspirations for the future will find its body within persons called children, but this does not change the identity construction itself; historicity lives within the perimeters of the identity but cannot shape or call it into question.

8 Jonathan Todres and Shani M. King, "Children's Rights in the Twenty-First Century: Challenges and Opportunities," in *The Oxford Handbook of Children's Rights Law*, ed. Jonathan Todres and Shani M. King (New York: Oxford University Press, 2020), 720.

Looking at time, Paul Ricoeur asked, "How can time exist if the past is no longer, if the future is not yet, and if the present is not always?"[9] The identity of the child sits in the soft spot of time without its history, a situation ahead of the past and "not yet" the future. There is a distinction between saying that childhood's purpose is to transition a person into adulthood and that the child as an identity is to be transitioned through. To say that the purpose of childhood is to lead to adulthood is to diminish the value of childhood and the value of the child itself, but to describe how all adults at one point were children is a statement of fact that binds all humans together into a universal construction. Childhood itself has its own meaning and importance, and persons classified as children are not lesser persons because they are not classified as adults.

4.6 THE SPLIT: THE PLACE OF RADICAL CRITIQUE

In *The Souls of Black Folk*, W. E. B. Du Bois posits a social theory of the making of the black identity that illustrates why it is necessary to establish whether the child-rights identity is its own regime, or if children are one part of the universality of all persons as discussed at the beginning of this book. Du Bois describes three crucial concepts. First is that the overarching shared value is the universal aspiration toward freedom. Second is that the structure of the color line exposes the shortcomings of the United States in living up to its ideal of freedom for all by still holding onto the social structures of slavery. As he states, "The Nation has not yet found peace from its sins."[10] It is the contradiction between the aspirations of the modern nation of the United States and the social reality of persons of color that Du Bois is able to confront the double standard of the nation and its history of slavery when he writes, "The problem of the twentieth century is the problem of the colorline."[11] The Swedish economist, Gunnar Myrdal, would echo Du Bois in his classical work *An American Dilemma*, where he concludes that there is a split in white Americans' conscience caused by an intertwined relation between the faith in all persons having equal value on the one hand and a belief in racism on the other. Instead of a double consciousness, he calls it the "American dilemma" and stems out of what he believes is a moral value of equality, and he calls the American creed, in contrast to how Americans live their lives upholding Jim Crow laws, which for Myrdal causes a split consciousness. Myrdal's

9 Paul Ricoeur, *Time and Narrative*, vol. 1, trans. Kathleen McLaughlin and David Pellauer (Chicago: University of Chicago Press, 1984 [1983]), 7.

10 See chapter 1, "Of Our Spiritual Strivings," in W. E. B. Du Bois, *The Souls of Black Folk* (New York: Oxford World's Classics, 2008 [1903]), 10.

11 See chapter 2, "On the Dawn of Freedom," in ibid., 15.

conclusion is that the American people will not be able to sustain this contradiction and one day will choose to align its society with the equality principle.[12]

Du Bois' third concept is how this structural contradiction constructs the black identity, by forcing upon people a double consciousness. This comes from an internalized conflict, to both embrace freedom and equality as the American creed, while the lived experience embodies what Du Bois terms "the negro problem."[13] This embodiment of a nation's contradiction of freedom and the color line in the everyday experience of subordination and abuse is also what ties individual black healing to a nation being able to finding its peace; it interlinks not only a shared history of slavery but a future of peace beyond the color line. To Du Bois, black identity is a socially constructed identity giving rise to an individually experienced double consciousness among black people, mirroring the paradox of a freedom-loving nation holding slaves.[14] It is this double consciousness and the exposure of the contradiction that will force change, according to both Du Bois and Myrdal.

How can one translate this process of socially constructing an identity to another setting where the identity is not socially constructed? Even Du Bois, when it comes to the child, seems to place her outside the color line; in fact, Du Bois seems to place the child in a time before she is subordinated by the color line, before she has become black. It is necessary to identify whether it is freedom and equality that guide the child-rights regime – if it is, then freedom of speech must be a foundation of child rights advocacy. If freedom and equality are not the center of child rights advocacy, but rather care and protection are, then the principles of the right to be heard and the best interest of the child are the given guiding principles. Because if it is the right to be heard and the best interest principle that are the overarching values of the CRC, then these cannot support the breaking open of a split between the concept of the child and the child's own agency – in that they are not principles that can challenge the concepts themselves, as neither the right to be heard nor the best interest principle recognizes the legitimacy of an agency that would contradict and split open the monist identity construction of the child, since the final scope of the rights themselves is dependent on the power of someone other than the child holding the right, in other words it is a question of scope not derogation of a right. If children do not have the power

12 Gunnar Myrdal, *An American Dilemma*, vol. 1 (London: Routledge, 2017 [1944]).
13 See Du Bois, *The Souls of Black Folk*, 14.
14 See ibid., 136.

to challenge and disrupt the smooth identity they have been given, how are we to explain social justice for children?

The monist child-rights identity construction with its individual focus renders disharmony and makes radical critique of its regime an impossibility. However, by taking a few steps back, one can see that there is radical potential in the monist child-rights identity, if we are willing to shift the field of vision from the individual claim of the child-rights identity to instead see the group identity construction through monism. In the words of Fred Moten when addressing the philosophical use of discontinuity as resistance: "It makes you linger in the cut between them, a generative space that falls and erases itself."[15] In this sense, the child-rights identity in its monist form might be an impossibility and an act of disruption, but only if it is possible to demonstrate the distance between what the CRC establishes as the child-rights identity and what the child herself declares herself to be.

This radical potential of child rights is too easily forgotten when children and child rights become equated with cuteness and helplessness or are vilified as bundles of violence as exemplified in Chapter 3. It is possible to level criticism at this monist view of child-rights identity that is akin to the subject critique Spivak directs toward Foucault and Deleuze. In Spivak's retelling of their conversation about the Maoist and workers' struggle, she calls these subjects monolithic and anonymous, which means that they are not able to recognize the actual lives of the persons they have created in their minds as categories and concepts of persons.[16] The child as an identity is a radical proposition because it theoretically cannot be explained in line with other identity constructions. The challenge is how to manage a transformation of monism into a bifocal identity critique where the child can launch a resistance and gain power over her own construction, when the child-rights identity no longer rests in the hands of only adults but is also embodied by children themselves and thus gains a new form of unity through its split of both time and self, bringing the bifocality of the child and childhood into the same body.

4.7 THE TIME OF HUMANITARIAN CRISIS

Unlike the fixed nature of the child-rights identity, the child as a person is constantly undergoing a temporal transformation: The child is not supposed to

[15] Fred Moten, *In the Break: The Aesthetics of Black Radical Tradition* (Minneapolis: University of Minnesota Press, 2003), 89.

[16] Esteania Peñafiel Loaiza and Gayatri Chakravorty Spivak, *Can the Subaltern Speak?: Two Works* (London: Afterall Books, 2021), 9.

be the same child today as she was even a year ago as she is developing in harmony with her surroundings and, eventually, will one day no longer be a child. One single year of a child's life is seen as being so significant and transformative that a large part of society is organized around children from toddler age moving through one new grade in school every year – all the way until adulthood. Thus, the rights-based identity of the child remains fixed, yet unlike an adult, the inhabitant of the identity is herself transient.

To think of time and the child takes on a different dimension when one thinks of situations of harm and risk. In these situations, time creates urgency to act before the harm has become a part of the person without the possibility of challenging it through identity construction. Women and black people have been able to articulate how violence has been part of making their identity. By recognizing how violence has been part of shaping the woman and the racialized identity a language and a discourse have developed to counter both the violence and its purpose to designate through subordination a social hierarchy of categories of persons.

The role of time in the formation of the child is only further exacerbated in times of violence when the present is disrupted, the past obscured, and the future uncertain. Peace does not have a place in the memory of a child who has only lived through war.[17] If one has never experienced peace, it cannot exist within one's temporal memory; instead, war serves as the past, the present, and the future. In the context of narrating one's identity with recourse from the past, we can draw on Paul Ricoeur when he asserts that "expectation is the analogue to memory."[18] For younger children, there is no memory of a time of peace upon which to build an expectation of a return to the normal; peace or a nonviolent family becomes that unknown. To continue, Ricoeur writes, "by entrusting memory the fate of things past, and to expectation that of things to come, we can include memory and expectation in an extended and dialectical present which itself is none of the terms rejected previously."[19] In the case of the child refugee, there might be limited memory prior to armed conflict or before the journey to a new life in and out of refugee camps.

Without a past and only fragments of experiences to make up one's memory, it is difficult for the expectation of peace to take hold. This impossibility for a child to hold on to time is even more remarkable considering that it

[17] Ricoeur, *Time and Narrative*, 7.
[18] Ibid., 11.
[19] Ibid., 11.

is only in early and the very late years in life that each year has such a dramatic impact on one's personhood and capabilities and relationship to the future.

Not only is violence part of constructing childhood in the private sphere but time also plays a distinct role for children living in a humanitarian crisis. Consider the experience of a child growing up in a constantly changing, insecure environment – an environment that presents damaging experiences that are then blocked out, so that the child is prevented from defining the formation of the self. These circumstances make it so much harder to create a memory and that also can help bring together an identity with a consciousness that is anchored in a body that matches its age. In these environments, the goal is to keep the effects of time and place away from freely forming the child, to be replaced by a conscious effort to help shape how memories of harm are to become a part of a child's life with the least possible harm, for the rest of her time on Earth. This is to prevent memories of harm from finding a place in a child's personhood and from informing her identity without control. Instead of wanting historicity to influence the development of the child, in times of war and humanitarian crisis the aim is to keep these damaging influences to a minimum of harm. Instead of letting time in, the focus is on keeping time out.

In contrast, in an environment that is nurturing and caring for the child, historicity is supposed to become a part of one's personal identity, a process essential to the formation of the core of self to develop into a person who is able to construct one's own individual and collective interests and agency. This process is called "child rearing," as it appears in Principle 6 of the Declaration on the Rights of the Child: "The child, for the full and harmonious development of his personality, needs love and understanding. He shall, wherever possible, grow up in the care and under the responsibility of his parents, and, in any case, in an atmosphere of affection and of moral and material security." The fixed points in life that normally help orient the constantly changing and developing child are, in times of war and refugee crisis, in constant flux: "Moral and material security" is unavailable; the very atmosphere is impossible to maintain. This flux presents an additional challenge to defining yourself as an individual and to articulating your rights: the right to be seen as a full human and to know yourself as the full human you are now, not as you were one or two years ago. A child who is fourteen years old is very different from a child who is sixteen years old, the personal identity in childhood is a constant evolution, while the child-rights identity remains static until the age of majority when it ends. Not only is there a dissonance between how time works for the child-rights identity and childhood but also between individual identity and the child-right identity.

4.8 THREE FORMS OF VIOLENCE

Violence is intimately linked to the origin of child rights as manifested in international law and already addressed at the beginning of this chapter when examining the relationship between time, childhood, and violence. This section addresses three forms of violence: (1) violence in war among adults as it affects children in a systemic, general way, (2) violence that is directed toward children in particular, and finally (3) violence in the name of love.

In times of war and armed conflict, violence affects children in ways that differ from its effects on adults for a variety of reasons. There is first the form of general, indiscriminate violence, such as bombs being dropped, violence that physically impacts children as collateral damage as it also affects adults. The effects might differ; for example, a child will have to live with the trauma and memories of war for the rest of her life while an adult will have experienced a time – before the war – that was not affected by such violence. Children will live more days and years with the memory of war than adults for the simple reason that they have more days to live ahead of them. A second form of violence is where its harm to children is strategic in the war effort itself. One such example is the effects of landmines. Landmines can be intriguing to young children, who can mistake them for toys.[20] Landmines are one example of violence that when it affects children also harms the whole community both in the actual war effort but also negatively affects the community's future recovery and its transition from a time of war to a time of peace. In this respect, landmines do longer-lasting physical and psychological damage to children. Landmines can be found in areas where children are important contributors to the family farm life as they help with chores, which is important for both the child and the family at large in these settings.[21] Amputation and the related physical injuries that prevent children from participating in providing for the family cause lasting mental harm.[22]

Violence that specifically targets children is in itself twofold: Not only are there forms of general targeted violence such as by landmines, but there are

[20] M. A. Hemmati, H. Shokoohi, M. Masoumi, et al., "Mental Health Disorders in Child and Adolescent Survivors of Post-War Landmine Explosions," *Military Medical Research* 2, no. 30 (2015), https://doi.org/10.1186/s40779-015-0052-3.

[21] The study assessing the effects of landmines on children living at the Iran-Iraq border found an increase in mental disorders among these participants when compared against rates in the general population. Hemmati et al., "Mental Health Disorders in Child and Adolescent Survivor of Post-War Landmine Explosions."

[22] Ibid.

also forms of directed violence as well. For example, the recruitment of child soldiers is a form of directed violence, which takes advantage of the fact that a child is being recruited by adjusting the recruitment process to strategies that are most effective for enlisting children. The International Committee of the Red Cross (ICRC) has identified that children's need for security and protection as well as their lack of formal education all contribute as indirect factors in the recruitment of child soldiers. Other factors are family and friends who persuade the child to join or, alternatively, the absence of family, which can also push the child into the arms of the military.[23] This twofold violence means that guarding against violence and struggling to prevent violence wholly depends on the kind of violence affecting the child.

A third form of systemic violence that I want to address is the violence committed in the name of love, violence inflicted on children during a violent crisis by their own side, by the people that love them, making violence an expression of love. This is a form of violence that connects to care and power. An example borrowed from the literature is the character Beloved in Toni Morrison's novel of the same name. *Beloved* is inspired by the true story of Margaret Garner, an escaped slave. When Garner was captured, in 1856, she opted to kill her child instead of having the child sent back to slavery.[24] Building on this story, Morrison's main character Sethe kills her child to prevent her eventual capture and enslavement. This echoes W. E. B. Du Bois, who describes when, in the midst of his deep grief over the death of his son, at the same time he finds his son's death to be an act of liberation. Morrison's carachter Sethe goes further in her novel than Du Bois in his writing about how is deepest sorrow over his son's death describes the mixed feelings of one part of relief, that his son will never have to experience racism and the pain it causes. Sethe crosses the line from out of love as Du Bois express relief over that racism will not be able to touch his son, into the murder by the hands of the mother in protecting her daughter from the pains of slavery. The child, Beloved, later reappears in her house as a spirit. While Du Bois expresses the pain of not being able to protect one's child from the violence of racists in *Beloved* it is the mother murdering her child out of love. Examples from the real world of caregivers putting children in immediate danger, purportedly out of love and care, are multiple; for example, the American saying, "spare the rod spoil the child," is a perversion of parental love.

[23] Kristin Barstad, "Preventing the Recruitment of Child Soldiers: The ICRC Approach," *Refugee Survey Quarterly* 27, no. 4 (December 2008): 143–144.

[24] Pelagia Goulimari, *Toni Morrison* (London: Routledge, 2011), 81.

A much closer and ongoing humanitarian crisis concerns unaccompanied minors fleeing to Europe, mostly from Afghanistan and Syria. What is not often discussed is that many of these children arriving at migration offices are today's Beloveds, castaways, and others' loved ones, who have been sent away by their families to find a better life and placed in danger in an effort to ensure their own and their families' future security. The child is sometimes sent away because of love, to protect the child from the abuses in the sender country, either from the State, criminal organizations, or sometimes male relatives who want to earn an income by selling a girl for marriage. At other times, the children are sent away to Europe to secure finances for the family in the sender country. These children are sent to Europe alone, unaccompanied by their caregivers, but often in the hands of smugglers, who take them through areas of war and through refugee camps via trafficking routes. These violent contexts that drive migration, trafficking and smuggling – which often take place under the auspices of "protection" – also make the child different from the adult: The child's exposure to violence and war presents an additional vulnerability toward those placed in charge of the law or custom to protect them because they do not as children have the power to refuse.

I do not believe that the only reason for condemning violence against children is its direct harm on the child. Violence against children should also be condemned the additional burden it places on a child to manage through adulthood too: To make a happy life for herself despite the violence is an additional burden to carry throughout a whole life.

In connection with these forms of systemic violence, the inevitability of dehumanization might be a question of perspective. From the perspective of Sethe, the escaped slave in *Beloved*, the question is not a choice between dehumanization or maintaining one's humanity, a question often left to white abolitionists and white slaveholders. To Sethe, the binary is between slavery and not-slavery, which leads her to choose her child's quick death over the child's life as a slave. Sethe kills Beloved to prevent the child's re-entrance into slavery, yet interestingly, she does not choose to kill herself but follows through on her own escape. From the perspective of subordinated people, subjugation is not necessarily a choice between humanity, dehumanization, or resisting subordination. The choice might rather be a question of whether to exist or not. It is, at times, a question of choosing between life over death or death over life, where in some cases, resistance is death, as for Sethe in the act of killing her daughter. Saidiya Hartman offers a historical perspective on similar choices made by people captured to be shipped off as goods across the Middle Passage.[25] Hartman describes how captured people, not yet categorically marked as slaves, made the similar choice of death over life to resist becoming someone's property. Jenny Edkins, referring to Primo Levi when addressing the concentration camps, writes, "just because resistance is impossible, it does not mean that the person who has drowned has no worth. To be outside relations of power, to be beyond resistance, that is to be one of the drowned."[26] What is telling in *Beloved* is that when Sethe chooses death for her child and life for herself, it is Sethe as an adult mother who makes the decision to resist slavery through the death of her child. Her daughter Beloved must reappear in the shape of a ghost, a thought without a body, one that can only exist in Sethe's mind. The child Beloved herself remains out of reach, out of touch, manifesting not as a body, but rather as a mind within another's body, unable to speak.

When I was sent away from my original country to Sweden by my caregivers I had no choice or agency in a decision that was to fundamentally shape me as a person from that moment on, a decision that transformed who I am and who coming generations to follow will become, shaped by both the pain it caused to be sent away, but also by the fact of growing up as a person of color in an increasingly racist Sweden – to forever belong to a racial minority at the bottom of the social hierarchy, but also appreciating the parts of my life I consider good, such as my friends and family. This in one way was an act of love, to save me from a life as a child born out of wedlock in my birth nation. However, I had no possibility of agency in a decision that has now made me into what I am. Instead of protecting me from harm in my native country, my caregivers decided to protect me by sending me away. This story half a century ago is similar to that of the unaccompanied minors that arrived in Sweden 2015: To live for the rest of one's life in a society formed by racial violence and discrimination.

Regardless of whether dehumanization is the process that makes systematic violence possible (Hannah Arendt) or it is considered the effect of systematic violence (Johannes Lang), it can be agreed that humanity is at stake in moments of systemic violence.[27] But the burden of humanity must rest on the perpetrator

[25] Saidiya Hartman has addressed this phenomenon in the history of the Middle Passage, see Saidiya Hartman, *Lose Your Mother: A Journey along the Atlantic Slave Route* (New York: Farrar Straus Giroux, 2008).

[26] Jenny Edkins and Véronique Pin-Fat, "Introduction, Life, Power, Resistance," in *Sovereign Lives, Power in Global Politics*, ed. Jenny Edkins et al. (London: Routledge, 2004), 9.

[27] On dehumanization as enabling violence, see Hannah Arendt, *On Violence* (New York: Harcourt Publishing Company, 1970 [1969]). For a developed argument for understanding dehumanization as an effect rather than cause, see Johannes Lang, "Against Obedience: Hannah Arendt's Overlooked Challenge to Social-Psychological Explanations," *Theory & Psychology* 24, no. 5 (2014): 649–667.

and those who have the power to prevent violence, not on the victims of this violence. For these victims, systematic violence is more a question of being alive or not being alive, where resistance against violence presents either the choice of one's own death or engagement in a systemic critique of one's subjugation. Much as the rights-based identity of the child creates a glitch in time between a disavowed past and a future unable to take shape, the child also becomes a glitch between dehumanization and humanity when the child becomes a victim of harm and possible death as a choice made by adults.

4.9 THE SILENCING OF WAR

Speech in times of danger and war is often contested. Indeed, silence is often encouraged by patriotism and nationalism. It is in the context of war that the child's right to freedom of speech is first addressed by the United States Supreme Court as a civil right in the case *Tinker v. Des Moines Independent Community School District*, 393 U.S. 503 (1969). There the question for the Court was whether the Des Moines School District had violated their students' First Amendment rights in preventing some students from wearing armbands in symbolic protest of the Vietnam War. The school took this symbolic act of protest – wearing an armband – as a violation of an implicit patriotic duty to remain silent. The Warren Court held that the school district had indeed violated the students' First Amendment rights by prohibiting the armbands and thus preventing their peaceful protest.[28] It should be noted that the armband is a "silent" protest. Not only is acting on one's freedom of speech to protest in times of war seen by the State as dangerous, unpatriotic, and possibly treasonous, free speech can also challenge a "soft" version of silencing – namely, the silencing associated with civility, and often related to the importance of showing gratitude. In this view, refugees should be grateful for being granted entry into a country or for being provided protection in refugee camps; in exchange, they are meant to remain silent, to not complain.

Two important questions are raised in the reports to the Office of the United Nations High Commissioner for Human Rights (OHCHR) concerning how children's freedom of speech is protected in refugee camps. What right does a child have to free speech in a space where their speech is not actively facilitated? And how safe is it for children to protest against conditions within these camps without retaliation from the authorities providing them with shelter? This factor, the physical embodiment of the speaking subject, is

[28] Catherine J. Ross, *Lessons in Censorship: How Schools and Courts Subvert Student's First Amendment Rights* (Cambridge, MA: Harvard University Press, 2015).

illustrated in the difference between the ghost of Beloved that can only manifest as the thought of Sethe, and the silenced female subaltern of Spivak. The Spivakian subaltern is embodied, capable of annunciation, to be heard but without the ability to "be understood when speaking."[29] To protect the child in the name of its identity when speaking freely allows for the opening of a split in the identity anchored within its thinking body and is to create a place in time: to move from being constructed by age to attaining a location to be anchored to the world.

4.10 MIND AND BODY

The CRC encompasses civil-political rights, socioeconomic rights, and humanitarian and refugee laws as noted earlier. In other words, the CRC not only covers every person under the age of eighteen years but also almost every situation of every child imaginable.[30] The treaty is applicable to a child of one day just as to a child of seventeen years, eleven months, and twenty-nine days of age. Accordingly, in each situation, choices must be made about which of the several articles within the CRC should be given weight and how much weight in any given application of a right. The intention is that the CRC should be applicable to every child's situation wherever the child is, instead of the child having to adjust to the CRC. The challenge for adults interpreting the CRC is to decide which rights to apply at any given moment, and the challenge to lawyers when it comes to the CRC is that the articles guiding the convention's application are often individual and contextual, instead of general and objective, which is what law is normally required to be. The individual child's best interest (article 3(1)) and the right to be heard based on the child's maturity (article 12) are supposed to guide the application of the rights, when the child's identity is abstract and universal. Therefore, the CRC in its concrete application is, on the one hand, entirely nonsubjective and hyperformalized with its use of age as the sole constituting factor of subjecthood, and age being completely delinked from society, but. on the other hand, the CRC is all-subjective in its application of a particular right with a specific child in a set moment.

It is not the child who determines how much weight should be granted to her opinion, or what is in her best interest, and this has no effect on the subject construction itself, only on how different rights and circumstances should be

[29] Loaiza and Spivak, *Can the Subaltern Speak?*, 101.

[30] Articles 24 (health) and 29 (the purpose of education) include elements of environmental concerns. The environment is an underrepresented concern in the CRC.

weighted. This is how the child-rights identity lacks the duality that Paul Ricoeur associates with being a subject who both speaks and hears.[31] This is the duality that contains the ambiguity of being a person with both heart and mind, capable of making both good and bad decisions affecting both the self and others, shifting over time and place. This duality is absent in child rights. The monist child-rights identity in the CRC can only make responsibly good decisions because when the decisions are not good or responsible, they are immature and not to be taken into consideration in accordance with the CRC. This occurs because weight must be given to the decisions, based on maturity and best interest, and bad decisions are neither mature nor in the best interest of the child, they cannot be made by the child within the scope of the CRC. This places the child under a higher and different standard than the one for adults when it comes to the enjoyment of actual rights. Adults have their human rights to the fullest even when they might be held by a person that for one reason or another is not acting rationally because every adult benefits from the formal presumption of being rational. For a child, the substance of one's rights is determined based on whether what you will do with the said right is to be accepted as responsible and in your best interest, a rather unique form of right.

4.11 FREEDOM TO SPEAK

The CRC states that States parties are prohibited from using unlawful force against children: "[N]o child shall be subjected to torture or other cruel, inhuman or degrading treatment or punishment."[32] In addition to prohibiting States parties themselves from using violence against children, the CRC obligates States parties to take measures to prevent private actors from using violence against children: "States Parties shall take all appropriate legislative, administrative, social and educational measures to protect the child from all forms of physical or mental violence."[33] These specific provisions reflect the strictest norm in international law, the *jus cogens* prohibition against torture. Yet these provisions present a resounding dissonance between the stern voice of international law and that of lived experience and social reality. Children have been victims of torture and of degrading, inhumane treatment in times of previous wars, and those of today.

[31] Paul Ricoeur, "Philosophical Anthropology," in *Writings and Lectures*, ed. Johan Michel and Jérôme Porée, vol. 3, trans. David Pellauer (Cambridge: Polity, 2016 [2013]), 218.

[32] CRC, article 37(a).

[33] CRC, article 19(1).

As articulated in article 13 of the CRC, children have a right to speak without fear of retaliation or punishment from States parties. This right to freedom of speech is especially important for children in particularly vulnerable situations, such as during armed conflicts or while living in a refugee camp, situations where the child's dependence on others is at its highest. These are moments when the adult obligation to protect children has failed and where the child's ability to speak freely might be their most important defense against abuse directed toward them and others. Adults should not be granted so much power over children as to both fail to do their job in protecting children and, at the same time, circumscribe a child's ability to protect herself by being able to speak freely about what happens to her.

For adults, the ability to speak freely is one of the most important forms of protection from violence. The power of freedom of speech is targeted by authoritarian regimes, which fear the free word. In uneven power relationships, where one party controls the military or has a monopoly on violence, it is free speech that can serve the weaker party's side. This is an important lesson from the civil rights movements. Against overwhelming State powers, these movements adopted a policy of nonviolence in which free speech served as an alternative tool against the overwhelming violence deployed by the State against the protestors. This obligation to protect the free word should also be a basic routine within the child rights movement itself. The movement should put in place measures to guarantee that the children encountered in its projects shall be able to speak freely and to critique the treatment that they encounter while in the care of the various projects sponsored by the child-rights advocates. The atrocities that took place under the UN flag, where children were being forced and recruited into the sex trade, is one such example where children's freedom of speech could have an important effect on the activities of the UN presence in a region.[34] Skye Wheeler has reported on the rapes of children under the UN flag taking place in Haiti, the Central African Republic and the Democratic Republic of Congo, and also taking place under the flag of the African Union in Somalia.[35] As a response to the reports of sexual abuse of children by UN employees, the UN has adopted measures to control and combat the abuse.[36] For adults to be able to commit

34 Skye Wheeler, Opinion Contributor, "UN Peacekeeping Has a Sexual Abuse Problem," *The Hill*, November 1, 2020.

35 Ibid.

36 United Nations Action on Sexual Exploitation and Abuse, G.A. Res. 71/278; 71/297; Enhancing the Participation of Indigenous People's Representatives and Institutions in Meeting of Relevant United Nation Bodies on Issues Affecting Them, G.A. Res. 72/312; and Resolution to Prevent Sexual Exploitation and Abuse, G.A. Res. 73/302.

sexual abuse against children, adults need access to these children; as a consequence, it is not simply an abstract theoretical debate when I critique the child rights movement for its lack of internal critique. The culture of infallibility is a dangerous culture to children and a movement. Yet freedom of speech has a value in and of itself, not only as a tool for bearing witness or mending a wrong. To speak is part of being human, a part of fighting violence but also of resisting its pernicious effects; so far, this has theoretically been done through the manifestation of time in the split between description, performance and agency – through the speaking subject.

4.12 CONCLUSION

The very existence of a child-rights identity is itself a radical theoretical suggestion, considering it is being made out of time and not matter. The challenge is to either develop the possibility of challenging the monistic construction of the child identity or opting to bring the child-rights identity into the duality of identities forged through a process of subjugation.

To create a critical theory of the child identity within its dual perspective will mean reassessing the role of time, especially when it comes to taking age as the sole constituting element of the child. This is a fundamental challenge to the child-rights projects since the adoption of the CRC. It is worth considering what the gains and losses would be in comparison with the current monist construction. Even if, at the end of the day, a monist child identity is preferred, at least its blind spots and costs would be examined, and hopefully, we would be able to develop the safeguards needed to limit the downside of monism.

5

The Child in the Child Rights Movement

For the larger part of my adult life, I have proudly described child rights and its movement as a child-political and nonideological movement. Every time I said these words, I meant them and believed in their truthfulness. Within the past decade, I have come to see both naïveté and arrogance in this statement.[1] Ideological neutrality was never the case in any ontological sense with respect to the child rights movement. A more correct description is that during the 1990s, there was a historical period in which there was a Swedish party ideological consensus on children's rights. The politics surrounding children in the Swedish child rights movement of which I was a part did not in practice need to distinguish between ideology and child rights politics, thanks to a general consensus between the different political parties in the national parliament. As a member of the national board of Save the Children Sweden in the 1990s, I could see what I thought were nonideological practices, instead of what I now understand was an ideological consensus, played out in board meetings. Members of the national parliament from the major political parties, the Social Democrats, Conservatives, Liberals and Centrists sat on this board, all able to agree without falling into party ideology on issues concerning child rights. Karin Söder, the then Swedish vice prime minister and president of Save the Children, told me upon several occasions that politicians working with the same practical issues such as child rights often had more in common between each other across party lines than with a member of their own political party in the national parliament responsible

[1] Samuel Moyn describes a similar development for human rights in general. The similarities might be general but the root causes might vary; I am not making the wider human rights claim here. See Samuel Moyn, *The Last Utopia, Human Rights in History* (Cambridge, MA: Harvard University Press, 2012 [2010]), 213.

for a different area of the government. By way of example she would use the finance department, with which, she would argue, everyone is angry, regardless of party membership, because the minister of finance will always want to say no to calls for more money. I genuinely believe that she gave a truthful description of the fault lines existing within the Swedish national parliament in the first decade after the end of the Cold War. As Swedish society and politics became more binary, I then came to understand that it was not that the social suggestions we advocated when interpreting the meaning of child rights were nonparty ideological, but rather that there was a consensus around their interpretation in the Swedish parliament at that time. Instead of party ideological conflicts, the conflicts played out in a binary over how much you believed in child rights or not. Removing the ideological element of child rights interpretation in my experience created a binary relationship between those who were for child rights (they agreed on the child rights interpretation as ideology-neutral) and those against child rights (they did not agree on the social solutions suggested as interpretations of child rights). This binary view made it tempting to feel as if there were easy answers to complex and nuanced social questions. Either you were for children or not, and approval of child rights meant you were for children. It was by closing off any critique of the interpretations and by dismissing such as not child friendly, or even worse, to not be in support of child rights, that this consensus could be maintained as ideologically neutral.

I now understand that this was an unfortunate foreclosure as to diversity, diverse opinions and life perspectives, all of which could have enriched child rights and have had practical, positive effects for a diverse set of children. It becomes difficult to have disagreements when the norm is binary, either you are for children (and the platform proposed) or against children. In the long run, this binary risks hampering the evolution of a homogenous social movement towards a movement adjusted to a world of heterogeneity and complexity. It is through the internal critique, as discussed in previous chapters, for example, with critical race theory, that social movements keep pushing themselves to evolve and adjust and thus remain relevant in addressing the social concerns of the present time. The idea that what was considered good for children could be disconnected from wider social views was not addressed. Neither was the fact that children are not a homogenous group, not by age, but, further, children live in the same society as adults and their experiences will to some extent be shaped by the very same social inequalities as their parents. The use of age as the constituting element of the child identity was supposed to help the child-rights identity to escape social structures of discrimination and inequalities but whether this strategy has been successful is not discussed.[2] How is it then possible to argue that the age-based identity of the child can override the conflicting interests of other identity groups and categories such as gender, race, sexual orientation and class, to which children also belong?

I was invited to speak in 2022 by the Center for Child Rights Studies at the University of Linköping. During lunch, Dr. Jonathan Josefsson asked me what I meant by "the child rights movement" and which people did I refer to with that term.[3] His question highlighted the core of the dilemma with calling anything a child rights movement because in truth, the child rights movement is a loose term without clear externality. Social engagement has, in large part, moved from the regular organizational meetings, on different levels from local, regional, national and international levels to events and online manifestations. In its early history, these types of meetings still occurred in person between people in real life often on a weekly or bi-weekly basis, and the people showing up to these meetings were the bedrock of its movement. A large part of social organizing has moved from the regular meetings where everything was planned to a fleeting Internet presence. Jonathan's question made me wonder whether the child rights movement itself has become as immaterial as its identity subject.[4]

If the agenda of this possibly immaterial child rights movement is to advocate for the rights of children, such a movement should be able to explain why and how an age-based identity can take precedence over other forms of identification that might be more pressing – for example, the identification of black children in the Black Lives Matter (BLM) movement. Yet, this possibility of one identity taking precedence over another in the movement raises another question: Who in the child rights movement has the legitimate authority to make the call for children with conflicting identity-based interests to stand back and let others speak? To decide when the interests of girls

2 Karl Hanson asks the important question whether adults representing children is a reflection of the already established global status quo, or if in fact adults advocating for children is a necessity. See Karl Hanson, "Children's Representation in the Transnational Mirror Maze," in *The Politics of Children's Rights and Representation*, ed. Bengt Sandin, Jonathan Josefsson, Karl Hanson and Sara Balagopalan (London: Palgrave Macmillan, 2022).

3 For an examination of child representation and global justice, see, Jonathan Josefsson and John Wall, "Empowered Inclusion: Theorizing Global Justice for Children and Youth," *Globalizations* 17 (2020): 1043–1060.

4 For a study on the use of the Internet to drive child and youth participation, see Frida Buhre, "Child Figuration in Youth Climate Justice Activism: The Visual Rhetoric of the Fridays for Future on Instagram," in *The Politics of Children's Rights and Representation*, ed. Bengt Sandin, Jonathan Josefsson, Karl Hanson, and Sara Balagopalan (London: Palgrave Macmillan, 2022).

override the interests of boys or vice versa? Jessica Clarke has argued for law to take the non-binary identity of trans people seriously.[5] Who can decide when, for example, trans rights should override the rights of boys and girls alike as the primary identity to advocate for within the child rights movement? These types of choices within a movement are often represented by different interests and positions within the movement itself, where the participants demand that their representation be respected and acknowledged. Who within the child rights movement is authorized to argue that the child-rights identity of the child exists outside, for example, the gender binary?[6]

This chapter examines a theoretical understanding of group consciousness and the possibility of forging a democratic link to collective actions that can make up the parts of a child rights movement. I draw from the Google searches conducted in Chapter 3 to claim that in some instances, a child-specific identity was, in fact, exhibited, one formed outside considerations of race and gender. Beltrán has found that it is possible to construct a pan-Latino national identity in the United States, despite different and, at times, conflicting cultural and historical experiences and narratives.[7] I similarly argue that the intersections among various identity categories in individual children could be considered alongside a rights-based identity of the child if children as agents within their own movement are taken seriously.

5.1 TO BE THE INTERPRETER OF CHILDREN

The early child rights movement found legitimacy to be derived from the efforts of individuals across several professions. The White House Children's Conference served as the meeting point for professionals working with children between 1909 and 1971.[8] These conferences gathered teachers, pediatricians and social workers representing every US state to debate the federal government's policies toward children and young people. The conference met once every decade at the White House and was hosted by the sitting president, regardless of whether Republican or Democrat.[9] Yet these

5 Jessica A. Clark, "They, Them, and Theirs," *Harvard Law Review* 132, no. 3 (2019): 894.

6 Ibid., 990.

7 Christina Beltrán, *The Trouble with Unity, Latino Politics and the Creation of Identity* (Oxford: Oxford University Press, 2010), 42.

8 The first conference was called to order by President Theodore Roosevelt at the White House at 2:30 pm on January 25, 1909; Maria Grahn-Farley, "How Children Got Rights" (Doctoral diss., Harvard Law School, Cambridge, MA, 2013), 22; see also Children's Bureau (DHEW), "The Story of the White House Conferences on Children and Youth" (1973), PS 006 506.

9 For a full description of the conferences, see Grahn-Farley, "How Children Got Rights."

conferences were not only places where professionals met; they also became meeting places for children and young people to debate and influence the nation's agenda concerning their lives. By the 1930s, children and young people had already become an integral part of these conferences. It was during this period that children, for the first time in the United States, constituted themselves as a discrete youth identity.[10]

The experiment of joint child and youth governance came to an abrupt end in the years 1970–1971 with the last White House Children's Conference.[11] During this period, the conference was divided into two separate meetings, one focusing on children held in 1970 and the other focusing on young people held in 1971. The 1971 youth conference hosted 1,318 delegates; 915 of them were young people between the ages of fourteen and twenty-four years, representing every state.[12] By 1971, children and young people had become a significant force within the structure of these conferences, where they argued for the end of the draft and for lowering the age of majority from twenty-one years to eighteen. They proclaimed their own Declaration of Independence and the expansion of the Bill of Rights with four new rights: (1) the right to food, clothing and a home; (2) the right to one's own things as long as this was not interfering with the rights of another; (3) the right to cultural heritage; and (4) the right to whatever is necessary to preserve these rights.[13] Participants also expressed their opposition to the Vietnam War, with the conference organizers describing the war as "abhorrent to the majority of Americans."[14] The young people decided to address the conflict within the formal conference protocol with an official statement that read as follows: "The fear of youth identifying with adults and vice versa, the fear of people identifying with themselves, the fear of people identifying with their race, the fear of people identifying with a country – all create a climate of fear which permeates this nation. Internal divisiveness has contributed to a loss of national purpose."[15] During these formative years, the tension between generations was strong, but it was recognized and addressed.

[10] Remarks of James E. West, Youth Outside of Home and School, Section III – Committee G, WHC 1930, 247–248.

[11] White House Conference on Children Program (December 13–18, 1970); 1971 White House Conference on Youth, Washington, DC.

[12] White House Conference on Children Program (December 13–18, 1970), 2.

[13] The Preamble: Recommendations and Resolutions, WCH 1971, see Grahn-Farley, "How Children Got Rights," 136.

[14] The Resolution: Recommendations and Resolutions, WCH 1971.

[15] Ibid., 21.

If the White House Children's Conferences served as any indication of what a child rights movement would look like if it were run by children, it is clear that it would not be the same as a child rights movement led by adults on behalf of children. The agenda most likely would be different (not necessarily "better"), as would possibly the choices at the nexus of conflicting interests between different movements. Even if the agendas remained similar, the ability to speak freely and without fear would give the agenda additional meaning. One example where the agendas between adults and children diverged in the White House Conferences was that the young people took the lead in arguing for racial desegregation and solidarity, an argument that would presumably not have been issued from the conference if it had been led by adults alone. This crucial distinction demonstrates the disparity between the child's assertion of her rights and her rights as articulated by someone purportedly speaking on her behalf.

It is appropriate here to disrupt the tempting conclusion that children will always be more ethical and more progressive than adults. That narrative stems from a very specific time when a whole generation of male youth were sent to fight a war in Asia on behalf of a cause they did not feel was theirs to fight. The Vietnam War is not a clear predictor of how children and young people will position themselves as a group in relation to their adult generation. What the Vietnam War provided was a common interest among a specific set of people in one society – it provided the children and youth of the United States with a commonly constructed identity through shared interests. Just as important was the fact that the draft was also age-based and affected the older children and youth groups of the population.

5.2 THE ACCOUNTABILITY GAP

Today's rights-based child rights movement is neither required to be led by children nor built on the specific knowledge of professionals concerning the unique conditions children face. Nor, for that matter, are parenting or family ties considered in the movement to be a legitimate ground for speaking on behalf of children. Instead, the child rights movement is open to anyone who feels like participating, as long as they are explicitly committed to *child rights*. What creates a common interest is child rights itself and not an interest forged out of the experience and agency of the group identified. The qualifier for participation is not self-representation nor is it knowledge or even care for the condition of children, even if a large proportion of participants in this movement deeply care for children. This is not to say that child rights activists do not care for children, most of them certainly do care. But it is not what gives legitimacy to speak for children; instead, it is solely based on a self-appointed and professed commitment to the child rights regime.

This approach differs from other forms of constituency-driven agendas. For example, labor unions typically demand that their members have (or have had) employment in a given profession to be members.[16] Laura Carlson makes an interesting observation in her comparative study on the accountability of trade unions toward their members: In the United Kingdom and in Germany, the accountability of unions toward their members is regulated through statutes, case law, or internal documents, while Swedish labor unions only have regulation of their obligations through internal documents, if addressed at all, as interpreted by the union. The only recourse Swedish labor union members have with respect to violations of any obligations is to vote with their feet and leave the union if it does not fulfill its duties toward its members.[17]

It should be noted that none of the above-mentioned forms of demanding or exercising accountability are available to children in the child rights movement. This lack is because children's participation within a child rights movement is not seen as a necessity for the movement to be able to legitimately speak for children. In this respect, it is not possible to leave a movement of which one is not a participant. Most importantly, it is not possible for children to hold their advocates accountable for the lobbying and legislation on behalf of children. One example of the accountability gap is to be found on the official website of Save the Children International. The website demonstrates this dilemma of accountability when they define how they seek to be accountable to their subjects – that is, how they hold themselves accountable through self-policing: "We are committed to holding ourselves accountable for the promises we make to our supporters, partners, staff, and most of all, children."[18] In much the same way, only the child rights movement itself can evaluate whether it is serving children well. If the rights-based child identity upon which a movement is built cannot anchor its consciousness within its body to announce its identity, accountability becomes a theoretical impossibility.

[16] Carlson weaves a narrative of collectivism and special interest and guarding of boundaries in her book, drawing on the historical context within the guilds to the present day. See Laura Carlson, *Workers, Collectivism and the Law* (Cheltenham: Edward Elgar Publishing, 2018).

[17] See ibid., 176, 178 (UK), 202 (Germany), while Swedish labour unions do not have legally codified and regulated duties towards their members, 221.

[18] See the website of Save the Children, Accountability, available at www.savethechildren.net/about-us/accountability, accessed on July 14, 2020.

5.3 GROUP CONSCIOUSNESS

In contrast to the self-appointed approach, ties can instead be created in a movement through "group consciousness." This is linked to the idea that a specific group of individuals who possess common external traits such as markers of race, class or gender will also share common experiences that correlate to their shared traits.[19] In the existing literature, indicators that lead to the formation of group consciousness are experiences of external threats directed toward a specific group of people that, when taken in such a consistent and coherent manner, establish an identifiable group as a putative target of these threats.[20] To aid in understanding how the formation of group consciousness is produced by external threats, Arthur Miller makes a distinction between "group identification" and "group consciousness."[21] Group identification occurs when a person self-locates their individual place within a larger social stratum, an act accompanied by a psychological feeling of belonging to that stratum.[22] Natalie Masuoka and Jane Junn presume that once individuals within a group have identified themselves as belonging to that group, they will exhibit strong loyalty to it.[23] Yet as suggested by the distinction between the terms, group identification does not necessarily lead to group consciousness, the latter of which entails some understanding of interconnectedness on the basis of being threatened.

The child rights movement is not building its legitimacy to speak for children on an exhibited interconnectedness, as would presumably be expressed through solidarity between individual children themselves. At the very least, this solidarity is not part of the child rights agenda as articulated by the movement if one looks to the large established organizations such as Save the Children and UNICEF. One possible exception is the climate justice

[19] Colette Guillaumin describes this as a system of marks, see Colette Guillaumin, *Racism, Sexism, Power and Ideology* (London: Routledge, 1995).

[20] Magnus O. Bassey, "The Place of Group Consciousness in Black Autobiographical Narratives," *Journal of African American Studies* 11, no. 3–4 (December 2007): 214–224; and Ritchie P. Lowry, "Leadership Interaction, Group Consciousness, and Social Change," *The Pacific Sociological Review* 7, no. 1 (Spring 1964): 22–29.

[21] Arthur H. Miller, Patricia Gurin , Gerald Gurin and Oksana Malanchuk, "Group Consciousness and Political Participation," *American Journal of Political Science* 25, no. 3 (August 1981): 494, 495.

[22] Ibid., 494.

[23] Natalie Masuoka and Jane June, *The Politics of Belonging: Race, Public Opinion, and Immigration* (Chicago: University of Chicago Press, 2013), 92.

movement, where children have taken the lead in bringing their States to court with references to the intergenerational principle.[24]

More recent studies caution against drawing parallels between the experiences of people of color when studying other groups: for example, suggesting a parallel between the experiences of Latinos and Asian-Americans, or commonalities in their formations of group consciousness.[25] Accordingly, we might revise the definition of group consciousness that appears in the opening to this section: Group consciousness is a process of group identification combined with an ideological understanding of the group's placement within the social structure, which often yields a political commitment to collective acts on behalf of the group's larger interests.[26] Masuoka and Junn note that individuals within a socially identified group might feel they contribute different strengths and build their attachment to the group on different grounds: Even if a group of individuals identify as belonging to a specific social group, their individual motivations and identifications with and within that group can and do vary on an individual basis.[27] Similarly, in her studies on what has led women to become active in the women's rights movement, Lauren Duncan argues that it is too limiting to presume that identity groups have coherent motivations for their participation. Within these groups, she argues, one should instead apply a combined approach between individual psychological experiences and identification with a group consciousness.[28]

There is a body of scholarship on group consciousness that is not forged out of disadvantage, but rather of privilege, namely, critical whiteness studies.[29] This strand of research follows a similar method as that developed by black

[24] Maria Grahn-Farley, "The Human Rights Claim in Climate Justice: An Argument for Reintroducing the Principle of Anti-discrimination and Strengthening the Anti-domination Principle When Children Go to Court," *Journal of Gender, Race & Justice* 439 (2022): 25. See also, Buhre, "Child Figuration in Youth Climate Justice Activism."

[25] Dennis Chong, Reuel Rogers and Alvin B. Tillery, "Reviving Group Consciousness," *Politics of Democratic Inclusion*, ed. Christina Wolbrecht, Rodney E. Hero, Peri E. Arnold and Alvin B. Tillery (Chicago: Temple University Press, 2005), 45, 46. See also Gabriel R. Sanches, "Latino Group Consciousness and Perceptions of Commonality with African Americans," *Social Science Quarterly* 89, no. 2 (June 2008): 428–444; and Natalie Masuoka, "Together They Become One: Examining the Predictors of Panethnic Group Consciousness among Asian Americans and Latinos," *Social Science Quarterly* 87, no. 5, Special Issue on Ethnicity and Social Change (December 2006): 993–1011.

[26] Miller et al., "Group Consciousness and Political Participation," 494.

[27] Masuoka and June, *The Politics of Belonging*, 93.

[28] Lauren E. Duncan, "Motivation for Collective Actions: Group Consciousness as Mediator of Personality, Life Experiences, and Women's Rights Activism," *Political Psychology* 20, no. 3 (September 1999): 611–635.

[29] Pamela Perry and Alexis Shotwell, "Relational Understanding and White Antiracist Praxis," *Sociological Theory* 27, no. 1 (March 2009): 1.

scholars. Yet instead of focusing on disadvantage as a form of group identification, this scholarship focuses on how whiteness is built on group privilege, which creates a common identifier and motivates a scholar's willingness to practice self-awareness in order to work against the racist structures that make white privilege possible.[30] Gearey makes a similar observation regarding the recognition of shared privilege as a marker of group consciousness: A privileged lawyer can work within herself to push against societal oppression by sharing her own experiences of an oppressive space, rather than claiming to speak on behalf of the people who actually live in these spaces. As Gearey writes, "they can speak for themselves," and speaking about one's own privilege is to acknowledge the authority of personal agency in contrast to the power of definition as exhibit when speaking for the experiences of others.[31]

Clearly, there are differences between various forms of social movements. Both the women's rights movement and the civil rights movement offer deliberate strategies of introspection and consciousness raising for individual members to address the legitimacy of the authority to speak for others as if they are the self in order to resist the place that the greater social hierarchy has assigned them. The strategies are themselves up for evaluation and subject to internal critique from both a practical and an ideological approach.[32]

Perhaps the most striking difference emerges when we consider the links between the civil rights movement and the women's rights movement, on the one hand, and the environmental movement, on the other hand. The clear difference is that the subject and the object largely coincide within the civil rights movement and women's rights movement, whereas the actors participating in the environmental movement are distinct from the movement's actual purpose,[33] with probably children being a significant exception to the

30 Ibid., 34.

31 Adam Gearey, *Poverty Law and Legal Activism: Lives That Slide Out of View* (London: Routledge, 2018), 101.

32 There are several strategies to fight "system justification," such as those witnessed in the "black is beautiful" and "women can" campaigns. One serious effect that comes with system justification is how African American university students had lower self-confidence than white students, as discussed by Elle Shockley, Ashley Wynn and Leslie Ashburn-Nardo, "Dimensions of Black Identity Predict System Justification," *Journal of Black Psychology* 42, no. 2 (2016): 105.

33 The landmark case addressing legal injury and personhood when it comes to the environmental movement is *Sierra Club v. Morton*, 405 U.S. 727 (1972), where the Court held that the Sierra Club lacked legal standing because they had not suffered the injury and because the environment as such did not have legal personhood.

more general rule. Children in the climate justice movement are relying on a direct connection between their identity and their claim, due to age.[34]

In contrast, the environmental movement coalesces around a shared purpose, but not with the authority gap of who legitimately speaks for others. It is widely accepted that the environment is not the self but rather one of the interests of the self (except when it comes to children, where there is the direct link between the self and the universal through the inter generational principle). The child rights movement is not like the civil rights movement and the women's rights movement struggling with the legitimacy of authority to speak or the adult environmental movement without the ethical dilemma of legitimate authority to speak. Yet the challenge is that neither is it a movement in which the actors and its purpose coincide, as they do for the civil rights movement and women's rights movement.

At the core of its ideological self-image, the child rights movement sees children as subjects, not objects, and believes that children are capable of forming their own view. (To take the previous example: Only a more radical actor within the adult environmental movement would argue the same for trees.) Nevertheless, this understanding of the self-ideation of children as advocates occurs at the same time that the child rights movement fails to provide any argument for why one set of adults – who belong to the movement – would be in a better position than other adults – who are not part of the movement – or children themselves to decipher the needs of children and to know what is in the best interests of individual children.

Both marginalization and deprivation are described in the literature as factors that aid in constructing group identity. When experiencing either, it is in one's interest to join together with others to take part in collective action in order to achieve political change.[35] This presumption that marginalization and deprivation drive group consciousness is questioned by Arthur Miller who

[34] See, for example: *Ali v. Federation of Pakistan* (Paktistan Punkab Lahore High Court) Constitutional Petition No. 1 of 2016; *Armando Ferrao Carvalho and Others v. The European Parliament and the Council of Europe* (European Court of Justice) Case No. T-330/18; *Duarte Agostino and Others v. Portugal and 32 Other States* (European Court of Human Rights) Communicated case – 39371/20; *ENVironnement JEUnesse v. Canada* (Canada Quebec Superior Court) 500-06-000955-183 (2018); *La Rose v. Her Majesty the Queen* (Canada Federal Court) T-1750-19; *Neubauer, et al. v. Germany* (Germany Federal Constitutional Court) (24 March 2021) 1 BvR 2656/18; and *Sacchi et al. v. Argentina et al.* (UN Committee on the Rights of the Child) CRC/C/88/D/104/2019.

[35] Ritchie P. Lowry connects the idea of group consciousness to the Marxist theory of change through a feeling of being lost through disenfranchisement, a feeling that finds its structure though group consciousness. When this more structured self-and-group understanding meets resistance and conflict with other social interests, only then are leadership and solidarity formed, which, in the final stage, can lead to a political agenda taking control over the

argues that any strong connection to these processes in the anatomy of a particular group consciousness persists solely in their connection to an idea that the author traces back to a Marxist presumption "that fundamental differences exist between the interest of one's own group and those of the domination group."[36] In this respect, Miller adjusts group consciousness theories that place marginalization and deprivation at the center of the understanding of group consciousness, instead arguing that group consciousness can also be formed when one identity group finds justification in maintaining its privileged central position over a deprived group and supports the said group's further marginalization.[37] It is not deprivation in itself that constitutes group consciousness, but rather the favoring of one group's position over another – a sense of internal group interests constituted against external threats against these interests, regardless of whether the group is privileged or deprived.[38]

If it is not the self-interest of individual children that governs the child rights movement and its agenda, and if there is no professional link to children among actors taking part in the movement that explains subject knowledge upon which the movement is speaking and acting on behalf of children, then I must ask: Who today inhabits the child rights movement, and where do they derive legitimate authority to set international and national agendas for it? Neither are parents an authorized group in the child rights movement: While motherhood used to provide women with a legitimacy to speak on behalf of their children, this is no longer the case. The argument is not that this outdated view of the role of women should be a way of restoring legitimacy. The point is that old and often for good reason rejected forms of legitimacy were replaced by a commitment to child rights itself, without any substantial debate over what would constitute the power to talk and interpret child rights on behalf of children.

In a functional democracy, collective action has been an instrumental tool for ideologies to marshal politics in order to provoke changes in law. When it comes to child rights, however, the law is no longer the tool of politics; instead, law is the ideological expression of rights transposed to, and secured by, metaphysics. Pierre Schlag describes this change as a form of pre-scripted discourse that excludes participation in advance.[39] Another way of viewing this

processes of power in a community. See Lowry, "Leadership Interaction, Group Consciousness, and Social Change," 22, 24.

36 Miller et al., "Group Consciousness and Political Participation," 494, 495.

37 Ibid., 494, 497, 507.

38 Ibid., 494, 496.

39 Pierre Schlag, "Normative and Nowhere to Go," *Stanford Law Review* 43, no. 1 (1990): 170.

pre-scripted discourse is by way of a question: What collective action is there to participate in when the outcome has already been decided? If the child rights regime is without a clear sender, without a coherent politics, and without a cohesive movement claiming authority to interpret the group's essential purpose, the question of who serves as legitimate authority to represent and speak for children presses for an answer.

5.4 "THE BEST INTEREST"

The closest the child rights movement comes to making its source of authority known is when making arguments on behalf of children using an interpretation of the "best interest" of the child. The international child rights regime mirrors this invisible subject with its open-ended "best interests," like an invisible hand that generates an expansion of child rights norms without a real subject actually generating them.[40] As a result of this invisible subject, the regime is often in conflict about whether or not controlled reception of these "best interests" into the regional and national regimes can even be promoted. To argue in the form of interest, rather than through action, is not unique to child rights: For example, scholars have noted that the political mobilization of a Latino vote is dependent on the possibility of establishing a unifying interest to subsequently decipher and represent.[41]

Yet when it comes to child rights, the "best interest" argument challenges both the possibility of uniting a movement around "interest" as well as the notion of translating a common interest into "best interest." This issue of translation is particularly difficult when the "best interest" established by the CRC is a concrete evaluation based on the individual child, which would mean that it cannot be used as the foundation for a unifying claim for a movement covering children as a whole. The "best interest" is thus a principle of proportionality, balancing opposing interests in concrete situations. However, proportionality presumes that the interests to be balanced are between the interests of children and those of adults, rather than between the interests of children themselves. This division of interests again raises questions: On what legitimate authority can adults constitute the child rights movement, especially when the said adults do not have professional knowledge about children nor serve in a caregiving role as parents? How is a

40 For an example in Swedish of a study of the use of best interest, see Louise Dane, "Den reglerade invandringen och barnets bästa" [Regulated Immigration and the Best Interest of the Child] (Doctoral thesis, Stockholm University, 2019).

41 Beltrán, *The Trouble with Unity, Latino Politics and the Creation of Identity*, 101.

self-proclaimed supporter of children's rights to obtain the legitimacy to balance the best interest on behalf of children against one singular child, or one group of children against another group of children, or against other adults? Where does this authority come from? One place to begin looking for a source of authority is in the concept of solidarity rather than in the belief in child rights as constituting this authority because it is not representation, nor specific knowledge, or association to a child or children. For solidarity to be the legitimating source, one must decide what one is in solidarity with and also acknowledge that it is a legitimacy that comes as an action of choice freely given – but equally that there is a freedom on the other end to either accept or reject the offer.

5.5 NARRATIVE IDENTITY

In the contest of distinguishing between the interests of one particular child and the interests of children in general, we must recognize a difference between narrating and retelling. When heard, the child is not providing a narrative, but rather a form of retelling, one that only concerns that specific child and her unique experiences. Narrative, on the other hand, puts together fragments of a person's experiences, so that these separate acts of telling come together to represent the cohesive experiences of an identity.[42] Ricoeur describes the function of narrative as a device that "integrates into one whole and complete story multiple and scattered events, thereby schematizing the intelligible signification attached to the narrative taken as a whole."[43] In short, narrative helps to build a group identity out of singular, personal experiences by turning them into a collective memory.[44] For children to be able to build a common narrative, they must be able to speak; it is not enough for them to be heard by adults, they must also be understood.

The success of the women's rights movement and the civil rights movement, which are both based on the self-interest of their participants as a group,

[42] This is a different form of narrative from the one used by C. Wright Mills, using narrative to expand the social imagination for the possible. See C. Wright Mills, *The Social Imagination, Fortieth Anniversary Edition* (Oxford: Oxford University Press, 2000 [1959]).

[43] Paul Ricoeur, *Time and Narrative*, vol. 1, trans. Kathleen McLaughlin and David Pellauer (Chicago: University of Chicago Press, 1984 [1983]).

[44] In this text, "collective memory" is referred to in a narrow sense based on the work of Maurice Halbwachs, *On Collective Memory*, ed. and trans. Lewis A. Coser (Chicago: University of Chicago Press, 1992 [1941]), this before collective memory gained its more normative role within, for example, Holocaust studies and later in studies of redress. See, for example, Michael Rothberg, *The Implicated Subject: Beyond Victims and Perpetrators* (Stanford: Stanford University Press, 2019).

ultimately depends on narrative to achieve their respective degrees of authenticity and community – that is, whether or not each movement is accurate and thus legitimate in its representation of women or of minorities, respectively. These concerns for authenticity, legitimacy, and authority to represent the experiences of other people, as already addressed in the introduction to this book, were raised by Derrick Bell as part of a self-reflective suspicion from within the civil rights movement. A former National Association for the Advancement of Colored People (NAACP) lawyer, Bell reexamines whom a lawyer actually serves when arguing for integration in American schools.[45] He questions if it is possible to serve the larger civil rights agenda that ideologically stands for integration when, at the same time, it is in the interest of his client as a black child to actually win a case against a school so racist that they are brought to court by the NAACP. Bell's famous article "Serving Two Masters: Integration Ideals and Client Interests in School Desegregation Litigation" initiated a method of self-reflection within the civil rights movement, a process that has come to grow into critical race theory and to spin off into multiple critical schools advocating for women, gay, lesbian, and trans rights. Bell's self-reflective critique and use of a narrative method for examining his experiences gave the civil rights movement the energy to transition and adjust to our present-day concerns for authenticity, leading the NAACP to maintain its position as one of the most relevant organizations in the United States protecting black and African American citizens against racism.[46]

One way to prove the veracity and thus legitimacy of any representation of someone else's lived experience is through narrative authentication. Narrative not only serves as a means of threading together fragmented experiences into collective memory but also authenticates representation because it begins with the personal: Whereas the truth is typically guarded and left to its manipulation in the eyes of the beholder, through a narrative approach, the truth is kept by the person telling the story. For Miranda Fricker, this process could be understood as managing a credibility deficit that stems from the power deficit of one's identity.[47] When the center of a movement presents clear, legitimate

45 Derrick A. Bell, "Serving Two Masters: Integration Ideals and Client Interests in School Desegregation Litigation," *The Yale Law Journal* 85 (1976): 470.

46 Tommy J. Curry expands on Bell's now almost fifty-year-old critique to a contemporary, internal critique over the silencing of black males based on the fear that to address the social reality of black men in the United States will make invisible and question the authority of the black female narrative. See Tommy J. Curry, *The Man-Not: Race, Class, Genre, and the Dilemmas of Black Manhood* (Chicago: Temple University Press, 2017), 229.

47 Miranda Fricker, *Epistemic Injustice: Power and the Ethics of Knowing* (Oxford: Oxford University Press, 2007), 17.

authority to speak on behalf of others in the movement, the precise location of the place of solidarity can be more clearly defined. While the fragments are personal and truly unique only to the individuals who experienced them, when they are shared, they can be recognized by others who occupy the same place in the social hierarchy and can be taken as representative of others' experiences, too. This process of drawing from the fragments of a personal history is how narrative identity emerges from collective memory. In a movement, collective memory locates the place from which solidarity has the legitimacy to act by making a common imaginary possible to all. Collective memory creates an image of the future for those who do not share the fragments of a personal history. The narrative allows for this sharing of the imagination, an inclusive participation in a future based on something wider than the authentic yet singular self.

At the periphery of the women's rights movement and the civil rights movement is the potential for cross-identity solidarity. Of course, the designation of periphery and centers are themselves interlinked with identity. What for the individual is the center begins with where one stands; the center and the peripheries are constituted by the hierarchies of identities. What is peripheral for a white feminist is not the same as for a feminist of color. The intersection between race and gender constitutes the center point for a critical race feminist orientation, while for a mono-feminist orientation, it is peripheral. For someone claiming legitimate authority to represent a particular group in a diverse movement, a certain amount of discomfort as well as resistance from others will always result, yet the discomfort also protects against co-option. To find oneself caught in this bind between representation and authenticity is what Adam Gearey describes as a "creative anxiety."[48] Gearey's term refers to the fact that even without a sense of self-interest based on self-representation, one can take part in a movement through solidarity.[49] However, taking part in a movement that entails someone else's representation leads to a form of participation that cannot be pursued without a sense of doubt because it is, ostensibly, to ride on someone else's life narrative.

The discourse within the child rights movement has by and large been spared this "creative anxiety" between representation and authenticity that the civil rights movement, the women's rights movement, and movements built on class solidarity of which Gearey writes have had to confront from within their own ranks, with the interesting exception of Sandin et al. in *The Politics*

[48] Gearey, *Poverty Law and Legal Activism*, 23.

[49] Gearey uses the figure of what he has identified in the civil rights movement as the "White Ally" within black Marxism – see Gearey, *Poverty Law and Legal Activism*, 33.

of Children's Rights and Representation, where the various authors begin to grapple with child representation.[50] The authors take on the distinction between an objective telling about something, and the possibility to speak about an issue of concern.[51] Interestingly, the tension through which other social movements encounter their ethical binds while establishing their means of self-accountability is not a central theme within the child rights movement: Without children in the movement, no one can challenge the legitimacy or authenticity of those speaking on their behalf or, for that matter, produce the "creative anxiety" that maintains a self-reflective suspicion. For example, men can take part in the women's rights movement out of solidarity, and white people can be part of the civil rights movement or Black Lives Matter through solidarity, but they would never claim that their agency within the movement is based on self-representation. On the contrary, there is often an explicit understanding that any agency to act as part of the movement outside self-representation has to be granted by others within it. Gearey calls this moment of granting agency "the open-hearted pause," which takes place in the meeting between two people recognizing each other as human beings.[52] There is no such tension between self-representation and granting agency within the child rights movement. The child is the most recent subject to be transformed from being treated as an object of law to a subject of rights. The very idea of the child as being a rights holder, as late as 1989, was a radical idea, and there is still no discourse of recognition within the movement itself. After all, this radical call for identification between generations was expressed at what was to be the last White House Conference in 1971.

Even the argument for solidarity is difficult to make without the requirement of children as members of a movement claiming to be a child rights movement. It would be difficult for two reasons to make solidarity a building block for what one wants to call a child rights movement: First, there is no self-representation within the movement to associate one's solidarity with, and second, there is no method for expressing solidarity when the will of the subject (in this case, children) remains a nonconstituting requirement, and will thus remain unknown. It follows that there is no means of establishing a form of solidarity between adults and children that can legitimize the former's claim to authority to represent children. For the child rights movement, the argument for solidarity is instead built on claiming to know what is in the best

[50] See Bengt Sandin, Jonathan Josefsson, Karl Hanson and Sara Balagopalan (eds.), *The Politics of Children's Rights and Representation* (London: Palgrave Macmillan, 2022).

[51] Jonathan Josefsson et al., "Representing Children," in Sandin et al. (eds.), *The Politics of Children's Rights and Representation*, 2.

[52] Gearey, *Poverty Law and Legal Activism*, 45.

interest of children based solely on that the adult making the claim is a participant in the movement, and on insisting that this knowledge can guide the agenda of the movement. This is a different form of knowing since the rights-based identity of the child, anchored as it is in age, cannot in itself generate knowledge about the child in the world. This posthumous or belated form of knowing is not connected to anything external because it has lost the experiential link to childhood that representation would otherwise provide. This form of knowing can only be granted through actual rights, not by knowledge of the child in the world.[53] The rights-based identity of the child thus presents a conundrum: It is to see without the possibility of knowing what one is watching.

5.6 THE MOVEMENT GOES GLOBAL

A geographical expansion of the push for children's rights, what was later to be loosely defined as the child rights movement, occurred during the twentieth century in the aftermath of World War II, with the focus of the movement shifting from a Western, US and European span to a wider span, interlinking with national, regional and local movements and actively expanding beyond its Western roots.[54] The expansion of the movement to Africa and Asia followed in the wake of European countries' expansion of foreign influence through the development of aid networks and the agenda to build an international welfare state, as argued by Alva Myrdal as a director at the United Nations Educational, Scientific and Cultural Organization (UNESCO).[55]

The expansion of the public role of States when it came to children was also the result of the efforts of the newly constituted United Nations and its project of nation-state building throughout the twentieth century.[56] Within this larger historical narrative, child rights have mostly been seen as a parallel project to the development of a general human rights regime. In fact, the Child Rights Declaration of 1959 is often considered an extension of the UN's international welfare state project.[57] These efforts were markedly different from advocating

[53] For the distinction between a rights discourse and jurisprudence see, for example, Alexander LeFebvre, *The Image of Law: Deleuze, Bergson, Spinoza*, (Stanford: Stanford University Press, 2008), 86.

[54] See, Maria Grahn-Farley, "How Children Got Rights," 176.

[55] Alva Myrdal, "A Scientific Approach to International Welfare: America's Role in International Social Welfare," (New York: Columbia University Press, 1955) at 1. Alva Myrdal was Director of the Department of Social Science, UNESCO.

[56] Grahn-Farley, "How Children Got Rights," 175.

[57] The drafting of the Declaration on the Rights of the Child began in 1950.

for general human rights, which are typically seen as negative rights and as more or less agnostic regarding the role of the welfare state in maintaining them. Instead, in this new postwar context, human rights served as a vehicle through which to carry the general child rights agenda across multiple countries and across cultures.

It is in this international and intercultural setting that the child takes on an ethnic and cultural otherness. Bourgeois women are no longer directly involved in saving children; their task instead becomes fundraising in order to pay for professional staff stationed abroad. For that matter, it is no longer just a woman's task to save children, but rather part of a larger international affairs agenda. The agents of the child rights movement are no longer actual physical persons, but are now instead policy decisions applied over several regions and cultural contexts. This is what Kaarlo Tuori would describe as the beginning of a legal culture changing its horizon and through experts striving for the universal.[58] The mainstreaming of human rights policies becomes important in the creation of coherence across these different projects analyzed by a professional class around the world. For this shift, the monist child-rights identity of the child is well suited as it is the only conception of the child from which it is possible to build a coherent human rights–based approach. The policy document is an important tool of governance for the organization over its staff in various parts of the world, and for this, a context-detached child-rights identity is needed. To delink the legal life of the child from its social and biological life creates a child unit that is comparable to each and every other child, regardless of where in the world one is operational, and this in turn makes it possible for donor organizations with projects across multiple regions to compare and demonstrate results in an accountant-friendly manner.

This is not to be easily dismissed as something bad even if it can be distant and abstract in relation to individual children. Its advantages are that it provides both accountability and the possibility to be questioned, not just by children but instead by the boards located in the headquarters of the organization. The accountability and the questioning of what is done in their name do not fall solely upon the children.

When the child rights regime itself cannot be questioned or altered from within, the goals of the regime cannot be questioned either, and the only area of debate becomes whether and, if so, how countries and societies are failing to meet the goals established by the rights regime, not whether the goals are desired or even correlate to the social outcome they claim to promote. This

[58] Kaarlo Tuori, *Ratio and Voluntas: The Tension between Reason and Will in Law* (London: Routledge, 2016 [Ashgate, 2011]), 288.

leads to a discrepancy between the social experiences of children and the child rights regime. In reality, both biology and social structures shape childhood even if not the child-rights identity, a discrepancy made possible because the social and the legal are not linked to each other, as a matter of law. It also means that the discrepancy cannot be evaluated within the rights regime itself because it is dependent on the world outside the regime built on the monistic child-rights identity. This falls dangerously close to becoming authoritarian because the child-rights identity can only give the essence of an identity but not be a substantive part of the evolution of a legal regime for children based on how children live their lives. The delinking of the monistic child-rights identity from the social aspect of childhood makes the vulnerability of human rights clearer than a general human rights approach. To Lefebvre in his reading of Deleuze, human rights are a form of critique against philosophy by replacing problems with opinions.[59]

There is not only a delinking between the child-rights identity and the child in the social, but there is also a tension between the idealized adult, who is willing and available to protect the child of the CRC, and actual adults who behave in palpably different ways from this ideal when it comes to actual children living in society.[60] Harm inflicted upon children is usually committed by adults. And yet, it is also mainly adults who can provide the protection and advocacy that are needed to advance the situation of children and protect them from harm. This is why the CRC is a treaty about adults as much as it is about children. Or rather, the CRC is an expression of the relational and ideological conflict between different adults in their different relations to children.

The CRC has a conflicting relationship with the family as well. In article 5, it makes parental power the ultimate decider when it comes to children, and in article 9, it establishes the child's right to parental guidance.[61] This strong position in support of parental and family rights can be contrasted with the rights that are meant to protect the child from decision-making by abusive adults, most clearly expressed in the right to be heard (article 12) and the best interest of the child (article 3). These articles attempt to untangle the relationship between the parent and the child without setting the child fully free. The

[59] LeFebvre, *The Image of Law: Deleuze, Bergson, Spinoza*, 77.

[60] Again, see Pantea Javidan, "American Legal Discourse on Child Trafficking: The Re/Production of Inequalities and Persistence of Child Criminalization" (PhD diss., London School of Economics and Political Science, London, 2017), 296.

[61] For a developed study on the parental role and informed consent see Jameson Garland, "Informed Consent in Clinical Practice in Sweden," *Förvaltningsrättslig Tidskrift* 1 (2019): 49–78.

fundamental dilemma of child rights in relation to the social is that the family is both the greatest source of protection and joy to children while also the most dangerous place. The closeness of children to adults is both a blessing and a curse, but this dilemma of the social lives of children has no place from within the monistic construction of the child-rights identity of the CRC. The CRC in the end is an expression of a conflict between different attitudes held by adults toward children.

5.7 CONCLUSION

The way in which the child rights movement renders internal critique and ambiguity a theoretical impossibility can draw from what Christina Beltrán describes took place within the nationalist Latino movement. Beltrán provides a cautionary tale from the nationalist Latino experience by addressing what happens when unity is built on an abstract construction that does not allow for internal disagreement and critique. She writes, "Because unity was understood as a familial impulse crucial to the creation of a political agenda, little space existed for legitimate disagreement."[62] The force for internal unity made it difficult for both feminists and people of color to raise additional concerns and internal critique in their respective movements, which would threaten the presentation of a united external front for either movement.[63]

In conclusion, even if it might be possible to find an interest connected to an overarching rights-based identity of the child, this shared interest is not a concern that occupies the child rights movement today. A movement that has taken upon itself to self-evaluate and self-assess its own accountability does not need to worry about representation and legitimacy: It already has authority without having to take it or having been granted it. Children have a very limited part in the child rights movement today and therefore cannot provide the bifocal lens through which critical self-reflection can take place. In this way, the monist construction of the child rights movement mirrors the monism of the rights-based identity of the child on which it is built.

62 Beltrán, *The Trouble with Unity, Latino Politics and the Creation of Identity*, 45.
63 Ibid., 47–48.

6

The Child in the Exception

One central debate when the CRC was adopted by the UN in 1989 was how best to give force to this international treaty within its States parties and how to make the treaty reach the children it represented. The hotly debated question was whether transformation or incorporation would be the most effective method for guaranteeing the efficacy of the convention within States parties. The Swedish government at the time believed that transformation was preferable over incorporation because it forced countries to actively engage existing laws with the CRC, initiating the adoption of new laws and amendments of existing laws to fulfill the international obligations of the CRC. Incorporation was seen to risk making the CRC a token without teeth because it was easy to incorporate without fully engaging with its content. Neither transformation nor incorporation, however, can replace a lack of political will to make the CRC matter or the legal technical skills in mastery of either legislation (when it comes to transformation) or adjudication (for incorporation).

I moved to the United States at the end of the incorporation–transformation debate in the 1990s and thought that the transformation and incorporation discussion when it came to the CRC in Sweden was settled and that, as a party to the CRC, it had decided to follow the legal traditions established in the country of a dualist approach, where international treaties as a rule were transformed through domestic legislation rather then incorporated in the form of the whole treaty becoming domestic law as written.

Almost twenty years passed before I moved back to Sweden, and it was as if time had stood still. I arrived during a very similar heated national debate as I had left many years earlier. The difference this time, however, was that the Swedish government was now set on incorporation. The CRC was incorporated into Swedish law on January 1, 2020.[1] The incorporation did not follow the methods that are normally used when legal systems incorporate UN human rights treaties into national law. The Swedish incorporation did not put into place any of the mechanisms that safeguard the democratic legal order or an individual's legal security. The text of the CRC is wide and often open-ended, leaving the State party with wide discretion to interpret the concrete meaning of the treaty. Dinah Shelton points out that States usually deploy some form of mixture and a scale of gradation between incorporation and transformation.[2] Both approaches are usually balanced between each other even if a legal system favors one over the other. Shelton points out that States that normally incorporate international treaties into their domestic system have mechanisms for controlling this process through, for example, the doctrines of self-executing agreements and/or political question doctrines.[3] Another way for States to safeguard their democratic legal order when incorporating international human rights treaties is to regulate who within the domestic system is authorized to interpret the treaty in concrete cases. Sweden, when it incorporated the CRC, opted to not include any of the above-mentioned mechanisms, but instead incorporated the treaty directly as it was without any mechanism for application in a domestic setting and by making it open for interpretation in concrete cases by every civil servant within the public authorities regardless of place or training, as long as the person encountered children in concrete cases.

6.1 THE SWEDISH INCORPORATION OF THE CRC

As mentioned earlier, Sweden incorporated the CRC in 2020,[4] the first time the country had incorporated a UN human rights treaty into its legal system. Sweden had previously incorporated the European Convention on Human Rights (ECHR) in 1994, but that is a regional treaty under the Council of Europe with its own court, the European Court of Human Rights (ECtHR), and its guiding jurisprudence. The effects of the Swedish incorporations differ substantially between the two treaties as the ECHR has the ECtHR in Strasbourg, which interprets the convention and whose rulings guide the Swedish application of the treaty.[5] Within Sweden, the power to interpret

1 SFS nr: 2018:1197. Lagen om Förenta nationernas konvention om barnets rättigheter [The Statute on UN Convention on the rRghts of the Child].

2 Dinah Shelton, *International Law and Domestic Legal Systems* (Oxford: Oxford University Press, 2011).

3 Ibid., 4.

4 SFS nr: 2018:1197. Lagen om Förenta nationernas konvention om barnets rättigheter.

5 Prop. 1993/94:117, 37.

the ECHR remains primarily with the Swedish national parliament, followed by the two highest courts: the Supreme Court and the Supreme Administrative Court.[6] When it comes to the CRC, there is no authorized regional or international court designated to interpret the treaty. A UN Committee monitors the progression of a State party's implementation of the CRC,[7] but the committee does not have the power to issue legally binding decisions, and they are to measure progression and not violations.[8] The committee can deliver soft law general guidelines and Concluding Observations on State party progression.[9] For those States parties that have ratified the Third Optional Protocol (which does not include Sweden), the UN Committee can communicate nonlegally binding statements on individual violations of the CRC.[10]

In contrast to the ECHR, where parliament is the primary interpreter and, if not parliament, the two highest courts, following the Strasbourg Court's case praxis,[11] the government decided that the interpretation of the CRC should be conducted by everyone in a position of public authority. In practice, this means that a regular police officer on duty or, to take another example, a case worker in social services are obligated to make their own legal interpretation of a treaty that is notoriously open to multiple interpretations and where there would normally be a Supreme Court making the ruling on the meaning of such text if the national parliament had not already declared its interpretation. The Swedish government expressly abstained from providing any interpretive guidelines on the substance of specific articles of the CRC; instead, the government provided the rules for interpretation, specifying that it was to be interpreted as a dynamic international treaty through the Vienna Convention on the Law of Treaties (VCLT) and that this was to be done by not only the Supreme Court and the highest administrative court but by each person within public authority.[12] The differences between the incorporation of the ECHR in 1994 and the incorporation of the CRC in 2020 are, in other words, significant. With the Swedish incorporation of the CRC, in theory there is no limit as to the scope of who within the Swedish public authorities is

6 NJA, 2012, s. 211.
7 CRC article 43(1).
8 CRC articles 44 & 45(c)(d).
9 CRC article 44.
10 "Optional Protocol to the Convention on the Rights of the Child on a Communication Procedure," adopted December 19, 2011, entered into force April 14, 2014, G.A. Res. 66/457.
11 NJA, 2012, s. 1038. HD:s domskäl, para. 15.
12 Karin Åhman, *Vägledning vid tolkning och tillämpning av FN:s konvention om barnets rättigheter* [Guide for Interpreting and Applying the UN Convention on the Rights of the Child] (Stockholm: Regeringskansliet, Arbetsmarknadsdepartementet, 2019), 70.

authorized to interpret its legal meaning.[13] In practical terms, this means an enormous transfer of democratic legislative power to the executive on every level of public service – from police officers to social workers handling individual cases, a span that jeopardizes the legal certainty of the individual child that encounters the State in its executive capacity.

6.2 THE UN COMMITTEE

The UN Committee had two requests of Sweden in the two Concluding Observations predating the incorporation of the CRC in 2020. First, it wanted a formal incorporation, and second, the CRC was to prevail over any conflict with domestic law.[14] Sweden received the Concluding Observations of its most recent periodic report on March 7, 2023, in the aftermath of its incorporation of the CRC, and there, the UN Committee seems to have accepted the incorporation of the CRC as sufficient, but still insists on its requests that Sweden: "ensure that the Convention prevails whenever there is a conflict with domestic legislation or common practice."[15] This call, for an erasure of the autonomy of democratically elected parliaments in favor of a UN treaty that was not drafted to be applied in concrete cases and lacks the specificity to easily be directly applied to concrete cases, is a major benevolent authoritarian move. In other words, the UN Committee is asking Sweden to not only conduct judicial review in all concrete cases in line with Swedish law since the interpretation of the legal meaning of the treaty is now delegated down from parliament and the highest courts to individual civil servants, but the Committee goes one step further, requesting that in each case the CRC will be the superior law to the democratically enacted Swedish law. The Swedish legislative preparatory work has kept it open that this possibility that the CRC, because it is a human rights treaty, might be superior to Swedish regular law.[16] Sweden is a good example of a State blindly following the legal advice of the UN Committee and conflating democracy and human rights. The Swedish example is unique in the level of detail with which the State party adhered to legal commentary by the Committee. It should be remembered that the method through which Sweden incorporated the CRC followed the legal

13 Prop. 2017/18:186, 89.

14 Committee on the Rights of the Child, "Concluding Observation on the Combined Sixth and Seventh Periodic Reports of Sweden," June 26, 2009, CRC/C/SWE/CO/4, para. 10.

15 Committee on the Rights of the Child, "Concluding Observation on the Combined Sixth and Seventh Periodic Reports of Sweden," March 7, 2023, CRC/C/SWE/CO/6-7, para. 6.

16 See Prop. 217/18:186 s. 87 (Swedish preparatory work); also *Vägledning vid tolkning och tillämpning av FN:s konvention om barnets rättigheter* (Guide for interpreting and application of the UN Convention on the Rights of the Child), Ds. 2019:23, p. 72.

commentary of the Committee. This situation is worth studying for an understanding of other States parties since the Swedish method has its roots in the UN guidelines on how to implement the CRC into national law. The Swedish incorporation of the CRC goes further than what Sir Hersch Lauterpacht even in his wildest dreams could imagine ever happening:

> Undoubtedly, direct international judicial review is not the only conceivable effective procedure for implementing an international charter of human rights. There may be the alternative method: the obligations of the signatories may be limited to incorporating the International Charter as part of their constitutional law and to conferring upon their highest tribunal the full right of judicial review of legislation is not an innovation likely to prove acceptable to some States . . .. Moreover, such obligation, to be practicable, would have to include submission to some manner of international supervision, aided, in controversial matters of importance, by an opinion given by an international tribunal.[17]

This is why the Swedish case is of wider, international interest. It is an example of when a State has followed the methodology of the international human rights community to its fullest. In this case, instead of delegating judicial review upward toward an international tribunal or to the Supreme Court of the State as the only two methods of judicial review Lauterpacht could imagine, Sweden went even further and invented its own methodology for incorporation by deregulating the instrument completely and letting it free at every level of public authority. This resolved even the limitations Lauterpacht imagined to be a solid barrier toward an international bill of rights becoming the law of every individual. Lauterpacht calls the more timid move he suggests "a revolutionary departure in the status of human personality in the constitutional and international spheres."[18] It raises the question of whether child rights as a regime and especially children are best served with this legal turn of the UN Committee to insist on incorporation without limitations and as legal supremacy at each moment of judicial review, or whether it would not be a good reason for the Committee to maintain what Arne Vandenbogaerde describes a "legally soft" language, which is also why he finds that the "'Concluding Observations' do not lend themselves to deep legal analysis."[19] Instead of following this approach, Sweden decided to go all in and treat the CRC as a legal positive text and to treat public international

[17] Hersch Lauterpacht, *An International Bill of the Rights of Man* (Oxford: Oxford University Press, 2013 [1945]), 14.

[18] Ibid.

[19] Arne Vandenbogaerde, *Towards Shared Accountability in International Human Rights Law: Law, Procedures and Principles* (Intersentia, 2017 [online 2016]), 50.

law as Swedish domestic law and to treat the UN Committee as part of the national legal system.

6.3 TWO THIRTEEN-YEAR-OLD BOYS AND THE POLICE

The practical implications of the Swedish incorporation of the CRC on individual children can be illustrated in part by two distinct cases, both concerning thirteen-year-old boys. As a result, two separate complaints against the police were filed with the Swedish Parliamentary Ombudsman,[20] one in December of 2020[21] and one in May of 2021[22] by the parents of the two boys figuring in the complaints. Both boys had given the finger to police officers and been taken into custody by the police on the only legal ground available for police to take children into custody, that the police found the boys' life and health were in imminent danger under §12 of the Police Statute. The ombudsman found that the actions of the police in both cases were without legal grounds; giving the police the finger cannot be understood as a reason to think that the boys were engaged in behavior that would be an imminent danger to their life and health. The actions by the police were therefore subject to the critique of the ombudsman, but not found to be a violation of the law.

The ombudsman must ensure that public authorities uphold and operate under the Constitution and fundamental freedoms and rights when exercising power over individuals.[23] In addition to monitoring executive behavior toward private persons, the office has the role of promoting the quality of law. If an ombudsman finds that there is a deficiency in the legal regulations, she can choose to raise such concerns to the legislator.[24] The ombudsmen do not have lawmaking authority, but they have the power to issue decisions that can support legislative efforts as to the development of a coherent and purposeful legal application.[25] Private persons can request that the ombudsman review the actions of public authorities in their individual cases.[26] In the two decisions concerning the thirteen-year-old boys, the ombudsmen were requested to communicate whether the police in these two cases operated in accordance with the law.

[20] *Lag* (1986:765) med instruktion för Riksdagens ombudsmän, § 2 [Law (1986:765) with Instruction for the Parliamentary Ombudsman].

[21] Dnr. 2022-05-18, 9144-2020.

[22] Dnr. 2022-05-18, 4204-2021.

[23] *Lag* (1986:765) med instruktion för Riksdagens ombudsmän. § 3.

[24] Ibid., § 4.

[25] Ibid., § 6.

[26] Ibid., §§ 5 & 6, para. 1.

In one of the cases, the police justified its decision to apprehend the child for showing the finger by arguing that the CRC obligated the police to take the child into custody for this offense. The police invoked the CRC explaining that taking the boy into custody and filing the report with social services were acts in accordance with article 36 of the CRC: "States Parties shall protect the child against all other forms of exploitation prejudicial to any aspects of the child's welfare." The ombudsman found that the police should not have relied on article 36 of the CRC but on articles 3 (best interest), article 16 (the right to privacy) and article 37 (regulating the deprivation of liberty). The ombudsman also made the point that the principle of "the best interest" should be taken into consideration but it cannot compensate for police actions that lack support in police law.

The dilemma here relevant for this work is that both the police and the ombudsman are engaging in an interpretation of the legal meaning of a UN treaty law in a concrete case as obligated by the incorporation. One of the harshest powers of the state is interpreted by the police and the ombudsman through the CRC. Here, it can be argued that the case has crossed the lawmaking threshold since normally this type of interpretation would need either legislation or a decision by a court with lawmaking authority, which neither the ombudsman nor the police has. Interpreting the legal consequences of a UN treaty such as the CRC with such open-ended possibilities for a variety of outcomes and choices of which articles to rely on would normally fall within the responsibility of a national parliament, a supreme court, and/or a constitutional court to determine. Neither a police officer nor even the ombudsman would normally have this sort of authority.[27] In the decisions, the ombudsman does not disagree with the claim that regular police officers in the midst of taking someone into custody are supposed to interpret an international treaty like the CRC (and according to the government instruction via the VCLT), while applying per instruction a dynamic interpretation of the CRC for a concrete application in an individual case.

The CRC was not written to have legally binding effects in concrete cases. The CRC does not have any provisions referring legal disputes between States parties to the International Court of Justice (ICJ) or to arbitration. This is in

[27] An exception is the Convention on the Prevention of Torture (CAT) where ombudsmen have a delegated power to interpret the CAT in accordance with the Ombudsman Law, s. 5a. No formal delegation to interpret or to monitor ompliance with the CRC has been made through statute. The transfer is delegated through the preparatory works and a nonlegally binding guide issued by the government. Prop. 2017/18:186, 89; Åhman, *Vägledning vid tolkning och tillämpning av FN:s konvention om barnets rättigheter* [Guide for Interpreting and Applying the UN Convention on the Rights of the Child], 70.

contrast to CEDAW and CERD, which do provide for the possibility of referring a legal dispute to the ICJ or to arbitration.[28] In addition, Sweden has not ratified the Third Optional Protocol to the CRC establishing individual communication procedures – still not legally binding, but of morally binding character. To not be party to the Third Optional Protocol but to still want the police to interpret the CRC when making arrests clearly sends a mixed message to the entire Swedish public sector.

6.4 THE STATE OF EXCEPTION WITH A SWEDISH TWIST

The state of exception can be understood as a condition of the mind of the sovereign (the one that decides on the exception), with material characteristics that challenge the predetermined scope of authority and hierarchy of norms of the executive. Agamben's state of exception is influenced by two very disparate authors. The first is Carl Schmitt, who establishes the theoretical concept that the sovereign is the one who decides both the state of exception and what to do about such moments (the condition of the mind).[29] The second is the Swedish political scientist, Herbert Tingsten, who in 1930 presented a study on how constitutional democracies dealt with delegated emergency powers during and after war (the immaterial mind anchored in a matter of legal substance).[30] This is how Agamben describes the role of Tingsten in creating the concept of the state of exception: "We must also at least mention the book by the Swedish jurist Herbert Tingsten."[31] Agamben situates Tingsten with a span of authors that: "record for the first time how the democratic regimes were transformed by the gradual expansion of the executive's powers during the two world wars and more generally, by the state of exception that had accompanied and followed those wars."[32]

28 CEDAW, article 29; CERD, article 22.

29 Giorgio Agamben, *Homo Sacer: Sovereign Power and Bare Life*, ed. Werner Hamacher and David E.Wellbery, trans. Daniel Heller-Roazen (Stanford: Stanford University Press, 1998 [1995]), 11 – referring back to Carl Schmitt. Tracy B. Strong claims that the state of exception as Schmitt uses the term retains at its core an ambiguity – and this ambiguity is constructed by the fact that the sovereign decides both the state of exception and what to decide about it. See foreword by Tracy B. Strong in Carl Schmitt, *Political Theology*, trans. George Schwab (Chicago: University of Chicago Press, 2005 [1922]), xi.

30 The constitutions and emergency powers examined were: Switzerland, the United Kingdom, Belgium, the United States and Italy.

31 Giorgio Agamben, *State of Exception*, trans. Kevin Attell (Chicago: University of Chicago Press, 2005 [2003]), 6.

32 Ibid.

Agamben describes the state of exception and its relation to law as placed within law, while on the edge of the gap between law and politics. To him, "The state of exception is not a special kind of law (like the law of war); rather, insofar as it is a suspension of the juridical order itself, it defines law's threshold or limit concept."[33] Like Agamben, the use of the state of exception in this text draws on the juridical, and not the political, instrumentality of the state of exception by focusing on the instrument of judicial review exemplified by the incorporation of the CRC: the transformation of judicial review from an instrument of exception to becoming a routine necessity for governance, when the national parliament abstained from legislating and providing guidance to the public authorities on how to implement the CRC in their daily operations. The legal interpretation of the CRC in Sweden is left to individual public servants in a manner that affects almost every part of public life. The power, normally reserved for national parliaments to interpret an international treaty in the name of the State, is delegated in Sweden to the lowest level of public authorities in their routine encounters with individuals within the State.

Tingsten begins first by sorting through the pairing between the hierarchies of norms and the different levels of executive authority. He concludes that most democratic legal systems reserve the adoption of law statutes to the democratically elected parliament, and the authority to issue clarifying norms (not statutes but, for example, agency regulations) to the lower hierarchy of the executive.[34] Tingsten defines the emergency power as: "exceptional circumstances where the executive power is empowered to exceed its regular limited authority to issue norms concerning the interpretation of laws, and issue norms that in principle would require a legislative process, or constitutional amendment."[35] This is what Tingsten defines as the transfer of full-power laws from the legislator to the executives.[36] Tingsten found that broad delegated powers were not only delegated from the democratic legislator to the executive during the war, as had been the presumption, but also after the war, especially the regulating of inflation.

33 Ibid.

34 Herbert Tingsten, *Regeringsmaktens Expansion Under och efter Vārldskriget: Studies över konstitutionell fullmaktslagstiftning* (Falköping: Gleerup, 1930), 8–9. The version Agamben relies on is the French translation: *Les pleins pouvoirs/ l'expansion des pouvoirs gouvernementaux pendant et aprés la grande guerre* [The Expansion of Governmental Powers during and after the World War: Studies on Laws of Constitutional Transfers of Power of Authorities] (Librairie Stock, 1934).

35 Ibid., 9. Translation by author.

36 Ibid.

Tingsten's definition of the delegated emergency powers influences Agamben's understanding of the state of exception as seen in Agamben's book, *State of Exception*, where he writes: "By 'full powers laws' we mean those laws by which an exceptionally broad regulatory power is granted to the executive, particularly the power to modify or abrogate by decree the laws in force."[37] However, Agamben's reading of Tingsten in French differs from its original Swedish, a difference that might not change the understanding of the state of exception in itself but, I will argue, gives it a more ambiguous meaning. However, this difference between Tingsten as understood by Agamben and as he reads in the original Swedish shifts the weight between the "mind" toward the "substance" – it sets a material limit on what a state of exception might be. For Tingsten, there is still a limit on the delegation – each level of public authority must still use its already designated power to make laws; a lower-level authority cannot make law but must still use the decree to regulate a scope of authority that has previously been regulated by a higher level of authority. The original Swedish version of Tingsten's definition of full-power laws is centered around the hierarchy of norms and levels of authority, and not simply the scope of authority, as the English translation of Agamben's reading of Tingsten seems to indicate. In other words, to understand Agamben through Tingsten, the state of exception is when the executive can alter and create laws and norms beyond its authority outside the relationship between the hierarchy of norms and the proper level of public authority. It is not enough that it is the executive acting, it also has an element of wrong means for the designated level of the executive acting (this is where Tingsten and Agamben differ). For Tingsten the means must remain appropriate for each level of the hierarchy – even when its scope has expanded.

It is through this expanded delegated emergency power that the moment of emergency is transformed from an exception into a necessary routine in order for the public authority to uphold its governing function. Agamben relies on Tingsten to reach his conclusion: "A systemic and regular exercise of the institution necessarily leads to the 'liquidation' of democracy."[38] Tingsten himself in the Swedish original text does not seem as concerned with emergency powers as Agamben's reading might suggest. Tingsten in his Swedish text concludes almost the opposite to the interpretation Agamben makes of the

[37] Agamben, *State of Exception*, 7. Citing Tingsten in the French translation from 1934, p. 13; see original in Swedish published 1930, Tingsten, *Regeringsmaktens Expansion Under och efter Vārldskriget*.

[38] Agamben, *State of Exception*, 7 – referencing Tingsten in the French translation from 1934, 333; see original in Swedish published in 1930, Tingsten, *Regeringsmaktens Expansion Under och efter Vārldskriget*, 209.

same text. Tingsten acknowledges that there is a theoretical conflict between democracy and emergency powers, but he sees no greater real threat to democracy because of it – as he states, for the most part the parliaments of the countries included in his study, Switzerland, England, Belgium, the United States, and Italy, agreed with the decisions of the executive and the lawmaking relations were soon restored in accordance with the democratic order between the legislative and the executive. Tingsten makes one important exception to this: In Italy, he finds that the emergency powers were used to mask a fundamental revolutionary dictatorship.[39]

The key element Agamben draws from Tingsten is the almost routine voluntary transfer of democratic legislative power from parliament to the executive branch, not only limited to emergencies but to moments when the national parliament is unable to take necessary actions to govern the State in a way that solves its problems, such as inflation.[40] Agamben describes how Tingsten concludes that to permanently transfer power from the democratic legislative parliament to the executive, as a legal technical instrument, will lead to what Agamben describes as the "liquidation of democracy."[41] Tingsten takes a nuanced and cautionary view on the democratic effects of this transfer of democratic power to the executive. He writes that in general the executive manages to deal with the problem the parliament was unable to solve and that parliaments in most instances were satisfied and approved the acts of the executive.[42] Agamben has the advantage of already knowing as history what for Tingsten in 1930 was the unknown future, namely World War II, which was a full-scale global war between democratic and authoritarian ideologies.

When it comes to the interpretation of both the police and the parliamentary ombudsman in the two cases of the thirteen-year-old boys, they can be read almost as a mirror image of the reading of Tingsten and Agamben. If one reads the police and the ombudsman as not making law but merely interpreting the CRC due to finding the specific articles of the CRC clear and precise enough to constitute clear law, then both the police and the ombudsman have acted within Tingsten's understanding of full-power laws (where each level of public authority has communicated its executive power through the correct means for its level in the hierarchy). However, if one finds that the CRC is an international human rights treaty never meant to have the precision of directly applicable law, the police and the ombudsmen are making law. If this is the

39 Original in Swedish published in 1930, Tingsten, *Regeringsmaktens Expansion Under och efter Vārldskriget*, 210.

40 Agamben, *State of Exception*, 6.

41 Ibid., 7.

42 Tingsten, *Regeringsmaktens Expansion Under och efter Vārldskriget*, C.W.K., 209.

case, then they have acted within the reading of Agamben and not simply exercised executive power outside their hierarchy by normally designated scope but now also done through a means that would normally fall above them in the hierarchy of public authorities. The police attempted to make law through the arrests, and the ombudsman has made law through his decisions. If this is the case, then Agamben's warning as to the liquidation of democracy should be read as stronger then the warning delivered by Tingsten, and it should be added that the transfer of power from the legislator to the executive when it comes to the CRC is a permanent transfer.

6.5 JUDICIAL REVIEW AND PLACE

One more difference between the incorporation in Sweden of the ECHR in 1994 and that of the CRC in 2020 is that the instrument of judicial review has changed through the Constitutional Reform of 2010. In 1994 the power to conduct judicial review was preserved for only the highest courts, but this limitation was removed from the statutes in the 2010 Constitutional Reform with the motivation that case law had already eliminated this barrier to conduct judicial review.

Even though democratic concerns will be more fully explored in the next chapter when addressing the State's relationship to democracy and international law, it is not possible to fully separate democracy from the hierarchy of legal norms and sources. Judicial review, however, is one instrument available for managing the exception to the rule of the hierarchy of norms and its correlation to the correct levels of the executive. However, the standards and actors with respect to the institution of judicial review vary significantly across jurisdictions. Here, naturally the focus is on Swedish judicial review as a possible bar to the unconstitutional exercise of power. Judicial review has been debated in Sweden since 1941.[43] Interestingly, the chair of the governmental report investigating the question was initially held by Herbert Tingsten. His report is a comparative study of the constitutional use of judicial review, and in it Tingsten covers the American constitution, while Georg Andrén covers the German constitution during the Weimar Republic. One interesting point is the dismissive tone that Andrén takes when, in one short passage, he denigrates Carl Schmitt as having lacked grounding among

[43] For a clear demonstration of the tension between democratic values and democratic process as expressed in the tension between judicial review and the legislator, see Lars Vinx, "Republicanism and Judicial Review," *University of Toronto Law Journal* 59 (2009): 591; Lars Vinx and Samuel Garrett Zeitlin, *Carl Schmitt's Early Legal-Theoretical Writings* (Cambridge: Cambridge University Press, 2022).

his fellow legal scholars when arguing that the German constitution in no way could adjust, even when the provision in question allows for adjustments.[44]

Swedish judicial review by courts and lower authorities such as police and social workers was for the first time explicitly articulated as a set of separate procedures in the Constitutional Reform of 2010.[45] This separation was justified with the argument that, over time, there had been a movement of the review of administrative decisions from the lower authorities to the courts as understood to be required by the ECHR. Another argument was that the Europeanization of the Swedish legal system – powered by an expansion of EU law and a more active Strasbourg Court – called for a clarification of the authority of the lower authorities to conduct judicial review on the same terms as the higher levels, no longer bound by a correlation between hierarchy and norms and levels within the executive.[46]

In connection with the 2010 Constitutional Reform that clarified the equal powers of the lower authorities at all levels and the courts (including the lower courts) to conduct judicial review on all levels of norms, one formal change was made to the wording of the constitutional statute. The qualifying requirement – that the legal rule in question had to be prima facie in conflict with the Swedish constitution – was removed, motivated by a need to be in compliance with the EU Charter.[47] This alteration meant that the lower authorities are now authorized to suspend one law in favor of another law through judicial review of an individual public agency worker's interpretation of the conflict of law, as located at any level within the administrative hierarchy without having to consider whether the conflict meets the threshold of a prima facie conflict. If the prima facie rules had still been in place in the two decisions of the thirteen-year-old boys, neither the police nor the ombudsman would have been able to conduct judicial review on the police statute with the help of the CRC.

Until 2010, this expansion of judicial review had been taking place within a long-standing tension. On the one side, there was a need to protect democratic processes with the legislator as the primary representative of the people; on the other side, there was an explicit desire to protect human rights as being the primary value of the nation, not limited to fundamental rights such as liberal freedoms but instead unspecified human rights in general.[48] This idea of Sweden as bearing a special human rights responsibility is articulated by, for example, the government declaration in 2015: "We must be a strong voice in

44 SOU 1941:20, 60.
45 SFS 2010:1408.
46 Prop. 2009/10:80, 119.
47 Prop. 2009/10:80, 146.
48 SOU 1993:40, 227.

the world for freedom, peace, human rights and solidarity."[49] The effort to expand human rights protection at the expense of democratic legislative processes had, by 1978, already been met with mild attempts to dampen down the legislator's enthusiasm for transferring parts of its legislative authority to the lower authorities for judicial review. Instead of being guided by a set of clear values, for example freedom, Sweden decided to be guided by human rights in general, a normative regime without ever specifying which of the multiple values within human rights constituted fundamental values. The Legislative Council at the time emphasized that judicial review was not to be understood as a normal element of the application of the law and emphasized that the caution reflected in case law was to be continuously practiced.[50] Throughout this legislative history, the courts have been reluctant to receive the increased influence and power to control the legislator that parliament has wanted to hand to them.

Until the late 1970s, this duality of judicial review, serving as both a protection of parliament as the primary legislator *and* the instrument for checking parliament's legislation in favor of human rights, was seen mostly as a theoretical concern with limited practical implications.[51] However, it was noted in the 1978 governmental report that this tension would become more real if the Bill of Rights in the constitution were to be expanded, as it was in 2010 through amendments to the Bill of Rights in chapter 2 of the Instrument of Government.[52]

6.6 NECESSITAS LEGEM NON HABET

Swedish judicial review is not technically a judicial review but a *necessitas legem non habet* (necessity has no law) directed at "the one obligated to follow the law,"[53] as being distinct from the one that is obligated to make just law. The law is not what is meant to be interpreted in the Swedish judicial review; rather, what is interpreted is the *situation* that requires the nonapplication of a law. Swedish judicial review is of a pliable nature and can only be performed in concrete situations, not as an invalidation of the law, but rather as a review of the nonobservance of the law in that particular moment. Following

[49] The Swedish Governmental Declaration of 2015.

[50] KU. 1978/79:39, 13.

[51] SOU 1978:34, 104.

[52] SFS 2019:1408, 104 (1978:34).

[53] Thomas Aquinas, *Summa Theologica*, complete American ed., trans. Fathers of the English Dominican Province (Claremont: Coyote Canyon Press, 2018), Question 96 article 6 Obj. 3 reply Obj. 1. (I-II, Q. 96, Art.6).

Agamben's reasoning, what takes place in Swedish judicial review is a forced situation where individual public officials whenever they are making an administrative decision concerning a child in a situation that is covered by the CRC are asked to take a moment and assess whether this is a situation where the specific statutes or regulations adopted by parliament warrant the suspension of a law.[54] As the prima facie requirement no longer exists and the hierarchy of norms and sources is unclear, with the CRC covering almost every part of a child's public life in articles that are written to guide countries' child rights agendas, but never intended to be directly applicable binding law in concrete cases, there is hardly an act within the public sector concerning children that will not warrant a moment of judicial review after the incorporation.

6.6.1 *Constitutional and Judicial Review*

Under today's Swedish constitution, sections 11:14 and 12:10 of the Instrument of Government set out judicial review for the courts and government authorities, respectively. The substance of these two sections has three aspects. The first two are the defense of the hierarchies of norms and the rule of law. The constitution is the highest order, followed by regular law as enacted by parliament, then followed by governmental decree. This hierarchy has a long lineage dating back to King Magnus Eriksson (1316–1374) and Section V of the first collection of laws encompassing the whole kingdom under his rule. Section V bound the king to the law. Under today's Swedish constitution, the substance of the second paragraph in both sections 11:14 and 12:10 of the Instrument of Government is procedural and authorizes the courts and the lower authorities, respectively, to review the processes through which a legal rule has been adopted. The final and third area in the last paragraph of the sections is where the legislator, the parliament, directly addresses the courts and lower authorities by reminding them that it is parliament that is the highest authority in its role as the representative of the people and that the constitution takes precedence over regular law. This part of the section was emphasized in the incorporation of the ECHR and was suppressed with the incorporation of the CRC.

The Swedish construction of judicial review in the statute itself is called *lagprövning*, which in translation would be "legal review." This term means that it is a legality test rather than judicial review, which would be a legitimacy test. However, this is not the way that the Swedish government has interpreted

[54] Agamben, *Homo Sacer: Sovereign Power and Bare Life*.

the statute in its approach to human rights and specifically child rights. Instead of upholding the hierarchy of norms, the argument made by the government is that because the CRC is a human rights treaty, it *could* have a higher status than regular law, even when adopted as regular law.[55] In addition, to ask that a police officer, or ombudsman for that matter, is to interpret the CRC on their own in relation to other laws, *necessitas legem non habet*, established in the Swedish constitution has become a requirement for the regular function of the State since almost every law regulating children will be covered by the CRC as a topic in one of its articles.

The duality of judicial review is embedded within the question of law itself, as Thomas Aquinas poses it: "if law is to make men good or if law is to command, forbid, permit and punish within a jurist state."[56] His answer is that law is *not* to make men good, yet an effect of law is that it makes those who follow just law, by definition, good.[57] The Swedish parallel can be traced back to King Magnus Eriksson's law in Section V and later moves into § 16 of the 1809 constitution,[58] which contained a limited form of a bill of

[55] This form of reasoning is to be found already at the moment of incorporation of the ECHR, the first human rights treaty incorporated into Swedish law. See the discussion on the incorporation of the ECHR into Swedish law (in Swedish), Carl Henrik Ehrenkrona, *Europeiska konventionen om skydd för de mänskliga rättigheterna och de grundläggande friheterna, en kommentar* (Stockholm: Karnov, 2016).

[56] Aquinas, *Summa Theologica*, Question 92.

[57] Ibid., Question 92 obj. 3.

[58] Section V § 2: Andra artikeln är att han skall styrka, älska och vårda all rättvisa och sanning och undertrycka all vrånghet och osanning och all orätt, både med lag och med sin kungliga makt. Konungabalken i Magnus Erikssons landslag. [The second article is that he shall confirm, love and cherish all justice and truth and suppress all bad temper and untruth and all injustice, both by law and by his royal power. The King's Law in Magnus Eriksson's national law] (trans. by author).

1809 RF (1941:20) §16: Konungen bör rätt och sanning styrka och befordra, vrångvisa och orätt hindra och förbjuda, ingen förderfva eller förderfva låta till lif, ära, personlig frihet och välfärd, utan han lagligen förvunnen och dömd är, och ingen afhända eller afhända låta något gods, löst eller fast, utan ransakning och dom, i den ordning Sveriges lag och laga stadgar föreskrifva; ingens fred i dess hus störa eller störa låta; ingen ifrån ort till annan förvisa; ingens samvete tvinga eller tvinga låta, utan skydda hvar och en vid en fri utöfning af sin religion, så vidt han derigenom icke störer samhällets lugn eller allmän förargelse åstadkommer. Konungen låte en hvar blifva dömd af den domstol, hvarunder han rätteligen hörer och lyder.

[The king should strengthen and promote right and truth, prevent and prohibit perversion and injustice, no one should be harmed or be deprived of life, honor, personal freedom and welfare, unless by law decided and convicted, and no one should dispose of or allow to be disposed of any property, movable or fixed, without legal procedure and judgment, in the order prescribed by Sweden's law and legal statutes; no one's peace in one's house shall be disturbed or be permitted to be disturbed; no one is to be banished from one's place; everyone's freedom of conscience is to be protected, and everyone is free to exercise his religion, as long as he

rights.[59] The instrument kept its structure until the Constitutional Reform of 2010, when this division and the hierarchy of matching norms and levels of public authority were removed.

6.7 THE NEW NORMAL

As just mentioned above, the early definition of "necessity laws" divided instruments into two categories: one for kings and one for lower authorities.[60] Per the understanding of the necessity laws as described by Thomas Aquinas in his dissection of the principle of *necessitas legem non habet*, these two types of instrument follow different authorities and evaluations for when there is a necessity and for when the law can, or will not, be applied.[61] According to Aquinas, there are important distinctions to be made between the one who has the authority to interpret the law and the one who is obligated to follow it.[62] Kings have the authority to interpret the law and, through their interpretations, find a *necessitas legem non habet.*[63] Conversely, the lower authorities have the obligation to follow the law, not to interpret it.

When it comes to a state of exception, in relation to *necessitas legem non habet*, there is a significant departure from this state of affairs. To Aquinas, judicial review is not restricted only to the one with the authority to interpret the law; it also falls upon each individual who, out of necessity, is prevented from *applying* it. As Aquinas conceives it, lower authorities are not to interpret the conflicts of laws but rather they interpret the situation upon which the law is to be applied. Rather, it is an interpretation of the particular situation and its context in which the emergency is taking place.[64] It is the exception of the situation that leads to the actuality that the law, in that particular situation, will not be observed.[65] The nonobservance of the law in this moment of need is dependent on three requirements. First, the negative outcome that would follow the application of the law in the particular moment is *not* what was intended by the law. Second, there cannot be a doubt as to whether or not to apply the law in the moment. Third, if there is a doubt if the law should be

thereby does not disturb the peace of society or cause general outrage. The king will leave the conviction of a person to the court under which that person rightly belongs and obeys.]

59 (1941:20).

60 Aquinas, *Summa Theologica*, Question 96 (I–II, Q. 96, Art.6).

61 Ibid.

62 Ibid.

63 Ibid.

64 Ibid., Question 96 article 6 Obj.3 reply Obj. 1. (I–II, Q. 96, article 6).

65 Ibid.

applied or not, the person deciding on the exception has to consult those in power.[66]

This understanding of the declaration of a state of exception stands in stark contrast to Agamben's reading of Carl Schmitt's phrase: "Sovereign is he who decides on the exception."[67] This translation by George Schwab places the emphasis on the sovereign as the one who can through the power of the will construct the definition of each exception.[68]

Yet, the state of exception as a descriptive term rather than as a function is in many senses misleading. Because its function is not exceptional but for its name, the examples are many across time and space. For example, Marc de Wilde describes the medieval expansion of sovereign legislative and financial powers at the expense of local authorities and the church.[69] Wilde writes: "The meaning of *necessitas* thus gradually shifted from an outer emergency to an inner administrative need."[70] This alteration, Wilde argues, was done by shifting the legal interpretation of emergency power: While its meaning in the thirteenth century held that emergency power was only to be actualized when there was an actual necessity, by the end of the sixteenth century, its meaning held that necessity encompassed regular administrative needs.[71] The sovereign's use of emergency powers as a regular instrument of governance helped solidify what were to become constitutionally ordered States and the dawn of the modern State. This transformation was accomplished by a change from a state of *necessitas legem non habet* to a state of *necessitas perpetua*.[72] The state of exception thus switched from being invoked at moments of foreign invasion and domestic rebellion, to making possible the granting of power needed for the sovereign to administer justice – which was funded through taxation based on "public necessity and utility."[73] Vincent Brown demonstrates a similar temporal development but in a completely different location and context: the British struggle to maintain control over its slave colonies in the Caribbean through a militarization of the slave regime, justified and legitimized through martial law.[74] Brown demonstrates how the triggering of martial law followed

66 Ibid.

67 Schmitt, *Political Theology*, 5.

68 Ibid.

69 Marc de Wilde, "Emergency Powers and Constitutional Change in the Late Middle Ages," *Tijdschrift Voor Rechtsgescheiedenis* 83, no. 1–2 (2015): 26–59, 27.

70 Ibid., 46.

71 Ibid., 28.

72 Ibid., 49.

73 Ibid., 46.

74 Vincent Brown, *Tacky's Revolt: The Story of an Atlantic Slave War* (Cambridge, MA: Harvard University Press, 2020), 45.

an already widely shared sentiment in the slave colonies among the slave-owning class. The slave owners saw the need for martial law to be not only a question of property but also a battle for the identity of the "imperial colonial state."[75] It is through the legal location of the state of exception that slave owners and nonslaves were manifesting themselves as a community: "Martial law was intended to mobilize the entire non-slave male population, subjecting them to the strict discipline of the Articles of War. The result was the formal militarization of racial slaveholding."[76] The normalization of the exception is further shown by McBride when addressing the colonizing States' regular and necessary use of martial law to maintain colonial control and, with that, its imperial rule. The deployment of martial law contained within the place that Ngugi wu Thing'O describes as the stage of competing irreconcilable legal regimes, the imperial State expressed through its militarized colonial regime in tension with its own civilizing mission and with that the rule of law.[77] Examples of how emergency powers transition to regular governance are plenty.

It is worth returning to Tingsten's text to situate Agamben's understanding of the state of exception, especially as it pertains to a democratic State like Sweden.[78] Tingsten notes that it is understandable that a democratically elected parliament during war is willing to transfer emergency powers to an executive branch.[79] What seemed to have interested Tingsten more is the wide use of emergency powers granted to the executive *after* the war. The decisions made under these emergency powers after the war were not all of a temporary nature but led to permanent judicial legislative changes and reforms.[80] Tingsten gives the example of the emergency powers after the war that were granted in France, Germany, Austria, Hungary, Italy, and Belgium: All were able to address and manage inflation through currency regulation.[81]

There were only a few constitutions that involved parliament in the handling of the emergency powers – Germany, Austria, Switzerland, the United States, and Italy – and, he adds, the matter of delegation is important here, as

75 Ibid.
76 Ibid., 143.
77 Margaret Kohn and Keally McBride, *Political Theories of Decolonization: Postcolonialism and the Problem of Foundations* (Oxford: Oxford University Press, 2011), 1.
78 Olof Petersson, *Herbert Tingsten Vetenskapsmannen* (Stockholm: Atlantis, 2013), 234.
79 Tingsten, *Regeringsmaktens Expansion Under och efter Vārldskriget*, 209.
80 Ibid.
81 Ibid.

powers were granted to lower local authorities.[82] According to his findings, Great Britain and the United States practice a wide use of delegation of emergency powers, allowing for lower local authorities to make their own independent decisions based on the emergency powers granted to the executive. The Italian courts, however, had questioned this practice.[83] On the political implications of emergency powers within democratic States, Tingsten speaks to two sides: on the one hand, emergency powers have been critiqued for their dictatorial character, which some consider a threat to the democratic State, while, on the other hand, its defenders have argued that the granting of the power is harmless and that it is only a temporary sidestepping of the democratic order during moments of extraordinary circumstances. This latter position interprets emergency powers as symbolizing the flexibility and endurance of the legal order of the State.[84] Yet ultimately, Tingsten takes both sides as exaggerated generalizations: The true effects of emergency powers could only be understood and assessed on a case-by-case basis, he argued.[85]

6.8 THE DRIVE TOWARD MONIST HUMAN RIGHTS

The unclear order of how specific people became empowered to represent children while others are not is clearly exemplified by the way in which Sweden incorporated the CRC into its national law. In doing so, Sweden has expanded the executive power without proper checks or limitations in a manner not seen before in relation to human rights: Police officers are now empowered and requested to make an individual assessment in each particular encounter with a child whether, if they depart from the police statute or act without the legal support of the police statute, their action is justified by the CRC or not. Instituting an age-based identity results in a bar to challenging the decision and actions taking place in the name of children, since children are, by the very definition in the CRC, below the age of eighteen, the age of majority, and thus lack the right to vote in democratic elections. Nor can children ever challenge agendas that are interpreted in their names when the democratic order is suspended in the name of child rights through judicial review. This monistic identity has become the symbol of national identity touted by both the Conservative and the Social Democratic–Green Party governments in their efforts to maintain Sweden as a "humanitarian

82 Ibid., 202.
83 Ibid.
84 Ibid., 207.
85 Ibid.

superpower." Yet with respect to the fundamental tension between rights and law in what possible is a posthegemonic democratic-liberal era, the child-rights identity exceeds and escapes any democratic legislative proceedings due to the invocation of a perpetual state of exception by the system.

6.9 THE ORDER OF PREVIOUS TRADITIONS

The Swedish political and legislative drive toward monism – not only of the child-rights identity but toward a conflating of the democratically important distinction between the legislator and the executive – can be exemplified by its discomfort in differentiation, in this case between the authority to perform judicial review either through interpretation of the law or its suspension based on the understanding of the circumstances of law's application. The equal power of the court and of the lower authorities to conduct judicial review was addressed in the 1973 legislative preparatory work to Sweden's new constitution.[86] The legislative bill confirms that the power to conduct judicial review in case law has been established to include both courts and lower authorities without distinction.[87] It is not before 2010 that this implosion of a distinction is codified in the Constitution. Already, in the legislative preparatory work of 1978/79:195, the government had clarified that judicial review was to be performed not only by courts, but also by lower authorities, using the terminology "public agencies." The government makes a point of clarifying that the use of the term "public agencies" was to make clear that the government did not want to limit the power to perform judicial review to only public authorities, but to also include nonpublic actors such as private individuals (*enskilda*).[88] From this moment on, Swedish judicial review is not only considered to be a right of the lower authorities, but also an obligation.[89] This view is deeply embedded within the Swedish legal tradition and was to be repeated throughout the historic development of judicial review, addressed already in a governmental report from 1963, but at each point successfully rebutted when discussed as a constitutional codification, until 2010.[90]

Thanos Zartaloudis describes the state of exception as a moment transformed as a continuous shock of normality: "Exceptionalism is transformed into a one-dimensional normality."[91] I argue that while the state of exception

86 Prop. 1973:90, 200.
87 Ibid.
88 Prop. 1978/79:195, 66; See also Prop. 1973:90, 200 for the same view.
89 Prop. 1973:90, 200.
90 SOU 1963:17, 154.
91 Thanos Zartaloudis and Giorgio Agamben, *Power, Law and the Uses of Criticism* (London: Routledge, 2010), 131.

begins as a temporary condition, over time, its original purpose risks blurring the distinction between the distinct elements of a liberal legal democratic order – the representative legislator, the parliament-appointed executive, and the independent judiciary. If anything, the state of exception is the moment when the blurring of who to hold accountable has been institutionalized as a lasting part of governance.[92] What seems to have its roots in urgent danger or evident necessity to be guided by law's purpose will, in Arendt's words, replace one order that over time has lost its common sense with another tradition that has come to make sense.[93] I argue that the state of exception is the suppressed order of the previous tradition – not a void in the current administrative order, but the very remnant that reveals its warp. In this reading, the state of exception is merely the incomplete end of one tradition and the lurching beginning of a new one, one that, when it has broken through, can be traced as the disrupting element of the tradition it has come to replace.

Clinton Rossiter describes a state of exception within a State as a dictatorial condition where the exception is for the protection of individual rights and freedoms.[94] In the context of the state of exception, it is hard to reconcile the idea that the protection of rights takes place through their suspension. This is today hardly contested, the Swedish Bill of Rights cannot be suspended but derogated, and it is the same with the EU charter. However, what used to be expressed as a formal function of the state of exception – to protect the State as a legal order – is now disconnected from the protection of individual freedoms and rights, and in the case of Sweden, it no longer serves as a guarantee of the preservation of a democratic legal order but rather its abdication.

6.10 THE LIQUIDATION OF DEMOCRACY

By incorporating the CRC, previous Social Democratic, Center Party, and Green Party governments delegated a task that is normally placed on the national parliament – that is, to interpret international treaty law, and transform it into national legal rules – to each individual civil servant in any encounter with anyone under the age of eighteen years. This makes the instrument of judicial review a necessity in the management of the everyday executive tasks of the State. This is a radical normalization of a legal instrument that was originally meant to be used sparingly and only during

92 Agamben, *State of Exception*, 7.

93 Hannah Arendt, *The Promise of Politics*, ed. Jerome Kohn (New York: Schocken Books, 2005), 40.

94 Clinton Rossiter, *Constitutional Dictatorship: Crisis Government in the Modern Democracies*, ed. William J. Quirk (Piscataway: Transaction Publishers, 2007 [1948]), 7.

emergencies. This power to conduct judicial review – granted equally to the lower authorities and to the Supreme Court without the limitations of a prima facie requirement – is at a minimum the transfer of power Tingsten has defined and is possibly the state of exceptions that risks undoing democracy itself, as Agamben warns. Only States that so strongly believe that their people are better and more child-loving than other nations contemplate delegating lawmaking and norm-giving down to individual civil servants encountering a child in their public duties. Only such States as this will consider this a democratically safe thing to do. Added to this expanded power is the fact that these civil servants – who are not trained in law – are supposed to interpret the CRC when its overarching values are unclear. In fact, we cannot clearly state that the CRC's overarching values are based on the idea of democratic liberalism, when no guidance has been provided. There is an unanswered question in light of the recent election when the Swedish Democrats gained the second most votes of all the political parties: Who does parliament imagine voted for this party with its roots in the neo-Nazi movement?

6.11 CONCLUSION

I argue that the way the CRC is incorporated into Swedish law can be understood through the lens of Giorgio Agamben's *State of Exception*,[95] with a Swedish twist derived from the writings of the Swedish political scientist Herbert Tingsten, the author alongside Carl Schmitt from whom Agamben builds his concept of the state of exception. Agamben covers several legal concepts under a theoretical nonlegal umbrella, analyzing the way that the State's monopoly as to the exercise of public power comes to be expressed in what he calls "the state of exception." This overarching concept gathers several different legal instruments, such as the transfer of full power from parliament to the executive, judicial review, emergency law, and martial law. One of the significant elements of Agamben's state of exception is that it demonstrates that through these legal instruments, something that begins as an exception in a particular moment easily becomes a necessity for the continuous administration of the duties of the State, despite the fact that the original need, based, for example, on emergency or war, no longer exists.

If anything, this chapter demonstrates why it is necessary to establish whether the CRC is guided by the same overarching values of equality and freedom as the other core human rights treaties under the UN umbrella or whether the

[95] Agamben, *Homo Sacer: Sovereign Power and Bare Life*; Agamben, *State of Exception*; Giorgio Agamben, *Where Are We Now? The Epidemic as Politics*, 2nd ed., trans. Valeria Dani (London: ERIS, 2021 [2020]).

CRC is guided by its own overarching values. Without these overarching values, a State is basically given free license to use child rights for any purpose it finds appropriate. The claim in this chapter is that the way the incorporation of the CRC in Sweden was done has expanded the executive's power to operate in individual cases concerning children that goes far beyond its previous scope. There is a conflict between the interest of promoting CRC as a regime and national democratic governance, where the CRC is promoted through an approach of benevolent authoritarianism, in conflict with the values that generate a democratic legal order within a State. Mechanisms exist to allow these two interests to coincide and work together. However, the CRC would then have to be subjugated by the national legal order and not by the UN Committee's views on how national democratic legal orders should be addressed when perceived to be standing in the way of the CRC. This is not a conflict between children and adult interests driven by the interest of children but a struggle between two authorities, the UN Committee on one side and the Swedish (or any other comparable State's) democratic legal order on the other. It does not serve the interest of children, in Sweden or elsewhere, to have a public administration free to arrive at its own legal interpretations of the CRC at each and every moment civil servants encounter a child in their decision-making at the expense of applying and following nationally and democratically enacted laws.

The effects of granting the authority of interpretation as to the legal meaning of the CRC to each and every civil servant – without any distinction as to the hierarchy of legal sources or norms or placement within the administrative hierarchy, or even education in law – is illustrated by the two decisions concerning the thirteen-year-old boys. The police officer in one case is interpreting the CRC to use a power not recognized in police law – and would even be in violation of police law. The ombudsmen are also dangerously close and possibly stepped over the line for lawmaking by demanding that the police should interpret the CRC in their regular police business when engaged with private individuals. The CRC was incorporated into Swedish law unfiltered as the UN Committee had requested in their Concluding Observations over several reporting periods, and after all that, the Committee still insists that Sweden continue to dismantle its democratic legal order even further in favor of the authority of the CRC and its Committee.[96]

[96] Committee on the Rights of the Child, "Concluding Observation on the Combined Sixth and Seventh Periodic Reports of Sweden," March 6, 2015, CRC/C/SWE/CO/5, paras. 6–8; Committee on the Rights of the Child, "Concluding Observation on the Combined Sixth and Seventh Periodic Reports of Sweden," June 26, 2009, CRC/C/SWE/CO/4, paras. 9–10.

7

The Monist Pull of Universalization

The Swedish line between the government and the child rights movement is traditionally fluid, which is not such a great surprise in a small country of about 10 million people located in the hinterlands of Scandinavia. Illustrating the closeness of this relationship is a memory I have from a meeting with Save the Children, probably around 1996. The drafting of an antimine convention was hotly debated in Sweden.[1] Sweden with its long coastline had quite a significant stockpile of land mines. I remember how one of the members of Save the Children told us at the meeting how she had called the Minister of Defense Thage G. Peterson and explained to him how horrible the use of land mines in the Swedish military defense was. The way she told the story was that she had said to him that he should immediately ban the use of land mines in the military and that he had agreed with her. Of course, a minister of defense cannot singlehandedly ban the use of land mines just because a child rights activist calls him up, but it was not only Save the Children that had lobbied the government and felt successful in its agenda. The peace organization, Swedish Peace, also claimed the land mine ban as their victory.[2] My retelling of this memory is more to illustrate the close relationship that not only child rights activists but also civil society in general had with Swedish politicians in the 1990s. In fact, the Swedish government proposed a ban of land mines in

[1] The convention was to be adopted as: "The UN Convention on the Prohibition of the Use, Stockpile, Production and Transfer of Anti-Personnel Mines and on Their Destruction," adopted in Oslo on September 18, 1997, entered into force March 1, 1999. Signatories 133, parties 164 as of April 10, 2023. United Nations, *Treaty Series*, vol. 2056, 211; C.N.163.2003. TREATIES-2 of March 3, 2003.

[2] Website: Om minor Is SVT Play, May 5, 2020, www.svenskafreds.se/upptack/fred-och-sakerhet/om-minor-i-svt-play/ accessed on April 10, 2023.

1996.[3] Sweden ratified the UN convention on July 16, 1997 and subsequently banned the use of land mines.[4] This close relationship between the democratically elected representatives and civil society has been productive and is an important part of a deliberative process in Sweden between civil society and its political representatives. However, the patterns of engagement have now moved from a political democratic deliberation between national politics and civil society, to a merger between international civil society and the national legal system. The lines between international and national legal regimes have become blurred, as well as the line between law and politics, and large gaps in accountability and legitimacy have opened up. It is unclear where the UN Committee finds its authority to demand that the CRC should overrule all Swedish laws when there is a conflict between laws. This not only risks affecting the legal certainty of individual children and adults but also the democratic order itself as the UN Committee cannot be held accountable by the Swedish people, and the CRC cannot be changed through Swedish elections. Adding to this accountability gap is the issue of who decides who speaks on behalf of children in Sweden (or any other national order) when decisions are being made between the nation's democracy and the CRC?

7.1 THE OBJECT OF SUSPICION

The American international law professor Louis Henkin famously explains that reciprocity is the reason why States in most instances follow international law obligations, despite the weakness of enforcement mechanisms.[5] In the same volume he makes a distinction between international law, on the one hand, and human rights law, on the other, when explaining why States follow human rights law in general. As he points out, the reciprocal incentive is not present with human rights since this regime mostly concerns internal affairs and not inter-State relations. Instead of reciprocity, he argues, it is international standing and reputation that States preserve by avoiding becoming the object of international political human rights critique.[6] In other words, it is the power of public shaming that makes States comply with most human rights provisions even if it might not be in their immediate interest in concrete cases. Here, he uses the same long-term interests reasoning as he does for his general international law argument – that States make the assessment that it is

3 Proposition 1996/97:145.

4 SÖ 1982:27. ISSN 1102-3716.

5 Louis Henkin, *How Nations Behave: Law and Foreign Policy*, 2nd ed. (New York: Columbia University Press, 1979 [1968]), 50–56.

6 Ibid., 235–236.

in their long-term interest to abide by human rights regulations even if they might be disadvantageous in concrete cases. Another way to explain the theory of Henkin is that he presumes that States value deferring more stable gratification over immediate more case-by-case gratification. Not only does Henkin provide a theory for why States follow human rights norms but he also illustrates the split within the sovereign State. Henkin's reasoning is illustrative in clarifying the bifocality between the State as a sovereign actor but also as a part of a community of sovereigns, and ultimately, how a State can be both the only violator of human rights and, at the same time, their guarantor.

The reason why Lauterpacht advocates for an international bill of rights with legally binding effects upon States is because he sees the State as an object of suspicion when it comes to individual human rights, while also believing that the international community of States will find an interest in establishing an international bill of rights.[7] In the context of the CRC, only the State can be held accountable for child rights violations. This means theoretically that there is a fundamental divergence of concrete interests between the State, on the one side, and on the other side, those individuals within it when it comes to human rights supported by the international community of States. It is safe to say that child rights, in line with general human rights, are premised on the idea of divergent interests between the State, on the one side, and the individual child backed by the international community, on the other.

7.2 GOVERNANCE INSTEAD OF COMPLIANCE

Sweden turned this presumption of States playing the long game upside down when it declared itself a humanitarian superpower. Instead of going through the pain of bridging the concrete short-term-State interest with a long-term alignment with international human rights, Sweden reversed the order and made communal international human rights interests its own. Other States have struggled with the conflict between sovereign self-interest and the communal good, while Sweden eliminated the conflict altogether by making the communal good the same as the sovereign interest. The closest to this on the international stage one can come is the Universal Periodic Review process (UPR), which is a State-driven human rights process when a State together with three supporting States, "troikas," jointly prepare the "outcome report."[8]

7 Hersch Lauterpacht, *An International Bill of the Rights of Man* (Oxford: Oxford University Press, 2013 [1945]), 14.

8 See United Nations Human Rights Council, Basic facts about the UPR, www.ohchr.org/en/hr-bodies/upr/basic-facts, accessed April 11, 2023.

This makes the line between governance and compliance not always easy to detect. Instead of fearing communal shaming – which is what Henkin thought was the driving force behind human rights compliance among States – Sweden was motivated by receiving communal praise for its governance through human rights. Instead of fearing critique for violation, it was seeking praise for leading the embodiment of human rights, which goes beyond compliance of child rights and becomes governance through child rights. The challenge is that there is no mechanism within international human rights for holding the State accountable for its governance through the CRC. The withholding of praise is not a recognized instrument within international law, even if it is only the withholding of praise that is available once a State decides to make the international agenda its own national agenda. The exception is where the governance of the State has become so severely criminal that it raises the question of compliance, as with the example of the International Criminal Court's issued arrest warrant for Ms. Maria Alekseyevna Lvova-Belova, the Commissioner for Children's Rights in the Office of the President of the Russian Federation suspected to be responsible for the war crimes of unlawful deportation of children and transfer of children from occupied areas of Ukraine to the Russian Federation.[9] This is when governance through child rights comes up against the limits of what can be explained by the child rights regime and transitions into international law violations, but almost up until this point, responding to State governance through child rights is a challenge. This is because each State according to international law has the authority to interpret the meaning of the provisions of the CRC as they see fit, as long as the interpretations are acceptable within the ordinary meaning of the words within the context of the treaty.[10]

7.3 THE SWEDISH EXCEPTIONALISM AS HUMANITARIAN SUPERPOWER

One consequence of national exceptionalism is that the State should explain why even when it behaves in its own sovereign interest in violation of international law and human rights, it is still in the long-term interests of the international community to permit the self-interested deviation from international norms. The Swedish exceptionalism is the opposite, for example, of American exceptionalism: the United States tried to bend the interest of the

9 Warrant of arrest of Ms. Maria Alekseyevna Lvova-Belova, accessed on March 17, 2023, ICC Pre-Trial Chamber II.

10 Vienna Convention on the Law of Treaties, article 31(1).

international community to align with its national interests, whereas Sweden decided to just bend its national interests to be aligned with the interests of the international community because that was the Swedish exceptionalism, to be the world leader in humanitarianism.

The Conservative Swedish government reflected in 2013 on the identity of Sweden by stating that Sweden is a humanitarian superpower.[11] Swedish people saw themselves as leading the world toward a more moral, humane path.[12] Public praise of Swedish humanitarianism can be followed through a variety of op-eds in national and local newspapers through the years, in addition to the opening statement by the prime minister at the annual government declaration.[13] This contributed to how unaccompanied minors between 2013 and 2015 interpreted the Swedish declarations of being a humanitarian superpower to be an invitation for them to come to Sweden. In a way, it was an invitation, but it was extended to the imagined child, like the imagined Maoist farmer that Spivak critiques Foucault and Deleuze for using, to serve their purpose almost as props, in advancing the story of their own agenda.[14] These grandiose gestures, in the name of being a humanitarian superpower, promoted Sweden as an immigrant-friendly nation. However, when the unaccompanied minors arrived in real flesh and blood and not as monist child-rights identities, they were nothing like the imagined vulnerable child that the country as a humanitarian superpower had invited. Males who are seventeen years old will often look and behave like adult men, and not as helpless five-year-old children that the pictures in the Google search populated when searching for "vulnerable children," as given in Chapter 3 of this book. Furthermore, these seventeen-year-old males will, within a very short period of time, become adults beyond the custody of the State, which also means beyond its control and beyond reshaping into model Swedish children. There is in Sweden today a major backlash against the previous humanitarian

[11] Swedish Government Declaration, 2013.

[12] Philip Boström and Elin Ylvarsdotter, "Sverige ska vara stormakt inom flyktingpolitiken (Sweden shall be a super power within the refugee policy)," *SvD (Swedish Daily News)*, April 3, 2017. For a rendition of the Swedish human rights awakening see Hans-Gunnar Axberger, Rättigheter (del I av II), Sverige, EKMR och EU:s Rättighetsstadga, *SvJT* (2018); Hans-Gunnar Axberger, Rättigheter (del II av II) Sverige och MR, *SvJT* (2018).

[13] Op-Ed, 233 Social Democrats in an. "Sverige ska vara en humanitär stormakt (Sweden shall be a humanitarian super power)," *Aftonbladet (Evening Post)*, July 4, 2020; Boström and Ylvarsdotter, "Sverige ska vara stormakt inom flyktingpolitiken (Sweden shall be a super power within the refugee politics)."

[14] Estefania Peñafiel Loaiza and Gayatri Chakravorty Spivak, *Can the Subaltern Speak?: Two Works* (London: Afterall Books, 2021), 9.

immigration policy Sweden held during 2013–2015. Today, no political party with self-preservation in mind will argue for open migration policies.

One thing that I was never able to fully grasp during my almost twenty years in the United States was the meaning of and the emotions surrounding the concept of *American exceptionalism*, debated and argued thoroughly, everything from whether it existed, what it was, and if it was a good or a bad thing. Intense debates were broadcast on CNN with Americans in suits (both women and men wear suits on American news shows) over the status of the United States and what they call the world stage. I watched these debates at times with some bewilderment, and I must admit, at other times with a sense of ridicule, and still other times with outright rage, as when the United States invaded Iraq and tortured prisoners in Gitmo – all this was always followed by heated debates over American exceptionalism. I could not understand why this was something important for people to debate; to me, American imperialism was clearly just wrong, and I could not understand American exceptionalism as anything different from a justification for imperialism and invasion. However, many Americans see American exceptionalism as something extraordinary and something to be proud of for making the world safe, while others do not, and the debates continue. The other day I was watching Philip Pullman, the author of the novel, *His Dark Materials: The Golden Compass*, as he addressed the Oxford Union, and about thirty minutes into the event, he made a comment about Britain, and what he called her "post-Second World War delusion that it's still a great power."[15] This became the liveliest moment for the audience during his full hour of discussion. In a way, it was a throwaway line, but it hit a nerve that sent an electric current of excitement throughout the audience. Peter Frankopan has written from a different angle a stand-alone series of books trying to engage British people with a multipolar thinking with the help of the gestalt of the Silk Roads.[16] All these are ways in which the justifications for the actions and decisions of the State as a bifocal unit can be questioned and debated. It allows for a democratically engaged deliberation over both the State's actions and decisions but also over the premises and the overarching values of such actions in the split between self-interest and international communal interests.

I no longer look down on the American obsession to debate and fight over its status or its role on the world stage, and I understand the importance of

[15] Philip Pullman, Lecture and Q&A, Oxford Union Society, People Who Shape Our World, June 14, 2019.

[16] Peter Frankopan, *The New Silk Roads: The Present and Future of the World* (London: Bloomsbury, 2018).

what Pullman and Frankopan are trying to do, to start a dialogue about national identity and its internal and external duality. The fact that questioning the status of one's country is socially allowed, from a position from within in both the United States and the United Kingdom – rather than being forced to treat it as something that cannot be discussed, as is the case with the Swedish identity as a humanitarian superpower – will hopefully permit people in the United States and the United Kingdom to keep challenging their countries' history and self-identity but also current actions and roles in the world. Because questioning the claims that are supposed to justify how a country acts and behaves makes it possible to participate in the production of a culture of democratic deliberation. Human rights and child rights cannot protect a democracy from internal authoritarianism – even when the authoritarianism is benevolent in that it means well with the best of intentions. The absence of human rights and child rights is a threat to democracy, but their presence alone does not guarantee democratic governance.

In contrast, it was rendered impossible among the left or liberals or even nonideologically affiliated people in Sweden to question its self-declared status as a humanitarian superpower. If a space had been created to allow for questioning and debate – and to deliberate among us what Sweden as a humanitarian superpower meant and would mean, and subsequently what actions were to be taken in its name – the Swedish people might have been more prepared for the outcome of its last election. They might have been able to reason about the Swedish role in the international community in a pluralistic way. This might have helped develop a sustainable path for how a small nation like Sweden could relate to the rest of the world without delusions of grandeur, but still understand that it matters when a small country with solid democratic credentials becomes the concern of the EU and the White House for having joined the authoritarians of the Western world when electing nationalistic political parties such as the Swedish Democrats" to prominence with their origin in the neo-Nazi movement. It turned out that people gave up without a fight any pretense of humanitarianism or humanism. Sweden as a humanitarian superpower was a self-image that was rapidly and easily abandoned by all political parties as soon as there was a new sheriff in town, and arguably, this is because the national identity as a humanitarian superpower had never been open for or anchored with any debate.

Returning to the child rights movement and the question of on whose behalf it speaks, one significant difference between when the United States or the United Kingdom attempts to bend the international communal will to align with their national interest is that any such project is deemed to fail – they will not succeed in erasing the distinction between them as sovereign democratic States within a community of sovereign States. When Sweden decided to align its interests with the community of norms, instead of developing a set of interests on its own, it will, of course, be successful because the only part that needs to change is Sweden and no other States. Sweden accomplished something new, it managed to eliminate the split between its singularity as a sovereign State and its role as a sovereign member of a community of sovereigns. This is a new form of human rights monism exemplified through the unrestrictive way in which it incorporated the CRC.

7.4 MONISM AND NATIONAL SELF-IMAGINATION

A majority of the values expressed in the CRC are both easy to support and uncomplicated to understand in the abstract. Examples here include the requirement that children should be protected from exploitation in article 36, protection against torture in article 37, or the requirement that the child should be cared for in article 18 and, if need be, have access to child care, and likewise, article 20 states that a child deprived of her family has a right to alternative forms of care. The problem, of course, appears when these principles are to be applied in concrete cases. In addition, some of the values of the CRC can be at direct odds with national views on families and children, which is the case for Sweden. An example of a discrepancy between the CRC and Swedish legally codified values are the parental right and use of spanking that is still upheld in the CRC, even if discouraged as a practice, which is not permitted in Sweden. Not to mention Swedish women's right to free and legal abortions, contradicted by the version of the interpretation of the Holy See as accommodated in the CRC by the unborn child's absolute right to life, as I have addressed in Chapter 2.[17] Judicial review alone cannot resolve the divergence between the CRC and national law because even the use of judicial review still presumes the State as the object of suspicion, when the State is presumed to fall short of its compliance with the CRC. This does not work when the law is to be directly applicable in concrete cases. Is it better for

[17] Declaration made by the Holy See on the ratification of the CRC:

> The Holy See recognizes that the Convention represents an enactment of principles previously adopted by the United Nations, and once effective as a ratified instrument, will safeguard the rights of the child before as well as after birth, as expressly affirmed in the "Declaration of the Rights of the Child" [Res. 136 (XIV)] and restated in the ninth preambular paragraph of the Convention. The Holy See remains confident that the ninth preambular paragraph will serve as the perspective through which the rest of the Convention will be interpreted, in conformity with article 31 of the Vienna Convention on the Law of Treaties of 23 May 1969.

the police to arrest a child contrary to the police statute but in what the police judge to be in accordance with the CRC, or is it better to not arrest the child in accordance with the police statute but what the police judge to be in conflict with the CRC? If one is to follow the request by the UN Committee, here the police should arrest the boys in accordance with the CRC but against the police statute.[18]

The distinctions between the CRC and Swedish democratically enacted laws are of great importance in other respects. United Nations treaties and Swedish law do not spring out of the same source. Rather, UN treaties are the result of multilateral negotiations among monarchies, dictatorships, theocracies, and democracies, while Swedish law originates in the Swedish people as they are represented through the legislative body of parliament. If one focuses on the CRC alone, rather than human rights in general, it is difficult to see how one can find its source to stem from anything but international legal positivism, as a treaty negotiated between the community of sovereign States, and not as a higher moral source able to overrule democratically enacted national laws. Within a democratic State, some discrepancy will exist between its domestic laws and an international legal treaty like the CRC. This is why by their very nature, international treaties will need to undergo some form of national interpretation for them to become part of the national law. This national interpretation is one of the steps that was not taken with the Swedish incorporation of the CRC.

7.5 HUMAN RIGHTS AND DEMOCRACY

To be able to describe what human rights are, one also must discuss their source. To discuss child rights, one must address whether they stem from the same source as human rights in general, or whether the CRC is constituted separately into its own almost universalizing regime through positive treaty lawmaking among all States, apart from the United States, which is not a party to the treaty. To illustrate the discourse on the sources of human rights, I draw on the discussion of whether human rights are man-made or if they are moral, universal, eternal norms. Samuel Moyn[19] and Martti Koskenniemi[20] are proponents of the argument that human rights are man-made and reflections

[18] Committee on the Rights of the Child, "Concluding Observation on the Combined Sixth and Seventh Periodic Reports of Sweden," March 7, 2023, CRC/C/SWE/CO/6-7, para. 6.

[19] Samuel Moyn, *The Last Utopia: Human Rights in History* (Cambridge, MA: Harvard University Press, 2012 [2010]), 210–211.

[20] Martti Koskenniemi, "Rights, History, Critique," in *Human Rights: Moral or Political?* ed. Adam Etinson (Oxford: Oxford University Press, 2018), 41–60.

of their own historical time and place, while John Tasioulas takes what he describes as an orthodox view that human rights are moral in their nature and that people hold these rights by virtue of being human,[21] and Brian Gran argues that children's rights are "even millennia-old," referring back to the Torah.[22] Mauro Zamboni and Tetsu Sakurai, in their work, ask the question if it is even possible for human rights to coexist with national sovereignty because national democratic law and human rights are in an embedded conflict with each other.[23] This argument is in line with the position of Lauterpacht who defends the natural law aspect of human rights: "To eliminate the ideas of natural law and natural rights from the consideration of the protection of the rights of man is to renounce the faculty of understanding their growth in the course of history and their association with that law of nations which is now to become its ultimate physical sanction."[24]

For scholars like Moyn, the rise of human rights is in part connected to the end of the decolonization process of the 1970–1980s and gained popularity as a utopian counterweight to the stale real politics of the Cold War.[25] Dependent on one's view of human rights as the expression of inherently human morality or politically constructed regulatory regimes, the view of the history of human rights and its lineage will, of course, differ. This is also where it matters whether child rights are part of the general human rights regime or if child rights within the CRC constitute their own regime. As its own regime, the legitimacy of the CRC on the international stage can be established through positive treaty law, while it is more difficult to argue its national legitimacy from treaty law since its domestic reach will be limited and the moral justification might be more easily explained within domestic law.

Being a democratic State depends on upholding certain human rights as codified in international treaties related to fundamental freedoms, while human rights can exist (and often have) independently of democratic systems. Regardless of whether one begins the history of human rights in the Enlightenment or in the postcolonial 1970s, human rights have not demonstrated an interdependency with democratic orders. For much of its history, the (human) rights canon has been protected by nondemocratic legal orders:

[21] John Tasioulas, "Philosophizing the Real World of Human Rights: A Reply to Samuel Moyn," in *Human Rights: Moral or Political?* ed. Adam Etinson (Oxford: Oxford University Press, 2018), 88–102, at 90.

[22] Brian Gran, *The Sociology of Children's Rights* (Cambridge: Polity, 2021), 24.

[23] Tetsu Sakurai and Mauro Zamboni, *Can Human Rights and National Sovereignty Coexist?* (London: Routledge, 2023).

[24] Lauterpacht, *An International Bill of the Rights of Man*, 3–4.

[25] Moyn, *The Last Utopia*, 214.

the most obvious example is the Magna Carta granted by King John of England in the thirteenth century (if we see human rights as the expression of universal morality, and not historically constructed because then the Magna Carta would predate human rights by a few centuries), while the Swedish equivalent is the *Landslagen*, Section V, as granted by King Magnus Eriksson in the fourteenth century. Historically, (human) rights have held a stronger connection to authoritarian rule than to democratically elected parliaments and democracy. Richard Tuck reminds the reader that, historically, rights have been advocated by authoritarian theorists in support of both slavery and the absolutist State.[26] An example already given at the beginning of this book is the Universal Declaration of Human Rights,[27] which was adopted by the UN General Assembly in 1948 including the United States, which still had apartheid laws in the South, as well as by authoritarian regimes such as the USSR and China. These historical examples warrant that continued vigilance must be maintained vis-à-vis contemporary rights and rights creation. "Rights" is not a magic word, and they do not become more magical if the word "human" is added in front of them. The authoritarian nature of the original parties behind the adoption of what has become the leading human rights instrument in the world suggests that the suspension of democratically enacted laws adopted within a democratic State in favor of authoritarian human rights regimes is not without its problems, even when it comes in the form of child rights.

Human rights are not only promoted and protected today through national constitutional provisions of democratic nation-states and, in this way, become part of a democratic legal order, but also through human rights regimes beyond the nation-state. As a result, human rights have been instrumentalized through multiple non-State actors, including public and private associations, intergovernmental organizations and regional associations such as the EU, a supranational organization. Human rights agreements are limited to describing democratic values. As such, the various treaties that codify these values cannot themselves serve as democratic expressions in and of themselves; they express some of the values that are of importance for democracies, but they do not guarantee democracy. In fact, the conditions for these agreements are at times *explicitly agnostic* toward the form of State governance. In the words of the Declaration of Friendly Relations: "all people have the right freely to determine, without external interference, their political status and to pursue

26 Richard Tuck, *Natural Rights Theories: Their Origin and Development* (Cambridge: Cambridge University Press, 1998 [1979]), 179, 3.

27 "The Universal Declaration of Human Rights," December 10, 1948, G.A. Res. 217 A.

their economic, social and cultural development."[28] The main challenge to international human rights, State sovereignty, is the same regardless of whether the State is democratic or nondemocratic. When major social changes are done in the name of child rights, without child representation, the question of both authority and legitimacy closely follows.

From the perspective of the UN Committee, the constitution in a democratic State can stand in the way of the CRC reaching individuals within that country as much as a constitution in a nondemocracy. To the international organization of these human rights regimes, it is irrelevant whether the State is a democratic republic, a democratic monarchy, or a dictatorship: All forms of sovereignty prevent the CRC from breaking through the sovereign veil. Of course, there is likely to be a difference in the level and quality of material rights that might be enjoyed within each of these nations, depending on whether they are built on a democratic legal order or not. Yet that difference is not connected to the governance structure of the treaties that these organizations are set to monitor and promote.

The connection between the CRC and democratic governance is more nebulous than the link between, for example, the International Covenant on Civil and Political Rights (ICCPR) and democracy. This is because the ICCPR's overarching value is freedom and equality – two principles strongly connected to democratic governance. The overarching values of the CRC are not as clearly defined. If the CRC is not a subcategory of human rights in general, the CRC will function under its own overarching principles, "the best interest" and "the right to be heard," and renders the link to democratic governance ambiguous.

7.6 THE SOVEREIGN VEIL

The foundation of the UN Human Rights Project was to protect against the crimes committed by the State against its own people; the problem with the sovereign veil is that we are asking the same sovereign State to serve as the protector of the same people whose rights it violates. It is fully understandable that international organizations, human rights activists and child rights activists, as described in this book, prefer the rule of UN Committees over the State. This follows a quite clear logic since the State is the only possible violator of human rights. It is equally understandable that the same

[28] "Declaration on Principles of International Law concerning Friendly Relations and Co-operation among States in Accordance with the Charter of the United Nations," October 24, 1970, G.A. Res. 2625 (XXV).

constituencies will promote an international human rights regime to take the form of universal positive law and a benevolent authoritarianism over a dysfunctional democracy. The CRC is the most widely ratified treaty within the UN system, with a deep expansion into the domain of the sovereign State, regulating education and child rearing, to name a couple of examples. These are areas of law that in many countries fall outside the public authority of the nation-state itself to regulate and are often left to the private sphere of the family, but nevertheless are encompassed by international child rights. Achille Mbembe describes a double movement of desires for contradictory things and for the incommensurables collected within what he calls "the same bundle of desire."[29] One such bundle of desires is the uninhibited international organization's power to legislate for sovereign States and, at the same time, the desire for such a State to be a fully fledged democracy.

7.7 THE SPLIT

The CRC and its incorporation became an important symbol for the Swedish government, as proof of Sweden's stature as a world-leading moral role model. The desire to make a humanitarian statement by incorporating the CRC also ended up eliminating any of the safeguards that normally follow the incorporation of a UN treaty into a national legal order. The importance of upholding a distinction between the obligations and the legal framework governing individuals' human rights claims against the States and the role of the State were lost. Instead, there was a presumption that the interest of the State was identical to the interest of the individual rights-holding person, who is supported by the international community of States. In this relationship, Sweden's national identity *merged* with the human rights treaties proffered by the UN, a merger that has led to a crucial misunderstanding and failure to remember that the human rights regime is founded on the healthy skepticism that considers the State itself to be an object of suspicion. To be an object of suspicion – a possible violator of human rights – does not fit well with Sweden's self-image as a humanitarian superpower. Instead of taking into consideration and safeguarding against this role as an object of suspicion, the Swedish State simply aligned its interests as being identical to the interests of the UN, with the result that no thought was given to any possible consequences to individuals and rights protection when the distinction between the State and its people imploded. The question is what happens when the State

[29] Achille Mbembe, *Necropolitics*, trans. Steven Corcoran (Durham, NC: Duke University Press, 2019), 29.

becomes the one possessing human rights not as claims but as entitlements for actions and decisions, instead of the individual holding the rights against the State?

One commonality among Western legal scholars is that law has a split, the difference between scholars is not of law's duality but where it is located and explained in various ways, either as a binary or as a bifocality; as two opposing units or as one unit with two sides. To Hans Kelsen, the law is binary; the split is fundamental and impossible to bridge even in the particular moment: "An *Ought* cannot be reduced to an *Is*, or an *Is* to an *Ought*; and so, an *Is* cannot be inferred from an *Ought*, or an *Ought* from an *Is*,"[30] governed by its hierarchy of norms and sources. Felix Cohen, who in contrast takes a bifocal view on the duality of law – at least from the perspective of Kelsen – takes a fundamentally different and conflicting approach, in violation of what Kelsen sees as the permanent separation of the binary of law, when for Cohen the prescriptive character of law is able to reach into its description, and vice versa.[31] Cohen treats the duality of law not as a binary of two separate independent concepts but as a bifocal interdependency where the normativity of the rule is subjugated to its function and manifestation: "[A] right is only the hypostasis of a property – the imagination of a substance supporting the fact that the public force will be brought to bear upon those who do things said to contravene it."[32] For Cohen, the ultimate split is placed between the law and society. A contemporary example of how the binary relationship of law transitions into the bifocal view on law can be found in Koskenniemi's writing. To Koskenniemi, the glitch between what he terms normativity and concreteness is the place of hope, the way to save law from falling into either apologism or utopianism is through an ethical interpretation.[33] To Koskenniemi, the lawyer must be aware of both; it is the interplay between the mind and the body of the interpreter and the facticity of the law that can resolve the disagreement between Kelsen and Cohen. The thinking subject located within the split is what has united the positivist view on law across theoretical schools over time. Its duality reflects that the law is man-made from a split subject, which is what makes democratic governance under the law possible.

Going back a little in time, for Morgenthau, the ad hoc decisions of sovereign States within a loose system of international law are the split. The

30 Hans Kelsen, *General Theory of Norms* (Oxford: Oxford University Press, 1991), 58.

31 Ibid., 76.

32 Felix S. Cohen, "Transcendental Nonsense and the Functional Approach: A Review of General Semantics," Winter 2, no. 2 (1944–1945): 97–98.

33 Martti Koskenniemi, *From Apology to Utopia: The Structure of International Legal Argument*, reissue (Cambridge: Cambridge University Press, 2005), 21.

question of enforcement, which is dependent upon the "balance of power as it operates in that particular situation," guides the bridging of the split. His duality is not within law, but rather between the dual incentive in front of the State to rely on the predictability of law and the interest in power.[34] For McDougal, however, the loosely connected international community is not law alone but a net of different actors and stakeholders guided by multiple decisions reflecting the multitude of actors and their interests. Within this plurality of forms of decisions, some are guided by communal expectations, made by established decision-makers within recognized structures of authority toward a communal interest, and backed by sufficient effective power.[35] According to McDougal, the split is occupied by the authority and control combined at the moment of the decision-making in the hands of the plurality of interests within the State.[36] To d'Aspremont, the duality of international law takes place in a trinity of what he calls ruleness, genealogy, and self-referentiality, where self-referentiality is the glue placed in the glitch providing the subjectivity to each element binding law together.[37] D'Aspremont's self-reflectivity belongs to the same tradition as Koskenniemi's lawyer. With Koskenniemi, it is the lawyer's power of imagination that bridges the duality of ascending and descending argumentative structures.[38] This split, which sometimes is simply a glitch and at other times results in the friction that comes with both being and representing, is the place where both suspicion and confirmation rest. D'Aspremont describes a critical approach to be "a self-reflective attitude or a mindset in the sense that it seeks to undo the 'false consciousness' of mainstream scholarship."[39] This is a form of suspicion that is more in line with the one on which Duncan Kennedy reflects, where the hermeneutic as a form of suspicion applied to law is better understood to show a direction of legal development, rather than to unveil legal errors in themselves.[40] Within rights it is in this glitch that the rights holder becomes an

34 Hans J. Morgenthau, *Politics among Nations: The Struggle for Power and Peace*, 7th ed., rev. by Kenneth W. Thompson and DavidClinton (New York: McGraw Hill, 2006), 301.
35 Myres S. McDougal, "Jurisprudence for a Free Society," *Georgia Law Review* 1, no. 1 (1966): 4.
36 Ibid.
37 Jean D'Aspremont, *International Law as a Belief System* (Cambridge: Cambridge University Press, 2018), 31.
38 Koskenniemi, *From Apology to Utopia*, 557.
39 Jean D'Aspremont, *Epistemic Forces in International Law: Essays on the Foundational Doctrines and Techniques of International Legal Argumentation* (Cheltenham: Edward Elgar Publishing, 2015), 196.
40 Duncan Kennedy, "The Hermeneutic of Suspicion in Contemporary American Legal Thought," *Law and Critique* 25, no. 2 (2014): 92.

individual. Schlag makes an almost weary comment in 2013 when he debunks the conflict between formalism and realism as foundational, instead he argues that "realism is thus already rhetorically indebted to formalism. A total triumph over formalism would be disastrous for realism as well."[41] The establishing of monistic rights, based on a monistic child-rights identity, is such an outcome, I argue. Schlag demonstrates a binary understanding in his descriptions of localized variations, while he takes a bifocal view on law from a bird's eye perspective.[42]

When the CRC is to be understood in relation to the State, it is confronted by two challenges. The first is possible to argue even though such an argument is a challenge. If the CRC is to be interpreted through the lens of a binary, its text cannot be both descriptive and prescriptive since the subject of the rights itself, the child, is monist in its construction, and there is a choice of either being descriptive or purely political. Instead this problem has to be resolved through hierarchy, although the CRC does not have any such clearly stated hierarchy since it sees the rights as indivisible and constituting a holistic singular unit. The CRC's two primary principles – the best interest of the child and the right to be heard – can possibly be seen to provide some sort of hierarchy, even though they are procedural principles and do not convey an overarching value, in addition Both the right to be heard and the best interest principles are to be given different weight for each individual child and in each particular case. The second challenge is how will it be possible to turn a monist child-rights identity into a conscious subject aware of the treaty's internal contradiction carrying the legitimacy to make the choice between a descriptive or a prescriptive interpretation in each concrete case?

7.8 IMPLOSION

Rights throughout history have served to straddle the balance between benevolent and malevolent authoritarianism, rather than to uphold democracy. One example of how authoritarian power is managed through law is the combination of exceptionality and rights. For instance, we can go back as early as Section V of Magnus Eriksson's *Landslag* from 1341, which continued to be the foundation of Swedish rules on judicial review until the constitutional reform of 2010. Here, the king is to be found as a combatant in the struggle between the order of God and the order of man. So also is the king in Thomas

41 Pierre Schlag, "Formalism and Realism in Ruins (Mapping the Logics of Collapse)," *Comparative Law Review* 4, no. 1 (2013): 19.

42 Ibid., 4.

Aquinas in Question 92.[43] The dilemma is that once one has accepted authoritarianism, what for some is a malevolent authority will for others be a benevolent authority. Related to the slave trade is the exercise of colonial power through military violence over the colonized, the expansion of executive power under the war powers in France, the United States and Switzerland in the First World War, or the Bush administration's enactment of the Patriot Act and Torture Memos in the wake of the attack on the Twin Towers. Sweden decided to dismantle its democratic safeguards, not for the sake of war but for the sake of children. Again borrowing from Duncan Kennedy's borrowing of Gramsci, by allowing for a critique of a false hegemonic consciousness of rights, one might open up a split within the child rights regime that will allow for a questioning of what is being decided for whole societies in the name of children.

Through the CRC, the political has been replaced by a discourse of human rights that cannot allocate the political sharing of power as is done in a deliberate democracy, even under the presumption that child politics is neutral with respect to party ideology, which I argue is not possible. This deliberation presumes a split of public power, of the making of the same law one is being ruled by, while the more general push toward eliminating ambiguity and doubt within authoritarianism not only has eliminated the split between the functional and what Kennedy describes as the Gramscian hegemony, the monism in the case of Sweden has also eliminated the Kelsean safeguard of hierarchies of norms and sources. It has done this by identifying with all systems of law equally, hard and soft law alike, whether originating from national legal institutions or the UN, or in the form of a UN committee's Concluding Observation, as if they originate from within the same source free of hierarchy.

7.9 UNIVERSALIZING POSITIVISM

If human rights law is to be able to function as a counterforce to malevolent authoritarianism, it must provide a space and a location from within that space for a democratic legal order to be able to find its function and legitimacy even in the face of a benevolent authoritarianism, such as when the UN Committee insists that the CRC should prevail in all concrete conflicts between Swedish law and the CRC.[44] This cannot be done simply through

[43] Thomas Aquinas, *Summa Theologica*, complete American ed., trans. Fathers of the English Dominican Province (Coyote: Canyon Press, 2018), Question 92.

[44] Committee on the Rights of the Child, "Concluding Observation on the Combined Sixth and Seventh Periodic Reports of Sweden," March 7, 2023, CRC/C/SWE/CO/6-7, para. 6.

the language of violation and compliance as the UN Committee insists, but must be founded in the possibility to change and to adjust and even to bend with the political will as expressed through the democratic legal exercise of power. This idea that human rights law constitutes a check upon democratic legal orders that have turned authoritarian presupposes an idea where the nation-state holds a self-understanding and views itself as a sovereign State among an external community of sovereigns. David Kennedy has, in multiple significant texts, addressed the role of the cosmopolitan professional in setting an international and human rights law agenda that is delinked from the one of the agenda produced from within the sovereign State.[45] The idea that an increase in benevolent authoritarianism, for example, by making each public servant, without guidelines, freely conduct a judicial review on every Swedish law in possible conflict with the CRC as suggested by the UN Committee, that such a license will counter the authoritarian antidemocratic push currently sweeping across Europe, needs empirical proof for it to become the dogma of our time. Finnish legal scholar Kaarlo Tuori expresses this presumption of the sovereign State as understanding itself as being both sovereign and communal in the language of globalization and transnational law, where international courts and contained regimes seemingly pierce holes in the divide between national and international legal regimes.[46] What for Tuori turns into a fragmentation of law is what this book describes as a positivistic universalization of human rights when the sovereign State merges its national identity of singularity with the international human rights communal identity, at the expense of its own democratic legal order.

If the State no longer sees itself as split and torn between being a unique sovereign singularity internally and a communal participant in the global and transnational arena of child rights, but instead completely merges its internal sovereignty with the external communal treaty law, there is nothing that stops it from also doing the reverse. Once its national view on law is monistic, the dilemma of law's duality disappears. Its form and its substance are no longer a source of tension.[47] This is a new form of monistic law in Sweden, and it is not clear how it will hold up against the antidemocratic pressure of authoritarianism, especially since this authoritarianism in some people's eyes will be seen as

45 See, for example, David Kennedy, "The Disciplines of International Law and Policy," *Leiden Journal of International Law* 12, no. 1 (1999): 9–134, 110; David Kennedy, "The International Style in Postwar Law and Policy," *Utah Law Review* 1994 (1994): 7–104.

46 Kaarlo Tuori, *Ratio and Voluntas: The Tension between Reason and Will in Law* (London: Ashgate, 2016 [Routledge, 2011]), 301.

47 For a reading on the foundational argument on form and substance, see Duncan Kennedy, "Form and Substance in Private Law Adjudication," *Harvard Law Review* 89 (1976): 1685.

benevolent, while others will see it as malevolent. Without a split in the argument, there will be no place from within the argument to open up for an ethics of ambiguity, a questioning or a willingness to engage in deliberate democratic practices. The problem is that child rights will not be able to provide the final say on what is what because the space of agency from within the CRC is closed through its monist subject construction.

The CRC, as the most ratified human rights treaty, comes close to being an example of something that is *like* natural law to be governed by a universal positive law.[48] The foundational idea of a democratic legal order is that its laws are the representation of the will of its subjects, who are able to adjust these laws through the legislative body of the democratic sovereign State. Yet a perpetual state of exception has been created in Sweden, which has delegated to the operations of independent treaties, courts, and UN committees on the international level, and to regular police officers and social workers on the local level, to determine and delimit the meaning of a human rights treaty. The CRC, on its own, does not possess the provisions needed for the concrete application of the public administration of power in individual cases. This is the delegation of what should be democratically held parliamentary decisions down to the individual civil servant. To give the police the authority to reinterpret the statutes regulating their power to deprive civilians of their liberty in the name of child rights might be understood but should never have been accepted even when the Swedish national identity was to be a humanitarian superpower. However, after the recent election, Sweden is now one of the countries in Europe flirting with nationalist authoritarian agendas by electing the Swedish Democrats as the second largest party in the country. The very construction of the CRC child-rights identity renders impossible any recognized discrepancy between the ways in which children might *want* to be represented and the ways in which they *are* represented through the incorporated treaty. Children are excluded from participating in the Swedish democratic legislative process per definition: At the very moment they gain the right to vote they are no longer children but plainly citizens with full civil and political rights, and any tension between their desired rights and their representation is removed beyond their reach.

7.10 THE MONIST CHILD-RIGHTS IDENTITY AND UNIVERSALISM

When it comes to human rights, the bifocality of the way you are in the social, and the way that law makes you into a legal subject, is typically afforded by

[48] For an expanded exposé of the nuances and the evolution of new, conflicting, and rival schools of natural law, see Tuck, *Natural Rights Theories*.

representation: Representation ensures a deliberately chosen connection between subjects and their reflection in the political body of the legal order of the State. Yet *without* representation, children have no part in the formation of a democratic legal order. In this way, the monist construction of the child identity of the CRC challenges the basic foundation of human rights as being a part of a democratic project. The child-rights identity is literally without the constituting moment of what Agamben defines as "bare life" – the idea that birth is what constitutes the human subject.[49] The monism of the child identity is not only without its bare life (since the CRC allows itself to be applicable from the moment of conception), but the child is also, by its very definition as a person under the age of majority, *unable to be included in the democratic legal process, as a body of the political.*[50] When it comes to the CRC and Swedish national identity, the question remains: Who has the representative authority to question the monism between the norms of the community of sovereign States in the shape of the UN Committee and the Swedish self-identification as the humanitarian superpower expressed through the incorporation of the CRC as being identical in the international and in the domestic legal spheres?

7.11 COMMENTARY AND CRITIQUE

The question raised against this background becomes: Is it possible to take a theoretical critical approach to child rights and advocacy? If the rights-constructed child is delinked from the social, is an internal critique even possible? What would a commentary on child rights sound like? The critique of law is dependent on the split in law, one of its splits being form and substance – and considering Duncan Kennedy's "conflicting considerations," this conflict comes to its expression as indeterminacy.[51] It is from this split between the law and the political that both are vulnerable to the accusation of being either ideological or strictly political.[52]

49 Giorgio Agamben, *Homo Sacer: Sovereign Power and Bare Life*, ed. Werner Hamacher and DavidE. Wellbery, trans. Daniel Heller-Roazen (Stanford: Stanford University Press, 1995), 127.

50 Disenfranchisement is unique to the child-rights identity in that it is directly connected to a rights identity, but factual disenfranchisement is a widespread condition in the largest democracy of all, the United States. See Amna A. Akbar, "Demands for a Democratic Political Economy," *Harvard Law Review* 134 (2020): 90, 94. Akbar does not stop at the ballot box and argues for a far more inclusive understanding of democracy, to include housing, health care the environment, economic say and self-determination.

51 Kennedy, "The Hermeneutic of Suspicion," 94.

52 Ibid., 101.

The possibility of an ethical approach to law is located in its ambiguity that constantly struggles against making the split permanent and independent of its other part. Instead of being vulnerable to the accusation of relying on ideology or falling into politics, following what Kennedy describes as a forbidden form of argument, law that is vulnerable to being described as ideology will be tainted by the political at the moment of application.[53] In discussing how legal theorists might be inspired by Gramsci as a thinker rather than by his commentary on law Kennedy makes a clear distinction between a general critical approach of law and a critical legal approach from within: "In Gramscian terms, the legal system is a complicated bloc, that is, it involves on the one hand an element of the use of force, of violence, of direct coercion and on the other hand it involves unmediated oppression by people against other people."[54] Kennedy continues, a Gramscian-inspired reading of law will on the other hand also hold an "hegemonic function."[55] For Kennedy's analysis of Gramsci, hegemony can be understood as ideology.[56] Kennedy argues that it would be helpful for lawyers to think self-critically about what he calls their part in "rights consciousness" and how their interpretation of these rights might be perverted by a false hegemonic consciousness.[57]

This is the challenge for child rights theory and advocacy because what is left is only the approach to law that relates to law as a bloc since rights themselves are monistically constructed in the CRC, to only be critiqued from the outside. This is because the child as she appears within law does not exist because of her inability to doubt and question her legally constructed identity. It might be possible to identify the hegemonic structure of child rights, but it is much more difficult to identify the critical self-reflecting subject from within child rights to expose a hegemonic false consciousness. Nor is there a space from within child rights itself for the legal interpreter or the lawmaker to rest on the ambiguity of law in the application of the CRC in concrete cases. The possibility for self-critique and questioning of monist positivist law can only take place from the outside, and when positive law becomes universal, even that space is filled not as an ambiguity but as a question of compliance and violation.

7.12 CONCLUSION

In the example of Sweden's embracing a monist understanding of child rights law, the juxtaposition between democratic legal order and child rights has

53 Ibid.

54 Duncan Kennedy, "Antonio Gramsci and the Legal System," *ALSA Forum* 6, no. 1 (1982): 34.

55 Ibid., 35.

56 Ibid., 32.

57 Ibid., 37.

taken the form of a perpetual condition of necessity. This raises the question of whether benevolent authoritarianism should be preferred over a stagnated democracy? I am advocating for choosing a democratic form of lawmaking over the benevolent authoritarianism the UN Committee is advocating. This question will become more urgent to address as the examples from the 1930s in Tingsten's study has shown that democracies are not all that capable of managing social crisis and that at moments like that, democratic political bodies have been quite comfortable with delegating its power back to the executive branch of the State. The human rights regimes coming out of the UN do not need to confront this question as democracy is not what constitutes their legitimacy, and the mandate of a treaty like the CRC granted upon the UN Committee set to monitor it is to guard and expand the CRC and not to take its democratic effects into account. This is as it should be seen from the position of the CRC as an international treaty; it is explicitly not the role of the UN Committee to engage in the governance of member States beyond the effects of the implementation of the CRC; it is only the democratic State itself that carries the responsibility to maintain its own democratic system.

The clearest example of this is the governmental argument for the executive to perform judicial review of national legislation in relation to the CRC on all matters, even those of life and death. All this might have remained a theoretical concern – until the second-largest political nationalistic party in Sweden came to perceive democracy as a hindrance to its agenda; this is now the political agenda for which the humanitarian superpower State has paved the way. All this power, delegated to the lowest level of public authority of the most open-ended of human rights treaties – with its monistic view on both the child-rights identity and its legal regime, risks making it theoretically difficult to locate where to place the possibility of a democratically led dissent or ambiguity over the ways in which the CRC is applied in concrete cases or is used as arguments for large democratic derogation.

8

The Monist Child-Rights Identity and Universal Positivism

This book has now come to its end. The motivation for writing this book was originally triggered by the social turn toward benevolent authoritarianism, which has led me to examine the interdependency between rights-based identities and the identity of the democratic State for the realization of rights.

8.1 LEGAL LIFE

With the CRC, law has shown itself capable of creating legal life independent of a social context. The delinking of law from its social context is made possible in child rights because, in contrast to CEDAW and CERD, the CRC is not constructed as a protection against discrimination. The child in the CRC is based on the legal definition of age alone. Contrary to what might be thought, the absence of legal life is not social death. Law casts its shadow over every aspect of modern Western life. Rather, to not have a legal life means to exist in the shadows of law. The consequences of law then will affect every part of your life, but you will not have the capacity to affect what is coming your way. The relation between the individual and the State is one made from law. Without legal life, you will not be a part of the only mode through which the State must engage with predictability and security in relation to individuals. This mode takes the form of claims as rights and obligations. It is therefore no small matter that adults fighting on behalf of children were able to create a legally binding treaty giving children legal life with the adoption of the CRC in 1989.

8.2 A MONIST IDENTITY

The CRC created its own legal life with the help of age, not from any reflection of social life as socially constructed identities are made, but rather from the movements of the Earth circling the Sun. The CRC came up with an identity independent of the social construction by relying on a place outside the control of the social. This identity relies only on one single data point – age – making the identity free from social life and thus achieving a monist identity construction, bringing the child out from the land of the shadows of law into its center. With the monist identity of the CRC, law on its own made a life and a relationship based on the rights of the child and the obligations of the State. The child identity – now free from abusive and harmful social and traditional practices for its definition – created a new field of both law and advocacy that came to be known as child rights.

8.3 SOCIAL CONSTRUCTION

Creating a rights-holding identity free of social construction is a way to avoid embedding the subordination that created a common identity in the first place into the rights themselves. However, there are unexamined ethical and social downsides to a monist construction. The monist construction precludes children's agency to shape their own identity. The strengths of the feminist movement and the civil rights movement have been the ways in which women and black people through social construction have been able to split open a critique of the social structures and practices that forms the group identities though which rights are being claimed. The reshaping of one's identity is a central part of the ethics of self-determination. There is no way for children to contest the use of age as the definition of their identity.

The split within identity construction is the site of both internal conflict and contradiction but also of resistance and hope. W. E. B. Du Bois has termed this internal conflict double consciousness. It is the place where one understands the larger social conflict of one's identity, that what you think of yourself might not be what others see in you, but through your ability to think and give meaning to the world around you, this insight will also help you reshape the society that both traps and makes you what you are. As painful as this is, it also gives resistance a place to anchor from within, to reshape, to challenge the social norms and to redefine oneself. This is what a monist identity construction precludes. What it gains is an indisputable identity and what it loses is an ethics of ambiguity where doubt and openness to be wrong and willingness to redo are made external to the identity construction itself.

8.4 A PERPETUAL STATE OF EXCEPTION

When Sweden decided that it was a humanitarian superpower with a mission to morally lead the world toward greater humanitarianism, the incorporation of the CRC became a symbolic act of significance. It also became important that the incorporation be done without any of the normal democratic safeguards in place that maintained a distinction between Sweden as a sovereign liberal-democratic State and its role as a humanitarian superpower in the international community. This meant the elimination of a correlation between the hierarchy or norms and levels of public authorities when interpreting the direct applicability and meaning of the CRC in concrete cases. As a humanitarian superpower, it was not possible to acknowledge that there could be any distinction between the interest of the UN Committee monitoring the CRC and the Swedish State as represented by the public authorities. This is how Sweden ended up with individual police officers conducting judicial review on the police statute with the help of the CRC.

The question of where the child rights movement gains its authority to represent children remains unanswered. Who granted this movement the legitimacy to argue for major social and political changes on behalf of children, especially where there is no requirement from within the child rights movement itself to have children as part of its movement? What makes one set of adults better equipped than another set of adults to argue for radical social change that carries large social costs, to prefer a benevolent authoritarianism to a democratic legal order? This freedom of individual police officers to conduct judicial review and individual civil servants in concrete cases is not only permitted but now also obligated as per the instruction for how Sweden incorporated the CRC. It might have been possible to turn a blind eye to this as it was a case of benevolent, and not a malevolent, authoritarianism when the Swedish commitment to democracy was considered unshakable. Now that Sweden has abandoned its identity as a humanitarian superpower with the last election and instead made the former neo-Nazi-associated Swedish Democrats the second-largest political party in Sweden, the dismantled democratic safeguards that were made in the name of child rights, remain dismantled even when Sweden no longer sees itself as a humanitarian superpower and the second-largest political party is questioning democracy as foundational for all people within Swedish society.

8.5 THE UNIVERSALISM OF POSITIVISM

One way to control and "win" an argument is by not making the counterargument possible to articulate, to eliminate any possibility of doubt or conflict via exclusion of the counterargument. At the center of the international community is the split interest of the sovereign State. The international order is characterized by the idea that the State compromises between its concrete short-term and abstract long-term interests to preserve human rights.

Where international child rights advocates will push for the eradication or at least drastic softening of the sovereign veil that prevents them from fully accessing the individual child within the State, they also risk dismantling the understanding that as a rights regime child rights is dependent on the State as an object of suspicion – both as the only recognized violator of rights and its protector. The CRC, with its monist child-rights construction that does not have any children (on whose behalf one argues) capable of articulating a different set of priorities, is exceptionally well suited to this type of universalizing positivist push, made possible not by natural law but by the positivist argument that the CRC is almost universally ratified, with only the United States standing outside the treaty today.

The question of whether child rights are a part of universal human rights or if child rights constitute their own universalism is important to answer from the perspective of democracy. If child rights are their own universalism, without the possibility of relying on the domestic constitutional and democratically established protected freedoms, we need to identify where child rights derive their source of authority. Ronald Dworkin's definition of positive rights rejects the idea that rights preexist legislation.[1] Kaarlo Tuori points out that it is the deliberate decision to make law that is the most significant characteristic of positive law.[2] Other characteristics of liberal positivist law are that law is both descriptive and prescriptive, both objective and subjective; in other words, dual and not monist.[3]

8.6 THE IDENTITY OF THE STATE

Just as I began this book about the child-rights identity the world took a sharp turn. At first, I thought it was a turn to the right, but I now think it took a turn into the right's side ditch of the road. Strongmen such as Trump, Orbàn, Modi, and Erdogan came to power. Sweden followed suite with the Swedish Democrats. Scholars and writers from a large spectrum of the Western world have in an amazingly short time begun the production of a self-critical archive in defense of democracy with a voice of urgency that the literature on democracy usually does not possess.[4]

1 Ronald Dworkin, *Taking Rights Seriously* (London:Bloomsbury, 1997), 6.

2 Kaarlo Tuori, *Critical Legal Positivism* (London: Routledge, 2002 [Ashgate, 2016]), 6.

3 Zartaloudis traces this duality of Western law to its Christian origin and a variety of metamorphoses, where its duality is the only constant. Thanos Zartaloudis and Giorgio Agamben, *Power, Law and the Uses of Criticism* (London: Routledge, 2010), 17.

4 Some significant examples of this rich literature, see William Davis, *Nervous States: How Feelings Took over the World* (New York: Vintage, 2019 [2018]); Ben Rhodes, *After the Fall:*

I initially did not understand how the authoritarian desire to elect anti-democrats was not limited to a right–left binary. The desire of this type of political agenda is in large part a politically right agenda, but there are also peculiar elements that are shared by the left and then often made in the name of human rights and in particular child rights. The benevolent authoritarian impulse that ended in the eagerness to comply with the UN Committee monitoring the CRC has been lingering for a long time outside the right–left binary; it instead cuts across with its own version of "us or them," measured in the dedication to the child rights regime itself. This takes the shape of the benevolent authoritarian. What is good and what is bad will be defined by the "us" or "them" binary, rather than by ontological definitions of what is good and what is bad, and democratic safeguards will be seen as bad when they go against an expansion of the child rights regime as defined by the UN Committee.

The turn into the ditch happened about the same time that my daughter was coming of age, and the youth literature taking place in futuristic fantasy lands and places became part of an imaginary world we discussed at home. What was striking in this literature was how the fight in these imaginary societies always seemed to take place between authoritarian good and authoritarian evil forces. It was seldom that the solution against oppression in the books was that people installed a democratic national parliament and called a national election to settle the issue. I asked my daughter if she did not think that it was odd that her books in general did not look to democracy as a method for settling conflicts between divergent interests addressing people's most fundamental rights, instead of everyone running out into the forest to fight. She explained to me that democratic processes would not make much of an action story. She is probably correct about that, but another thing is also correct, namely that legislation through national democratically elected parliaments for solving the social problems of the day is not seen as very capable in fulfilling its task, since the democratic legislative process is not only slow but also very often ambivalent. The challenge of the climate crisis is not only a factual challenge, but also the democratic challenge of our time. Democratic processes and parliaments are not necessarily well equipped to respond to crisis, as was demonstrated by Tingsten in his study of the 1930s when these parliaments transferred their power to the executives of the State. What

The Rise of Authoritarianism in the World We've Made (London: Bloomsbury, 2022 [2021]); Patrick J. Deneen, *Why Liberalism Failed* (New Haven, CT: Yale University Press, 2019 [2018]); Masha Gessen, *Surviving Autocracy* (London: Granta, 2021 [2020]); Francis Fukuyama, *Identity: Contemporary Identity Politics and the Struggle for Recognition* (London: Profile Books, 2019 [2018]).

Tingsten did not know when he wrote his study of the transfer of democratic powers to the executives in the 1930s was that a Second World War was to break out where the battle between good and evil was to shine brightly, and still the support for the Nazis in Europe was overwhelming. The climate crisis will not come to an end anytime soon and any such transfer of power from parliament to the executive or the Courts can easily be understood as benevolent and possibly a necessity. I am not comparing the Nazis with the climate crisis but I am comparing what might come in the wake of the reactions to the effort to fight the climate crisis. Democratic processes lend themselves to doubt and ambiguity in search of nuance while authoritarian acts that seem sure of themselves are not met with the same level of scrutiny – this despite the fact that the social problems that authoritarians were asked to resolve seem to persist even after their governance – Trump's America is not greater after the American people voted him out and, at the same time, the social problems that began under the Democrats' watch persist as well. I began to see that what authoritarianism abhors, regardless of whether benevolent or malevolent, is ambivalence, and that within this, there is an urge toward monism, not only in the creation of the child-rights identity but also in law in general. Democracy is an ambivalent process, as embedded within it is the idea that the counterargument might be correct.

I now believe that the move into the ditch cannot be measured within a scale of right-to-left, but instead is a fundamental shift in how we see the world, and it is much more connected to a sense of urgency and emergency than a straight line between right and left political positions. It is not only in child rights that one is trying to eliminate ambiguity, or the possibility for internal critique. The authoritarian wave currently sweeping across the world is not a movement between the right and the left, the unwillingness to accept ambiguity is not a right–left trait but rather a question of efficiency, absent the willingness to spend the time it takes on deliberation in the hope of identifying the nuances of a problem and having the courage to carry doubt and at times to be wrong – and to admit being wrong. The impulse to monism not only appears in the CRC, even though the CRC was the first clear human rights treaty to express this, and it is not an impulse that is seen only in Sweden but it is also an impulse invoked about rights and law in general, when ambiguity and deliberation are seen as standing in the way of the desired outcomes, regardless of whether they be right or left on the spectrum.

8.7 COMPLEX INTERSECTIONALITY

The monist child rights construction is effective, and it has a valid purpose to shield child from the harmful practices and traditions that serve to justify the abuse of children, whether that be child spanking or female genital mutilation. There are many good reasons for using a monist construction. However, the downsides to this construction must be addressed through policy and legislation. At the heart of the critique against a monist construction is the idea of inclusion. One important way in which agency and the structural social inequalities can become a part of the child rights movement is through the complex intersectionality between the monist construction of the child identity, by allowing for the socially constructed identities that comes with gender, race and sexual orientation. Child rights theory and advocacy can find agency through complex intersectionality without losing the important protection of the monist child-rights identity construction.

8.8 CONCLUSION

The adoption of the CRC by the General Assembly in 1989 is a historical statement of the hope and joy experienced by the world at the end of the Cold War.In this respect, it is a symbol of unity, one that reflects for the first time in generations a global gathering around a common agenda for children of the world, built not on religion but on human rights. It is in this spirit that one is to understand the monist construction of the child and the exclusion of cultural and sociological determinants in the construction of the child-rights identity.

However, before we begin to argue for any further expansion of the child rights regime, we must make a fundamental choice about power, whether it be authoritarian or democratic, before even getting to the point of arguing for a concrete child rights agenda. The monist child-rights identity makes child rights into a regime without a concrete body, absent a body for individual free will to anchor within and to legitimize both freedom and its limit. This also means that the child-rights identity cannot be adjusted by the very person holding the rights that come with the identity. This, the ability to define and contest one's assigned identity has been at the center of the evolving democratic national State during the whole of the struggles during the twentieth and the twenty-first centuries for social equality and against structural identity-based inequality of oppressed groups of people. This power to self-identify and to contest assigned belongingness is withheld from children – as defined by the CRC.

This lack of a required body and will for the identity construction of the child means there is no place from which the child rights movement – which purportedly represents children, yet is led by self-appointed adults – can open itself up to an internal critique and seek adjustment as a movement.

Invulnerable to the forms of internal critique that normally help other social movements to evolve and remain significant social actors for social justice and change over time, the child rights movement faces increasing irrelevance for the very subjects it intends to serve.

A grave consequence of the monist child-rights identity – and its difficulty of representation when confronted by the requirements of a democratic legal order – is that it becomes impossible to find the legitimate interpreter for the drastic societal changes it calls for. Once a nation abides by a legal definition of its subjects that is external to its own political process, the law can no longer be changed through political, democratic means. This tendency is further exacerbated when a nation-state such as Sweden decides to take on a monist approach to law itself by building its national identity on international human rights, rather than on its own democratic legal order.

My claim differs from what is often described as system fragmentation, wherein human rights break through the sovereign veil through national court systems or the regional courts. Rather, I am describing a paradigmatic shift in law itself: the elimination of the duality of the subject identity of the nation-state when it no longer distinguishes between moral rights and law. Even in theory, there is no place for democratic political expression through legislation or lawmaking within the CRC regime. The only way for human rights to be part of a democratic legal order is by being governed by democratic institutions that can challenge the monist subject construction, whether it be formed by national identity or by the CRC. Monism should be challenged so that it does not fall into authoritarianism and away from democracy.

Despite all the shortcomings of the CRC and its monist construction of the child-rights identity, its weakness is in a way also its very strength. Even if these children and young people in the underserved immigrant areas were never included in the imagining of who was to hold child rights, the children in these areas – regardless of what they have done or where they come from – are equal holders of rights with every other child. When all society's resources and goodwill are emptied out, it turns out that these rights are the only weak but possible resource that, if well mobilized, remain as a resource for the child who has neither individual capital nor communal status. Therefore, I will end this book by again calling for child rights scholars and participants in child rights advocacy to examine what from a Gramscian perspective would be a false hegemonic image of children, representing a very narrow span of children and interests. I want to refer to the original reason for my choice of using the narrative method and its historical link to critical race theory (CRT) as my methodology throughout this book. The origin of CRT is when Bell chose the concrete child over the dogma of the civil rights movement when he questioned whether they could serve two masters at the same time. Bell does not reject the civil rights struggle and its goals, but he is critical of the movement's blind spots to the downsides and costs of their agenda. When Bell asks if the movement could serve both his clients, the individual black children he represented as a civil rights lawyer, and the wider national interest to desegregate racist American schools, he responded with the hope of advancing a dialogue within the black and civil rights community for how to address this conflict between the children he represented and the nation. As a result, he sparked a whole new way of looking at law and social justice that rejuvenated the civil rights movement into what was to become a new way of looking at rights and intersectionality. My hope is that this book on child rights, legal theory and social advocacy, despite at times being critical, will be understood as mostly critical of the most significant blind spot within child rights, how monism precludes agency and self-identification for children to truly own their rights-holding identity. For adults to demonstrate to children the value of democracy, children must be able to reap its benefits. Central to modern democracy is the power of playing a part in the shaping of one's own identity as it relates to the larger society. As the CRC now stands, it does not allow for this.

Bibliography

Agamben, Giorgio. 1995. *Homo Sacer: Sovereign Power and Bare Life*. Stanford: Stanford University Press.

2005 [2003]. *State of Exception*, trans. Kevin Attell. Chicago: University of Chicago Press.

2021 [2020]. *Where Are We Now? The Epidemic as Politics*. London: ERIS.

Åhman, Karin. 2019. *Vägledning vid tolkning och tillämpning av FN:s konvention om barnets rättigheter*. [Guide for Interpreting and Applying the UN Convention on the Rights of the Child. Stockholm: Regeringskansliet, Arbetsmarknadsdepartementet.

Akbar, Amna A. 2020. "Demands for a Democratic Political Economy." *Harvard Law Review*.

Aquinas, Thomas. 2018. *Summa Theologica*. Cayton: Coyote Canyon Press.

Archard, David, and John Tobin. 2019. "Article 1 the Definition of a Child." In *The UN Convention on the Rights of the Child: A Commentary*, edited by John Tobin. Oxford: Oxford University Press.

Arendt, Hannah. 1970 [1969]. *On Violence*. New York: Harcourt Publishing Company.

2005. *The Promise of Politics*. New York: Schocken Books.

Ashburn-Nardo, Leslie. 2008. "Fairly Representing the Stereotyping Literature?" *Industrial and Organizational Psychology*.

Axberger, Hans-Gunnar. 2018. "Rättigheter (Del I & II), Sverige och MR" [Rights (Part I & II), Sweden and Human Rights]. *SvJT*.

Bains, Jasmine. 2020. "Search Engines and Algorithms Are Biased: Here's Why That Matters." *Information Outlook*.

Balton, David A. 1990. "The Convention on the Rights of the Child: Prospects for International Enforcement." *Human Rights Quarterly*.

Barstad, Kristin. 2008. "Preventing the Recruitment of Child Soldiers." *Refugee Survey Quarterly*.

Barthes, Roland. 2000 [1980]. *Camera Lucida*. New York: Vintage Classics.

Bassey, Magnus O. 2007. "The Place of Group Consciousness in Black Autobiographical Narratives." *Journal of African American Studies*.

BBC. 2016. "Migrant Crisis: Migration to Europe Explained in Seven Charts." March 4. Accessed June 23, 2022. www.bbc.com/news/world-europe-34131911.

Beauvoir, Simone de. 2009 [1949]. *The Second Sex*. New York: Vintage.

Bell, Derrick A. 1976. "Serving Two Masters: Integration Ideals and Client Interests in School Desegregation Litigation." *The Yale Law Journal*.

Beltrán, Christina. 2010. *The Trouble with Unity, Latino Politics and the Creation of Identity*. Oxford: Oxford University Press.

Bernstein, Robin. 2011. "Children's Books, Dolls, and the Performance of Race; or, The Possibility of Children's Literature." *PMLA*.

Bildt, Carl. 1993–1994. "Inkorporering av Europakonventionen och andra fri-och rättigheter" [The Incorporation of the European Convention of Human Rights, Proposition 1993/94:117]. Stockholm: Regeringskansliet.

Brown, Vincent. 2020. *Tacky's Revolt: The Story of an Atlantic Slave War*. Cambridge, MA: Harvard University Press.

Bueren, Geraldine Van. 1995. *The International Law on the Rights of the Child*. Dordrecht: Martinus Nijhoff.

Buhre, Frida. 2022. "Child Figuration in Youth Climate Justice Activism: The Visual Rhetoric of the Fridays for Future on Instagram." In *The Politics of Children's Rights and Representation*, edited by Bengt Sandin, Jonathan Josefsson, Karl Hanson, and Sara Balagopalan. London: Palgrave Macmillan.

Butler, Judith. 1997. *The Psychic Life of Power*. Stanford: Stanford University Press.

2007 [1990]. *Gender Trouble: Feminism and the Subversion of Identity*. London: Routledge.

Byrne, Seamus. 2020. "Reclaiming Progressive Realisation: A Children's Rights Analysis." *The International Journal of Children's Rights*.

Carbado, Devon, and Cheryl Harris. 2019. "Intersectionality at 30: Mapping the Margins of Anti-essentialism, Intersectionality, and Dominance Theory." *Harvard Law Review*.

Carlson, Laura. 2018. *Workers, Collectivism and the Law*. Cheltenham: Edward Elgar Publishing.

Castagno, Angelina E. 2013. "Multicultural Education and the Protection of Whiteness." *American Journal of Education*.

Cerda, Jaime Sergio. 1990. "The Draft Convention on the Rights of the Child: New Rights." *Human Rights Quarterly*.

Children's Bureau. 1973. "The Story of the White House Conferences on Children and Youth." PS 006 506.

Chong, Dennis, Reuel Rogers, and Alvin B. Tillery. 2005. "Reviving Group Consciousness." In *Politics of Democratic Inclusion*, edited by Christina Wolbrecht, Rodney Hero, Peri E. Arnold, and Alvin B. Tillery. Chicago: Temple University Press.

Clarke, Jessica E. 2019. "They, Them, and Theirs." *Harvard Law Review*.

Cohen, Felix S. 1944–1945. "Transcendental Nonsense and the Functional Approach: A Review of General Semantics." *Winter*.

Cooper, Frank Rudy. 2012. "Uncomfortable Conversation: Vulnerabilities and Identities – Experiencing Equality as Oppression: Why Vulnerabilities Cannot Replace Identities." Paper presented at Emory University School of Law, Atlanta, Georgia September 14–15.

Cott, Nancy F. 1997. *The Bonds of Womanhood*. New Haven, CT: Yale University Press.

Crenshaw, Kimberlé. 1989. "Demarginalizing the Intersection of Race and Sex." *University of Chicago Legal Forum.*

Curry, Tommy J. 2017. *The Man-Not: Race, Class, Genre, and the Dilemmas of Black Manhood.* Chicago: Temple University Press.

Daalen, Edward van. 2022. "Could It Be That They Do Not Want to Hear What We Have to Say? Organised Working Children and the International Politics and Representation of Child Labour." In *The Politics of Children's Rights and Representation*, edited by Bengt Sandin, Jonathan Josefsson, Karl Hanson, and Sara Balagopalan. London: Palgrave Macmillan.

Dane, Louise. 2019. "Den reglerade invandrigen och barnets bästa." [The regulated immigration and the best interest of the child]. PhD diss. Stockholm: Stockholm University.

D'Aspremont, Jean. 2015. *Epistemic Forces in International Law: Essays on the Foundational Doctrines and Techniques of International Legal Argumentation.* Cheltenham: Edward Elgar Publishing.

2018. *International Law as a Belief System.* Cambridge: Cambridge University Press.

Davidson, Julia O'Connell. 2011. "Moving Children? Child Trafficking, Child Migration, and Child Rights." *Critical Social Policy.*

Davis, William. 2019 [2018]. *Nervous States: How Feelings Took over the World.* New York: Vintage.

Deleuze, Gilles. 1968. *Difference and Repetition.* London: Bloomsbury Publishing.

Deneen, Patrick J. 2019 [2018]. *Why Liberalism Failed.* New Haven, CT: Yale University Press.

Dinstein, Yoram. 1995. "Human Rights: Implementation through the UN System." *Structures of the World Order. Proceedings of the American Society of International Law*, April 5–8.

Dommasnes, Liv Helga, and Melanie Wrigglesworth (eds.). 2008. *Children, Identity and the Past.* Cambridge: Cambridge Scholars Publishing.

Douglass, Fredrick. 1881. "The Color Line." *North American Review.*

Dowd, Nancy E. 2008. "Boys, Masculinities and Juvenline Justice." *Korean Law.*

Du Bois, W. E. B. 2008 [1903]. *The Souls of Black Folk.* New York: Oxford World's Classics.

Duncan, Lauren E. 1999. "Motivation for Collective Actions: Group Consciousness as Mediator of Personality, Life Experiences, and Women's Rights Activism." *Political Psychology.*

Dworkin, Ronald. 1997. *Taking Rights Seriously.* London: Bloomsbury Publishing.

Edkins, Jenny, and Véronique Pin-Fat. 2004. "Introduction, Life, Power, Resistance." In *Sovereign Lives, Power in Global Politics*, edited by Jenny Edkins et al. London: Routledge.

Ehrenkrona, Carl Henrik. 2016. *Europeiska konventionen om skydd för de mänskliga rättigheterna och de grundläggande friheterna, en kommentar.* [The European Convention on Human Rights on the Protection of Human Rights and Fundamental Freedoms, a Commentary], Stockholm: Karnov.

Ek, Simone. 2007. "The Legislative History of the Convention on the Rights of the Child." *United Nations High Commissioner for Human Rights.*

Falk, Richard A. 2000. *Human Rights Horizons.* New York: Routledge.

Faulkner, Elizabeth A., and Conrad Nyamutata. 2020. "The Decolonisation of Children's Rights and the Colonial Contours of the Convention on the Rights of the Child." *International Journal of Children's Rights.*

Fineman, Martha Albertson. 2008. "The Vulnerable Subject: Anchoring Equality in the Human Condition." *Yale Journal of Law and Feminism.*

Flacks, Simon. 2014. "Is Childhood a 'Disability'? Exploring the Exclusion of Children from Age Discrimination Provisions in the Equality Act 2010." *Child and Family Law Quarterly.*

Frankopan, Peter. 2018. *The New Silk Roads.* London: Bloomsbury Publishing.

Freeman, Michael. 2006. "What's Right with Rights for Children." *International Journal of Law in Context.*

2020. *A Magna Carta for Children: Rethinking Children's Rights.* Cambridge: Cambridge University Press.

Fricker, Miranda. 2007. *Epistemic Injustice: Power and the Ethics of Knowing.* Oxford: Oxford University Press.

Fukuyama, Francis. 2018. *Identity: The Demand for Dignity and the Politics of Resentment.* New York: Farrar, Strauss, and Giroux.

2019 [2018]. *Identity: Contemporary Identity Politics and the Struggle for Recognition.* London: Profile Books.

Gadamer, Hans-George. 1985 [1984]. "The Hermeneutics of Suspicion." In *Phenomenology and the Human Science,* edited by J. N. Mohanty. Alphen aan den Rijn: Kluwer.

Garland, Jameson. 2019. "Informed Consent in Clinical Practices in Sweden." *Förvaltningsrättslig Tidskrift.*

Garland, Jameson, and Santa Slokenberga. 2019. "Protecting the Rights of Children with Intersex Conditions from Nonconsensual Gender Conforming Medical Interventions." *Medical Law Review.*

Gearey, Adam. 2018. *Poverty Law and Legal Activism: Lives That Slide Out of View.* London: Routledge.

Gessen, Masha. 2021 [2020]. *Surviving Autocracy.* London: Granta.

Goulimari, Pelagia. 2011. *Toni Morrison.* London: Routledge.

Gragl, Paul. 2018. *Legal Monism: Law and Realism, Philosophy, and Politics (International Law and Domestic Legal Orders).* New York: Oxford University Press.

Grahn-Farley, Maria. 2008. "Neutral Law and Eurocentric Lawmaking: A Postcolonial Analysis of the UN Convention on the Rights of the Child." *Brooklyn Journal of International Law.*

2013. "How Children Got Rights" S.J.D. diss. Cambridge, MA: Harvard Law School.

2022. "The Human Rights Claim in Climate Justice: An Argument for Reintroducing the Principle of Anti-discrimination and Strengthening the Anti-domination Principle When Children Go to Court." *Journal of Gender, Race & Justice.*

Gran, Brian. 2021. *The Sociology of Children's Rights.* Cambridge: Polity.

Granger, Gilles-Gaston. 1989. "Les conditions proto-logiques des languages naturelles." *Philosphiques.*

Guggenheim, Martin. 2007. *What's Wrong with Children's Rights.* Cambridge, MA: Harvard University Press.

Guillaumin, Colette. 1995. *Racism, Sexism, Power and Ideology*. London: Routledge.

Hammarberg, Thomas. 1990. "The UN Convention on the Rights of the Child: How to Make It Work." *Human Rights Quarterly*.

Hans. J. Morgenthau. 2006. *Politics among Nations: The Struggle for Power and Peace*. London: McGraw Hill.

Hanson, Karl. 2022. "Children's Representation in the Transnational Mirror Maze." In *The Politics of Children's Rights and Representation*, edited by Bengt Sandin, Jonathan Josefsson, Karl Hanson, and Sara Balagopalan. London: Palgrave Macmillan.

Harris, Angela P. 1990. "Race and Essentialism in Feminist Legal Theory." *Stanford Law Review*.

Harris, Rosemary. 1996. "Interpreting Teenage Inter-ethnic Violence." *International Journal on Minority and Group Rights*.

Hartman, Saidiya. 1997. *Science of Subjection: Terror, Slavery, and Self-Making in Nineteenth Century America*. Oxford: Oxford University Press.

2008. *Lose Your Mother: A Journey along the Atlantic Slave Route*. New York: Farrar Straus Giroux.

Hearst, Alice. 2003. "Recognizing the Roots: Children's Identity Rights." In *Rethinking Childhood*, edited by Peter B. Pufall and Richard P. Unsworth. New Brunswick, NJ: Rutgers University Press.

Heise, Michael. 2005. "*Brown v. Board of Education*, Footnote 11, and Multidisciplinarity." *Cornell Law Review*.

Hemmati, M. A., M. Masoumi, and H. Shokoohi. 2015. "Mental Health Disorder in Child and Adolescent Survivors of Post-war Landmine Explosions." *Military Medical Research*.

Henkin, Louis. 2013 [1945]. *How Nations Behave: Law and Foreign Policy*. New York: Columbia University Press.

Hiedemann, Bridget, and Jutta M. Joesch. 2005. "Whose Sons and Daughters Are Treated Differently? (Re) Examining the Child Gender Literature through the Lens of Race and Ethnicity." *Seattle Journal for Social Justice*.

Humphrey, John. 1973. "The International Law of Human Rights in the Middle Twentieth Century." In *The Present State of International Law and Other Essays Written in Honour of the Centenary Celebration of the International Law Association*, edited by Maarten Bos. Deventer: Kluwer.

Imoh, Twum-Danso. 2022. "Adults in Charge: The Limits of Formal Child Participatory Processes for Societal Transformation." In *The Politics of Children's Rights and Representation*, edited by Bengt Sandin, Jonathan Josefsson, Karl Hanson, and Sara Balagopalan. London: Palgrave Macmillan.

Inter-American Court of Human Rights. 2002. "Judicial Condition and Human Rights of the Child." Advisory Opinion No. 17, August 28.

Javidan, Pantea. 2017. "American Legal Discourse on Child Trafficking." PhD diss. London: London School of Economics and Political Science.

Josefsson, Jonathan, and John Wall. 2022. "Empowering Inclusion: Theorizing Global Justice for Children and Youth." In *The Politics of Children's Rights and Representation*, edited by Bengt Sandin, Jonathan Josefsson, Karl Hanson, and Sara Balagopala. London: Palgrave Macmillan.

Josefsson, Jonathan, Bengt Sandin, Karl Hanson, and Sarada Balagopalan. 2002. "Representing Children." In *The Politics of Children's Rights and*

Representation, edited by Bengt Sandin, Jonathan Josefsson, Karl Hanson, and Sara Balagopalan. London: Palgrave Macmillan.

Kapur, Ratna. 2002. "The Tragedy of Victimization Rhetoric: Resurrecting the 'Native' Subject in International/Post-colonial Feminist Legal Politics." *Harvard Human Rights Journal.*

Kaya, Reifa. 2019. "Environmental Vulnerability, Age and the Promises of Anti-age Discrimination Law." *Review of European, Comparative, and International Environmental Law.*

Kelsen, Hans. 1991. *General Theory of Norms.* Oxford: Oxford University Press.

Kennedy, David. 1994. "The International Style in Postwar Law and Policy." *Utah Law Review.*

1999. "The Disciplines of International Law and Policy." *Leiden Journal of International Law.*

2005. *The Dark Side of Virtue: Reassessing International Humanitarianism.* Princeton, NJ: Princeton University Press.

Kennedy, Duncan. 1976. "Form and Substance in Private Law Adjudication." *Harvard Law Review.*

1982. "Antonio Gramsci and the Legal System." *ALSA Forum.*

1982. "Legal Education and the Reproduction of Hierarchy." *Journal of Legal Education.*

2002. "The Critique of Rights in Critical Legal Studies." In *Left Legalism/Left Critique*, edited by Wendy Brown and Janet E. Halley. Durham, NC: Duke University Press.

2014. "The Hermeneutic of Suspicion in Contemporary American Legal Thought." *Law and Critique.*

Kohn, Margaret, and Keally McBride. 2011. *Political Theories of Decolonization: Postcolonialism and the Problem of Foundations.* Oxford: Oxford University Press.

Koskenniemi, Martti. 2005. *From Apology to Utopia: The Structure of International Legal Argument.* Cambridge: Cambridge University Press.

2018. "Rights, History, Critique." In *Human Rights: Moral or Political*, edited by Adam Etinson. Oxford: Oxford University Press.

Kumm, Mattias. 2016. "Constituent Power, Cosmopolitan Constitutionalism, and Post-positivist Law." *International Journal of Constitutional Law.*

Lang, Johannes. 2014. "Against Obedience: Hannah Arendt's Overlooked Challenge to Social-Psychological Explanations." *Theory & Psychology.*

Lastowka, Greg. 2008. "Google's Law." *Brooklyn Law Review.*

Lauterpacht, Hersch. 2013 [1945]. *An International Bill of the Rights of Man.* Oxford: Oxford University Press.

League of Nations. 1924. Geneva Declaraton of the Rghts of the Child. Geneva: League of Nations, September 26.

LeFebvre, Alexander. 2008. *The Image of Law: Deleuze, Bergson, Spinoza.* Stanford: Stanford University Press.

Lindgren, Cecilia. 2010. *Internationell adoption i Sverige. Politik och praktik från sextiotal till nittiotal* [Adoption in Sweden. Policy and Practice from the 1960s to the 1990s], Stockholm: Myndigheten för Internationella Adoptionsfrågor.

Loaiza, Esteania Peñafiel, and Gayatri Chakravorty Spivak. 2021. *Can the Subaltern Speak?: Two Works.* London: Afterall Books.

Löfven, Stefan. 2017–2018. "Inkorporering av FN:s konvention om barnets rättighter" [The Incorporation of the UN Convention on the Rights of the Child, Prop. 2017/18:186]. Stockholm: Regeringskansliet.
Lowry, Ritchie P. 1964. "Leadership Interaction, Group Consciousness, and Social Change." *The Pacific Sociological Review.*
MacCormick, Neil. 2007. *Institutions of Law: An Essay in Legal Theory.* Oxford: Oxford University Press.
Macpherson, C. B. 2010 [1962]. *The Political Theory of Possessive Individualism.* Oxford: Oxford University Press.
Mägi, Erik, and Lina-leas Zimmerman. 2015. *Stjärnfamiljejuridik* [The Star Family]. Falkenberg: Gleerup.
Masuoka, Natalie. 2006. "Together They Become One: Examining the Predictors of Panethnic Group Consciousness among Asian Americans and Latinos." *Social Science Quarterly.*
Masuoka, Natalie, and Jane June. 2013. *The Politics of Belonging: Race, Public Opinion, and Immigration.* Chicago: University of Chicago Press.
Mbembe, Achille. 2019. *Necropolitics.* Durham, NC: Duke University Press.
McCluskey, Martha T. 2003. "Efficiency and Social Citizenship: Challenging the Neoliberal Attack on the Welfare State." *Indiana Law Journal.*
McDougal, Myres S. 1966. "Jurisprudence for a Free Society." *Georgia Law Review.*
Miller, Arthur H., Patricia Gurin, Gerald Gurin, and Oksana Malanchuk. 1981. "Group Consciousness and Political Participation." *American Journal of Political Science.*
Moten, Fred. 2003. *In the Break: The Aesthetics of Black Radical Tradition.* Minneapolis: University of Minnesota Press.
Moyn, Samuel. 2012 [2010]. *The Last Utopia: Human Rights in History.* Cambridge, MA: Harvard University Press.
Myers, John E. B. 2008–2009. "A Short History of Child Protection in America." *Family Law Quarterly.*
Myrdal, Alva. 1955. *A Scientific Approach to International Welfare: America's Role in International Social Welfare.* New York: Columbia University Press.
Myrdal, Gunnar. 2017 [1944]. *An American Dilemma.* London: Routledge.
Noble, Safiya Umoja. 2018. *Algorithms of Oppression: How Search Engines Reinforce Racism.* New York: New York University Press.
Oestreich, Joel E. 1998. "UNICEF and the Implementation of the Convention on the Rights of the Child." *Global Governance.*
Patterson, Orlando. 1982. *Slavery and Social Death.* Cambridge, MA: Harvard University Press.
Perry, Pamela, and Alexis Shotwell. 2009. "Relational Understanding and White Antiracist Praxis." *Sociological Theory.*
Peters, Anne. 2000. *Beyond Human Rights: The Legal Status of the Individual in International Law.* Cambridge: Cambridge University Press.
Petersson, Olof. 2013. *Herbert Tingsten Vetenskapsmannen.* Stockholm: Atlas.
Pink, Sara. 2001. *Doing Visual Ethnography.* Thousand Oaks, CA: Sage.
Posner, Eric A. 2014. *The Twilight of Human Rights Law.* Oxford: Oxford University Press.
Proulx, Michael G. 2011. "Professor Revisits Clark Doll Tests." *Harvard Crimson,* December 1.

Pullman, Philip. June 14, 2019. "People Who Shape Our World." Lecture and Q&A, Oxford Union Society.

Quisumbing King, Katrina. 2022. "The Global Color Line and White Supremacy: W. E. B. Du Bois as a Grand Theorist of Race." In *The Oxford Handbook of W. E. B. Du Bois*, edited by Aldon D. Morris et al. Oxford: Oxford University Press.

Radjenovic, Anja. 2021. "Vulnerability of Unaccompanied and Separated Child Migrants, Briefing." EPRS, PE 690.575. European Parliament.

Ramesh, Abhinaya. 2001. "UN Convention on the Rights of the Child: Inherent Weaknesses." *Economic and Political Weekly*.

Regeringen. 1941. "Betänkande med förslag till ändrad lydelse av § 16 regeringsformen" [Proposal to Changed Reading of § 16 of the Instrument of Government]. SOU 1941:20. Stockholm: Regeringskansliet.

1993. "Fri- och rättighetsfrågor: delbetänkande" [Questions on Freedom and Rights]. Draft SOU 1993:40. Stockholm: Regeringskansliet.

Reinfeldt, Fredrik. 2009–2010. "En reformerad grundlag" [Instrument of Government]. Prop. 2009/10:80. Stockholm: Regeringskansliet.

Rhodes, Ben. 2022 [2021]. *After the Fall: The Rise of Authoritarianism in the World We've Made*. London: Bloomsbury Publishing.

Ricoeur, Paul. 1970. *Freud & Philosophy: An Essay on Interpretation*. New Haven, CT: Yale University Press.

1984 [1983]. *Time and Narrative*. Chicago: Chicago University Press.

2016 [2013]. "Philosophical Anthropology." In *Writings and Lectures*, edited by Johan Michel and Jerome Poree. Cambridge: Polity.

Rigg, Andrea, and Jan Pryor. 2007. "Children's Perceptions of Families: What Do They Really Think?" *Children & Society*.

Roberts, Dorothy E. 2003. "Child Welfare and Civil Rights." *UIII Law Review*.

Rodrigues, José Noronha. 2021. "Refugee and Migrant Children in Europe." In *The Rights of Unaccompanied Minors: Perspectives and Case Studies on Migrant Children*, edited by Yvonne Vissing and Sofia Leitao. Cham: Springer. B. 2019. 5057-18 (Högsta domstolen, April 29).

Ross, Alf. 1957. "Tu Tu." *Harvard Law Review*.

Ross, Catherine J. 2015. *Lessons in Censorship: How Schools and Courts Subvert Student's First Amendment Rights*. Cambridge, MA: Harvard University Press.

Ross, Josephine. 2002. "The Sexualization of Difference: A Comparison of Mixed-Race and Same-Gender Marriage." *Harvard Law Review*.

Rossiter, Clinton. 2007 [1948]. *Constitutional Dictatorship: Crisis Government in the Modern Democracies*. Piscataway, NJ: Transaction Publishers.

Sakurai, Tetsu, and Mauro Zamboni. 2023. *Can Human Rights and National Sovereignty Coexist?*. London: Routledge.

Sanches, Gabriel R. 2008. "Latino Group Consciousness and Perceptions of Commonality with African Americans." *Social Science Quarterly*.

Sandin, Bengt. 2022. "Recognizing Children's Rights: From Child Protection to Children's Human Rights, the 1979 Swedish Ban on Corporal Punishment in Perspective." In *The Politics of Children's Rights and Representation*, edited by Bengt Sandin, Jonathan Josefsson, Karl Hanson, and Sara Balagopalan. London: Palgrave Macmillan.

Sandin, Bengt, Jonathan Josefsson, Karl Hanson, and Sara Balagopalan (eds.) 2022. *The Politics of Children's Rights and Representation*. London: Palgrave Macmillan.

Schlag, Pierre. 1990. "Normative and Nowhere to Go." *Stanford Law Review.*

2013. "Formalism and Realism in Ruins (Mapping the Logics of Collapse)." *Comparative Law Review.*

Schmitt, Carl. 2005. *Political Theology*. Chicago: Chicago University Press.

Scourfield, Jonathan, Bella Dicks, Mark Drakeford, and Andrew Davies. 2006. *Children, Place and Identity: Nation and Locality in Middle Childhood.* London: Routledge.

Shelton, Dinah. 2011. *International Law and Domestic Legal Systems*. Oxford: Oxford University Press.

Shockley, Elle, Ashley Wynn, and Leslie Ashburn-Nardo. 2016. "Dimensions of Black Identity Predict System Justification." *Journal of Black Psychology.*

Skinner, Quentin. 2012 [1997]. *Liberty before Liberalism*. Cambridge: Cambridge University Press.

Skivenes, Marit, and Karl Harald Søvig. 2019. *Child Rights and International Discrimination Law: Implementing Article 2 of the United Nations Convention on the Rights of the Child*. New York: Routledge.

Smith, Catherine. 2013. "Equal Protection for Children of Same-Sex Parents." *Washington University Law Review.*

Socialstyrelsen. n.d. *Ny kartläggning visar brister i stöd till adopterade*. Accessed January 4, 2023. www.socialstyrelsen.se/om-socialstyrelsen/pressrum/press/ny-kartlaggning-visar-pa-brister-i-stod-till-adopterade/.

Stafford, Ned. 2018. "German Doctor's Leader Condemns Support for Refugee Age Tests." *MBJ: British Medical Journal.*

Tasioulas, John. 2018. "Philosophizing the Real World of Human Rights: A Reply to Samuel Moyn." In *Human Rights: Moral or Political*, edited by Adam Etinson. Oxford: Oxford University Press.

Tingsten, Herbert. 1930. *Regeringsmaktens Expansion Under och efter Vārldskriget: Studies över konstitutionell fullmaktslagstiftning* [The Expansion of Governmental Powers during and after the World War: Studies on Laws of Constitutional Transfers of Power of Authorities]. Falköping: Gleerup.

Todres, Jonathan, and Shani M. King. 2020. "Children's Rights in the Twenty-First Century: Challenges and Opportunities." In *The Oxford Handbook of Children's Rights Law*, edited by Jonathan Todres and Shani M. King. Oxford: Oxford University Press.

Torehammar, Henrik. 2023. "Kraven svider i den svenska självbilden" [The Demands Stings the Swedish Selfimage]. *Svenska Dagbladet*. March 29.

Tuck, Richard. 1981. *Natural Rights Theories: Their Origin and Development*. Cambridge: Cambridge University Press.

Tuori, Kaarlo. 2016 [2002]. *Critical Legal Positivism*. Farnham: Ashgate.

2016 [2011]. *Ratio and Voluntas: The Tension between Reason and Will in Law*. London: Routledge.

United Nations General Assembly. 1948. Universal Declaration of Human Rights. Geneva: United Nations, December 10.

1959. UN Declaration of the Rights of the Child. Geneva: United Nations, November 20.

1965. Convention on the Elimination of All Forms of Racial Discrimination. Geneva: United Nations, December 21.

1966. International Covenant on Civil and Political Rights. Geneva: United Nations: United Nations, December 16.

1966. International Covenant on Economic, Social and Cultural Rights. Geneva: United Nations, December 16.
1979. Convention on the Elimination of All Forms of Dscrimination against Women. Geneva: United Nations, December 18.
1989. UN Convention on the Rights of the Child. Geneva: United Nations, November 20.
2011. Optional Protocol to the Convention on the Rights of the Child on a Communication Procedure. Geneva: United Nations, December 19.
Valdes, Francisco. 1997. "Under Construction: Lat-Crit Consciousness, Community, and Theory." *California Law Review*.
Vandenbogaerde, Arne. 2017 [2016]. *Towards Shared Accountability in International Human Rights Law, Procedures and Principles*. Cambridge: Intersentia.
Veitch, Scott. 2017. "The Sense of Obligation." *Jurisprudence: An International Journal of Legal and Political Thought*.
Vinx, Lars. 2009. "Republicanism and Judicial Review." *University of Toronto Law Journal*.
Wells, Karen. 2021. *Childhood in a Global Perspective*. Cambridge: Polity.
West, James E. 1971. "White House Children's Program (Dec 13–18, 1970)." White House Conference on Youth, Washington, DC.
Wheeler, Skye. 2020. "UN Peacekeeping Has a Sexual Abuse Problem." *The Hill*, November 1.
Wilde, Marc de. 2015. "Emergency Powers and Constitutional Change in the Late Middle Ages." *Tijdschrift Voor Rechtsgescheiedenis*.
Williams, Juliet A. 2013. "Girls Can Be Anything: But Boys Will Be Boys: Discourses of Sex Difference in Education Reform Debates." *Nevada Law Journal*.
Williams, Patricia. 1992. *The Alchemy of Race and Rights*. Cambridge, MA: Harvard University Press.
Wing, Adrien Katherine. 1999–2000. "Violence and State Accountability: Critical Race Feminism." *Georgia Journal of Gender and Law*.
2000. *Global Critical Race Feminism*. New York: New York University Press.
2003. *Critical Race Feminism*, 2nd ed. New York: New York University Press.
Woodhouse, Barbara Bennett. 2003. "Re-visioning Rights for Children." In *Rethinking Childhood*, edited by Richard P. Unsworth. New Brunswick, NJ: Rutgers University Press.
The Working Group. 1980. "Discussion and Adoption by the Working Group." E/CN.4/L.1542. United Nations.
Wyness, Michael. 2014. "Children, Family and the States: Revisiting Public and Private Realms." *Sociology*.
2019. *Childhood and Society*. London: Bloomsbury Publishing.
Yaqub, Nazia. 2022. *Parental Child Abduction to Islamic Law Countries: A Child Rights Analysis of the Legal Framework*. London: Bloomsbury Publishing.
Young-Bruehl, Elisabeth. 2012. *Childism: Confronting Prejudice against Children*. New Haven, CT: Yale University Press.
Zartaloudis, Thanos, and Giorgio Agamben. 2010. *Power, Law and the Uses of Criticism*. London: Routledge.
Zetterqvist Nelson, Karin. 2007. *Mot alla odds* [Against All Odds]. Malmö: Liber.

Index

For EU product safety concerns, contact us at Calle de José Abascal, 56–1°,
28003 Madrid, Spain or eugpsr@cambridge.org.

www.ingramcontent.com/pod-product-compliance
Lightning Source LLC
LaVergne TN
LVHW011814200926
848484LV00005B/1194
* 9 7 8 1 0 0 9 3 6 6 9 6 0 *